SMALL ARMS

SMALL ARMS

Children and Terrorism

Mia Bloom with John Horgan

CORNELL UNIVERSITY PRESS   ITHACA AND LONDON

First published 2019 by Cornell University Press

Printed in the United States of America

Library of Congress Cataloging-in-Publication Data

Names: Bloom, Mia, 1968– author. | Horgan, John, 1974– author.
Title: Small arms : children and terrorism / Mia Bloom and John Horgan.
Description: Ithaca [New York] : Cornell University Press, 2019. | Includes
    bibliographical references and index.
Identifiers: LCCN 2018040384 | ISBN 9780801453885 (cloth ; alk. paper) |
    ISBN 9781501709425 (pdf e-book) | ISBN 9781501712067 (epub/mobi)
Subjects: LCSH: Child terrorists—Islamic countries. | Child suicide bombers—
    Islamic countries. | Children and terrorism—Islamic countries.
Classification: LCC HV6433.I742 B56 2019 | DDC 363.325083/091767—dc23
LC record available at https://lccn.loc.gov/2018040384

Contents

The gallery follows page 96.

Acknowledgments

This book is the culmination of many years of research and immeasurable patience on the part of Cornell University Press and our editor, Roger Haydon. When I first approached CUP about writing a book on children and terrorism based on our field research in Pakistan, the so-called Islamic State (IS) did not yet exist. As a result, we watched in horror as the phenomenon of children coerced into violent extremism played out in real time in Syria, Iraq, Libya, Afghanistan, Yemen, and the Philippines.

The book would not have been possible without the support of the Minerva Research Initiative, Department of Defense Grant No. N00014-16-12693, and the program officers and support staff of the Office of Naval Research, Harold Hawkins, Erin Fitzgerald, David Montgomery, Annetta Burger, Chris Becker, Lisa Troyer, and others. While we are heavily indebted to the Department of Defense for its support of this research, we should emphasize that any opinions, findings, or recommendations expressed in this book are those of the authors alone and do not reflect the views of the Office of Naval Research, the Department of the Navy, or the DoD.

We are grateful to the members of our Minerva research team at Boston Children's Hospital and Harvard University. B. Heidi Ellis, Emma Cardeli, Beth Nimmons, and Sarah Gillespie have helped us flesh out the similarities and differences between children in gangs and those in terrorist organizations.

We thank our respective department chairs, Greg Lisby and Anthony Lemieux, for their support, with special mentions to Carol Winkler, who funded a research associate to work on the project; Lyshandra Holmes, who provided invaluable assistance with our Institutional Review Board; and Stacey Harrell, for her help with our budget. The revolving door of research associates who worked on the project allowed us unique access to materials in Arabic and helped the team to organize and archive hundreds of young martyrs eulogized by the terrorist organizations themselves.

We are indebted to our student research assistants over the years who helped collect and tag the raw data, especially Aaron Dicker, Ayse Lokmanoglu, and Kristian Warpinski at Georgia State University, who spent many hours analyzing IS propaganda and without whom this project would never have had verified data. We thank all of the researchers who joined our team over the years: Madhavi Devasher, Erin Kearns, and Gary Uzonyi, who helped us crunch the quantitative data and code the literature reviews; Cale Horne (when we were at Penn State), for his literature review on education in Afghanistan and Pakistan; Shaun Walsh and Suzette Abbasciano at the University of Massachusetts, Lowell; and Yannick Veilleux-Lepage, our project manager, who helped with the final stage of the project.

We are especially grateful to Tanya Zayed, who functioned as researcher, consultant, subject matter expert, adviser, and friend. Tanya ensured that our findings and assertions were valid beyond a handful of cases by drawing on a decade of experience reintegrating child soldiers in Africa, Latin America, South Asia, and the Middle East. Ian A. Elliott was vital for translating his research on child sexual abuse to the study of children recruited into the Islamic State.

We thank Feriha Peracha, who invited us several times to Lahore, Malakand, and the Swat Valley, Pakistan. Fia introduced us to some of the most impressive young men, who not only survived their experiences with the Pakistani Taliban but were able to lead productive and happy lives after their reintegration into society. We are also grateful to Raafia Reese Khan and the entire staff at Sabaoon, who graciously hosted us.

We appreciate the assistance of Scott Steadman, who helped integrate our divergent writing styles to create a more cohesive narrative. We extend our appreciation to the anonymous reviewers of the manuscript and to Eric Levy for his meticulous (and painstaking) editing, as well as to Emily Andrew and Susan Specter at Cornell University Press. Max Taylor, as always, helped elaborate the model of children's socialization into violent extremism, and Andrew Mumford organized a conference at the British Academy that instigated the six-stage model of children's socialization into the Islamic State. Our colleagues provided important feedback as we presented draft chapters at academic conferences or guest lectures; we are especially grateful to Scott Gates, David Rappaport, and John Mercer for comments on the theory chapter. The many experts working on IS have been generous with their time and exchange of ideas: Amarnath Amarsingam, J. M. Berger, Dan Byman, Simon Cottee, Raphael Gluck, Hassan Hassan, Bruce Hoffman, Laith Alkhouri, Nikita Malik, Malcolm Nance, Jessica Stern, Robert Tynes, Michael Weiss, Craig Whiteside (our hero who located our missing data), Graeme Wood, and Aaron Zelin, all of whom generously shared their own research and data over the years. I am especially grateful to Victor Asal and Jenna Jordan for their friendship and support during the extremely difficult final phase of publication.

Chapter 4 is based on an earlier draft of a paper by Mia Bloom and Ian Elliott presented to the Association for the Treatment of Sex Abusers (ATSA) in 2013, and an updated version presented on June 22, 2017, at the Lethal Aid and Human Security (LAHS) Conference at the University of North Carolina at Chapel Hill.

We are indebted to Dr. Elliott for his assistance with this material and his permission to use parts of the original draft.

While we hope this book sheds light on the phenomenon of children's recruitment into terrorist networks, we also hope for a future in which this book becomes irrelevant and groups stop exploiting children in this fashion. We echo the prayer from the United States Conference of Catholic Bishops: "For the people of Syria [and Iraq], that God may strengthen the resolve of leaders to end the fighting and choose a future of peace."

SMALL ARMS

WHAT IS A CHILD?

The time is now. Arm your women and children against the infidel!
Osama bin Laden, 2001, Tora Bora, Afghanistan

What is your most lofty aspiration? Death for the sake of Allah!
Kindergarten verse at a Hamas school, Gaza City

Children in violent extremist movements, disparagingly referred to as "child terrorists," are not born. Rather, they are made, and they learn to *want* to be a part of a violent group, either with or without the knowledge and support of their families.

On July 4, 2015, the Islamic State's (IS) propaganda channels released their most disturbing video to date. It began with claims of IS's "heroic" successes on the battlefield against the regime of the Syrian dictator Bashar al-Assad. In the video, adult IS fighters march bloodied and barefoot Syrian Arab Army prisoners in and out of jail cells. A caravan of Toyota trucks flying IS flags gather, as a *nasheed* (hymnlike musical prayer) begins. The colonnades of the ancient ruins of Palmyra, a two-thousand-year-old UNESCO World Heritage Center that served as the backdrop for *Indiana Jones and the Last Crusade*, are draped with the distinctive black-and-white flag. The twenty-five soldiers march onto the stage and fall to their knees, awaiting execution. The camera pans across the packed coliseum, whose audience includes adults and very young children.

In the next shot, twenty-five children march out as the *nasheed* commences again. IS calls these children Ashbal al-Khilafa, or Cubs of the Caliphate. The children sport matching uniforms, and some even smile for the camera. The condemned men (alternately referred to as either *murtadd*, *nusayriya*, or *kaffir*[1]), no longer blindfolded, look on with panic. After an announcer reads Qur'anic passages that describe both mercy and retribution, the camera pans across the faces of the children and those of the men condemned to die—such that the viewer can see the horror in the condemned men's eyes and the hollow stares of the youth. The Syrian soldiers understand precisely the fate that awaits them. The children, looking over their right shoulders (for a signal), raise their handguns in unison, and then each child shoots a Syrian soldier in the head. The scene is looped several times, lest anyone doubt that the children actually pulled the trigger on command. The final scene shows the aftermath: bodies with limbs akimbo, blood seeping into the sand.[2]

IS (also known as the Islamic State in Syria and Iraq, the Islamic State in Iraq, and the Levant, or Daesh, the Arabic acronym) uses children in ways that are markedly different from those of other terrorist groups and recruits them in ways different from how African child soldiers were recruited in the past. In previous conflicts, children were in the background, aiding behind the scenes or sneaking through enemy lines. In Iraq, children aided the insurgents fighting American soldiers and even operated on the front lines, though only occasionally and only in a handful of cities. But the trend of militarized youth grew during the Iraqi insurgency, with children playing a variety of roles in the battle of Fallujah, from snipers to armed fighters.[3] In January 2007, children played key roles in the kidnapping of Sunni merchants from Sinak Market in Baghdad, by engaging Iraqi police firing automatic weapons and forcing them to flee.[4]

According to the United States Marine Corps, "U.S. forces faced child soldiers in the past (Germany, Vietnam, Somalia, and Afghanistan), [and] it is inevitable that they will face them again in the future."[5] But in Palmyra, the victimized soldiers were not foreign "occupiers" and the children were not targeting US troops. These were children who had been groomed and brainwashed to carry out the most egregious acts of violence against their own countrymen.

Many of us have become accustomed to reports of child suicide bombers in places such as Afghanistan, Iraq, Pakistan, and Nigeria. According to the research we have conducted for this book, the median age of suicide bombers overall has been declining steadily, especially with the increased use of child bombers by IS and its affiliated groups (for example, Boko Haram). More children are participating in hostilities, and in more nefarious ways.[6] In the 1990s, child studies researchers observed that "more children and youth are bearing arms in internal armed conflict and violent strife than ever before."[7] In their analysis of child soldiers, Vera Achvarina and Simon Reich argued that this trend challenged the claim that international norms had positively influenced the rules of war.[8] An April 2010 news report by the journalist Erik Stakelbeck prophesized a future worsening of the problem of children not just as child soldiers but in terrorist organizations: "Islamic terrorists are always looking for new ways to escape detection and carry out their attacks. One of their latest ideas is using children as suicide bombers."[9] Our study of the Islamic State's Cubs of the Caliphate certainly dispels the myth that war is being fought more civilly; the chapters that follow will demonstrate how the problem is getting worse and metastasizing from one conflict and region to the next.

While the use of child soldiers in Africa is well documented and organizations such as the Liberation Tigers of Tamil Eelam (LTTE) have garnered international condemnation for recruiting children,[10] misconceptions persist about how children become involved in terrorist group violence or are recruited as front-line activists. The questions we answer in this book focus on the extent to which children are recruited and used differently from adults in terrorist groups. Over the past three years, the world has watched in horror as Syrian and Iraqi children, once just passive observers of extreme violence, have become fully committed activists personally involved in hostilities. These Cubs of the Caliphate have gone from viewing videos of beheadings, to leading prisoners onto a stage for execution, to passing out the knives used for execution, to carrying out the executions or beheading themselves (as was the case in Palmyra).[11] And since January 2015 they have acted as suicide bombers and *inghemasi*—commandos who fight and die alongside adults in high-risk missions in which their deaths are premeditated.

This book explores the extent of children's involvement in terrorist groups and examines their transition from victims to perpetrators, while demonstrating the interchangeability of these roles. It approaches children's involvement in terrorism from two complementary perspectives, one macro and the other micro. The macro lens examines under what circumstances and why terrorist organizations recruit children. This approach complements theories of international relations and civil war. For example, are children recruited because of a loss of manpower when adults are killed in battle, or during periods when adults cannot be mobilized? Alternatively, do children possess unique skills that adults might lack; that is, can they bring some new or innovative comparative advantages to the terrorist group, such as being able to gain access to sensitive or civilian targets that adults would fail to access? To this extent, this book borrows a framework from economics to determine whether children are a "complementary" or a "substitute" good for terrorist groups.[12]

We know little about the recruitment of children into terrorist organizations. Studies of child soldiers have traditionally approached the issue from a child rights framework, focusing on estimating the numbers of children involved, recounting individual experiences and stories, describing the legal instruments against their use, and evaluating disarmament, demobilization, and reintegration (DDR) programs.[13] According to the American University anthropologist Susan Shepler, we know more about the demobilization, rehabilitation, and reintegration of child soldiers than about why militants or governments use children in the first place.[14]

Is it conceivable that organizations might prefer to mobilize children because they are cheaper, more malleable, or easier to control than adults? This was certainly the case in Mozambique with the resistance group RENAMO (Mozambican National Resistance Movement), who evidence suggests preferred children to adults. One deserter conceded, "RENAMO does not use many adults to fight because they are not good fighters. Kids have more stamina, are better at surviving in the bush, do not complain, and follow directions."[15] From the 1980s on, RENAMO recruited children as young as six, seven, and eight years old, who were literally "programmed" to feel no fear or revulsion for the massacres and, according to Alex Vines, thereby "carry out these attacks with greater enthusiasm and brutality than adults would."[16] This preference for very young recruits was not limited to Mozambique. A senior officer in Chad's army explained, "Child soldiers are *ideal* because they don't complain, they don't expect to be paid, and if you tell them to kill, they kill." (emphasis added)[17] The same was true for the fifty-two-year civil war in Colombia.

We are witnessing something comparable in Syria and Iraq, where a generation of children has been entirely desensitized to extreme violence. According to a report by the international nongovernmental organization (NGO) Save the Children, children display signs of "toxic stress." The 2017 report explains that children have witnessed family members killed in front of them, dead bodies and blood in the streets, and bombs destroying their homes.[18] Joby Warrick summarizes the conflict as consistently pushing the boundaries of horror, and notes that children are not safe from being targeted:

> As ISIS dispatched suicide bombers into sports arenas and community soccer games as well as mosques, cafes, and markets even Iraqis inured to bloodshed expressed shock when an ISIS recruit drove an explosives laden truck into an elementary school playground in Nineveh Province in October 2013, killing thirteen children who were [playing] outside for recess.[19]

Other children shared stories about family members shot by snipers, blown up by landmines, or hit by explosives as they fled.[20] "The children are so deeply scarred by memories of extreme violence they are living in constant fear for their lives, unable to show emotions, and suffering from vivid 'waking nightmares.'"[21]

In conjunction with examining *why* terrorist groups recruit children, this book also examines the microlevel processes: *how* are children recruited and socialized into violence? Are children always coerced to participate, through institutional mechanisms (youth wings, summer camps, exposure to media aimed specifically at them) that facilitate their entry into violence and terrorism? Are the ways in which children are mobilized into a terrorist organization different from the ways in which adults are recruited, and if so, what distinguishes this process from the (stereotypically) coerced recruitment of child soldiers? This book focuses on the social ecologies of children's lives: parents, families, peer groups, religious leaders, and other community-based institutions, and how structural conditions pressure children to participate in hostilities. We also examine the varying incentives related to environmental (structural) conditions that might make involvement more or less attractive to children and their families.

The presence of children on the battlefield has additional unintentional consequences for the civilian population and the organization of power structures in a society. Using children for militant activities challenges existing age hierarchies and reflects the breakdown of the family unit.[22] In prisons, IS allegedly uses children to select who lives and who dies, at the same time empowering the children (who are made to feel that they have the power over life and death) and further humiliating and emasculating the adults, whose fates are decided by eleven- and twelve-year-olds.

Children's recruitment differs from that of adults in the degree to which they consent. Children may not have the same option to refuse mobilization into a terrorist organization as an adult does. In fact, actual accounts of children's recruitment by terrorist groups vary along a spectrum between co-optation and coercion. In some cases, like many involving child soldiers, children are forcibly taken from parents against their will, while in other instances they gravitate toward involvement over time, with the consent or even encouragement of their parents. Jamie Dettmer summarizes this spectrum:

> Since 2014, youngsters who joined ISIS were often coerced to do so in different ways, ranging from being cajoled by parents, to kidnappings from orphanages. Some parents were eager for at least one of their children to enlist because of the monthly payments ISIS paid the families of cubs; but others did so because they agreed with the terror group's ideology.[23]

We must consider that varying degrees of coercion play a role in how and why children become involved in terrorism and that each case might include a mix of inducements, luring, and coercion. Children may be forced or duped. The United Nations ruling regarding the international rights of the child (the United Nations Convention on the Rights of the Child [CRC]) is the most widely ratified treaty in history, with 196 states having endorsed it, and its contents help to delineate child soldier motivation. By 2017 only one country, the United States, had failed to ratify the convention.[24] The CRC sets out the civil, political, economic, social, health, and cultural rights of children but neglects to take into account the variety of ways in which children are mobilized.

Shepler highlights the fact that in Sierra Leone, there existed "historical continuities and cultural practices and meanings surrounding children and youth that make the participation in conflict . . . legible."[25] Understandably, there are different degrees of coercion involved in "forcing" an eight-year-old Nigerian girl to blow up a chicken market in Maiduguri and motivating a seventeen-and-a-half-year-old to behead an enemy of IS.

Once the children become part of a terrorist movement, they are groomed and exploited to victimize others. In turn, they are victimized and traumatized by their experiences as participants. Many children choose to remain in a terrorist or militant movement well after they reach adulthood. To understand the microprocesses at work, we examine the roles of parents, teachers, religious authorities, and coaches to ascertain how children become involved in the first place. Social ecologies and environment matter, as do the structural conditions of poverty, military occupation, and "cultures of martyrdom" constructed for the specific purpose of making involvement desirable.

Children may be exposed to cultures of martyrdom from an early age to normalize the idea of self-sacrifice; at the same time, parents are groomed to willingly hand over their children to the movement or provide the group unfettered access to the community's youth. Child soldiers by contrast have tended to be orphans—the deliberate destruction of the family unit is a key part of the recruitment process. Such a disruption of family cohesion is found only in cases where families are deliberately segregated from the terrorist operative physically and psychologically. In some cases, parents facilitate and/or encourage their children's involvement in militant activities. In order to fully understand how adults get children involved in what could certainly be considered deviant behavior, this book draws from the literature on child protection and studies of sexual exploitation.

The microprocesses at work also highlight which children might be most at risk; for example, one hypothesis suggests that groups target low-income middle children (not the oldest or youngest child) who have a history of behavioral problems. Such a model of children's recruitment into violent extremism may illuminate choke points in the process where intervention to prevent child mobilization is possible.

The issue of demobilization is especially salient given the increasing number of children involved in violent extremist organizations and the possibility that after IS is destroyed in the Middle East, there will be hundreds if not thousands of children who have been traumatized. As the Revolutionary United Front of Sierra Leone did with its policy of "bush wives," IS targeted young girls for recruitment and married them off to foreign fighters from the age of nine onward.[26] Male children as young as eight were given military training in the use of deadly weapons with the full acceptance and consent of their parents, who encouraged their participation through the Cubs of the Caliphate. This involvement is different from that of children we encountered who were involved with the Tehrik Taliban Pakistan (TTP), a.k.a. the Pakistani Taliban, most of whom were kidnapped and forcibly recruited after the terrorists extorted their parents to hand them over in lieu of ransom payments. In Afghanistan and Nigeria, the groups kidnap children outright. In contrast, terrorist groups such as the Provisional IRA, Hamas, and the LTTE follow a different trajectory of mobilization—they have formal youth wings to provide the next generation with the ideology and vernacular of the movement and prepare them to replace the adults (notably the fathers) lost in battle. However, unlike IS and its Cubs of the Caliphate, these youth wings rarely "permitted" the involvement of children until they reached an ideal age and were considered "old enough" to kill, usually around the age of sixteen.

What Constitutes a Child?

The age of majority is a social, religious, cultural, or legal device by which societies acknowledge a child's transition to adulthood. There is no correlation between the traditional age of adulthood (in some societies marked by coming-of-age rituals and religious traditions that occur as young as thirteen) and the Western understanding of what constitutes maturity and adulthood.[27]

In 1924 the League of Nations adopted the Declaration of the Rights of the Child.[28] The 1977 Additional Protocols to the 1949 Geneva Convention prohibited the military use of children under fifteen. In 1978 the UN Commission on Human Rights drafted the CRC. One of the most contentious issues the commission debated was that of what constituted the definition of a child. The United States advocated that the minimum age for military recruitment in hostilities should be fifteen, "in line with existing laws of war."[29] Until 2000 it was legal under international law to recruit children as young as fifteen. According to Jo Becker,

> the final text of the convention (adopted in 1989) combined economic, social, and cultural civil and political rights—one of the first international treaties to do so. . . . It emphasized four key principles [including] prohibiting violence and neglect, sexual and economic exploitation, and capital punishment, and outlined standards for juvenile justice.[30]

In 1991 the Swedish Red Cross organized a conference called "Children of War," in which the participants agreed "that the minimum age for recruitment into armed forces and for participation in conflict should be an unconditional 18."[31]

In 1998 the Rome Statute of the International Criminal Court addressed children in conflict, making it a war crime to conscript, enlist, or use children under fifteen in hostilities.[32] In 2000 the UN General Assembly adopted two optional protocols to the CRC, raising the minimum age for conscription or direct participation in armed conflict from fifteen to eighteen and prohibiting the recruitment of anyone under eighteen by nonstate armed groups.

As a result, child soldiers are defined as anyone under eighteen who is part of any regular or irregular armed force. These include youth who have been forcibly recruited as well as those who might have joined voluntarily. This definition encompasses all child or adolescent participants regardless of function, including cooks, porters, messengers, and girls recruited as "bush wives" or in other supporting roles. Rules of customary international humanitarian law provide that "children must not be recruited into armed forces or armed groups" and that "children must not be allowed to take part in hostilities" in either international armed conflicts or civil wars.[33]

Article 77(2) of the Additional Protocols I states that "the parties to the conflict shall take all feasible measures in order that children who have not attained the age of 15 do not take part in hostilities and, in particular, shall refrain from recruiting them into their armed forces."[34] Additional Protocol II, article 43(3)(c), adds that "children who have not attained the age of fifteen years shall neither be recruited in the armed forces or groups nor allowed to take part in hostilities."[35]

The United Nations and other international and nongovernmental organizations have determined that eighteen is the legal age for military involvement. This cannot be overstated, partly because of the universality of the age designation but also because it reflects a Western bias as to what constitutes a child. In other cultures, "child" and "teenager" are not uniform categories, and the life conditions for youth in these cultures are far from identical to those in the West. For example, Ali Akhbar Mahdi makes the point that the concept of the teen has no equivalent in Middle Eastern languages, "nor the conceptual autonomy in the theological, philosophical, and cultural domains of the society."[36] Instead, many cultures refer to prepuberty, pre-youth, or pre-adult, each with different age referents. In most Islamic contexts, childhood is understood simply as a period of time characterized by the absence of reason ('aql).

Although individuals under eighteen might not be mature enough to understand the consequences of their actions, this preset designation is problematic when compared to international, state, traditional, or religious laws, which may not conform to this definition of "adult." In some countries, youth participate in the political process by voting at sixteen (Brazil, Cuba, Iran, and Nicaragua) or volunteer to join the armed forces, with parental permission, at sixteen (Israel, Norway, the US, and the UK). Seven countries enforce compulsory military service for youth below the age of eighteen, including Afghanistan, Iran, the Lao People's Democratic Republic, Mexico, Namibia, Nicaragua, and South Africa.[37]

At some level, a legal age of responsibility may be intended to differentiate innocent youth from responsible adults. Shepler observed that child soldiering is worse than adult soldiering because of our beliefs about childhood, beliefs built on a modern ideology that sees children as innocent and separates childhood as a special time.[38] But this notion of the child as innocent has been shown to be illusory. The child psychologist Kate Douglas notes that the "assumption of innocence" has led to the development of a binary model in which children are innocent and adults are evil.[39] Nevertheless, as Chris Jenks writes, the fact that "children are [equally] capable of violence, of rape, muggings, and even murder, is an idea that clearly falls outside traditional formulations of childhood . . . [which] is supposed to be the age of innocence, so how could ten-year-olds turn into killers?"[40]

This debate engenders two basic questions: what constitutes a child, and to what extent are children responsible for their own actions? Answering them is anything but simple. Analyses of child militancy are complicated by the fact that different cultures have varied interpretations of what constitutes adulthood. Muddying the waters further, the actual age of children may not be known in some contexts. While children in Western cultures know their age from the time they can speak (and celebrate every birthday), in many countries childhood is an amorphous, undistinguishable mass. In rural areas in Africa, children's births are not always registered with the magistrate. In Guatemala, many of the rural poor lack identity cards because their births were not formally registered, or the registry was destroyed during the fighting, or because in some places, identity cards are not issued until one turns eighteen.[41] Such unregistered and undocumented children disappear more easily during times of conflict, are harder to account for, and tend to be at greater risk of military recruitment.[42] Their status is also unclear under international law, which fails to account for circumstances in which an individual might not know whether he or she is sixteen, seventeen, or eighteen years old.[43]

The division of youth categories that was codified into English common law involved three stages: infancy, childhood, and adolescence. Betsy Perabo, drawing from political theory, notes that

> [Thomas] Aquinas divided the three stages differently; he was more interested in an individual's ability to understand situations and make rational choices. Infancy, through age 7, was "when a person neither understands by himself nor is able to learn from another"; childhood, through age 14, [was] when "when a man can learn from another but

is incapable by himself of consideration and understanding"; and adolescence, the third seven years, [was] "when a man is both able to learn
from another and to consider by himself.[44]

The political scientists Robert Tynes and Bryan Early recommended establishing sixteen as the legal age for military mobilization in their large-N study
of insurgent groups.[45] The legal principles of *doli incapax*—the (in)capability of
children to commit crimes[46]—have determined the age of criminal responsibility
to be ten. Those below that age cannot appreciate the nature or wrongfulness of
their actions.[47] Under US law, children and youth are routinely held responsible
for their actions; for example, twelve- and thirteen-year-olds are occasionally
tried as adults. The average age across the United States of minor defendants
treated by the courts as adults is fifteen.[48] Although the criminal age of responsibility varies from state to state, we acknowledge that below a certain age, a
child cannot decide to voluntarily engage in violence, terrorist or otherwise. So
depending on the source or the organization, the age of "what constitutes a child"
changes radically.

Rather than determining maturity or age of responsibility chronologically,
many cultures use a different metric altogether, such as physiological indicators
that reflect the transition from child to adult. In some cultures, facial hair, body
hair, or coming-of-age traditions determine when a person reaches adulthood.
The ability to grow a beard is a sign of maturity in Afghan/Pashtun culture, as is
the appearance of body hair in Arab culture. Western biases do not always apply
to non-Western contexts; to quote the anthropologist Franz Boas, "Civilization is
not something absolute, but . . . is relative, and . . . our ideas and conceptions are
true only so far as our civilization goes."[49]

The average age for child soldiers is around twelve, but children as young
as five have been involved in some civil wars, such as that in Uganda.[50] Colombian guerrillas and paramilitaries recruited children as young as eight.[51] For the
purposes of this book, we have considered age-range categories based on developmental child psychology, whereby developmentally, sixteen to twenty-two is
considered to be the stage of early adulthood. Both the Iranian Penal Code and
the Iranian Civil Code agree that a child is defined as a girl under the age of nine
and a boy under the age of fifteen.[52]

Because the UN's additional protocols originally designated age fifteen in their
definition of child soldiers and article 38 of the CRC originally designated fifteen
as its cutoff point as well, it was appropriate for the purposes of this book to make
the distinction between children fifteen and under and those sixteen and older.[53]
This is validated by the cultural contexts of the research. According to Islamic
tradition, males are regarded as adults by the age of fifteen once they achieve

bolooq (maturity) and are *mokallaf*—responsible for performing their religious duties as adults.[54] In Islamic jurisprudence (*fiqh*), fifteen is further recognized as an important age of personal responsibility. Under the strict codes of gender segregation, a woman may not leave her home unless she is accompanied by a relative to act as a chaperone (*mahram*) to protect her and the family's honor. In determining the age at which someone can take on this important responsibility, Islamic scholars deemed fifteen to be appropriate. Thus, a fifteen-year-old can be responsible for the life and well-being of his sister or mother, thereby safeguarding the family honor. The implication is that a male of that age is old enough to distinguish right from wrong and make important decisions that have significant ramifications. Finally, IS itself designates fifteen as a special age; recruiters routinely call into crowds of children, "Who here is fifteen? You should be fighting the enemy." Thus fifteen is a culturally sensitive age for differentiating children from young adults, and this book distinguishes the actions of a ten-year-old from those of someone who is seventeen as inherently different with regard to motivation and the ability to comprehend one's actions.

The data on IS challenges the conventional wisdom that children are more likely to attack civilians and soft targets. The research for this book shows that children are not necessarily employed separately in dedicated children's units—on the contrary, they tend to be paired alongside adults in commando (*inghemasi*) units and attack the same targets as adults. Whereas children forced to be bombers for Boko Haram (the youngest of whom was seven years old) have been primarily directed against soft targets, civilians, and marketplaces, IS child martyrs attack hard (military) targets, other militias, and the police 61 percent of the time. In other words, the ways in which IS operationalizes its child bombers is decidedly different than those of other groups—even the ones that utilize young children and groups with whom they are formally affiliated (such as Boko Haram).[55]

What is most surprising is that unlike child soldiers, children involved in terrorist organizations are often enthusiastic participants, regardless of whether or not there are clear signs of coercion in their recruitment. Upon leaving, some even have positive recollections of their experiences, making reintegration all the more challenging.[56]

In chapter 4, we explore the nuances of coercion and how family members can encourage or coerce a child to join a terrorist movement. This is more common in cases where children live with their extended families, such as uncles and aunts, rather than with their biological parents. In conflict areas in which the terrorists impose a "tax" on the population that requires each family to provide at least one member as a conscript for the cause (a terrorist *levée en masse*), families faced with this difficult choice will more likely sacrifice nieces or nephews and save their own children. In these cases, nieces and nephews do not seek to participate but are forced into the movement against their will. There are numerous documented cases among the Tamils during the civil war in Sri Lanka (1987–2009), which generated many orphans who went to live with their extended families. As the Tigers demanded that every family provide at minimum one recruit for the LTTE, these children were often "given" to the group. After an initial period of transition, many such children acclimatize, becoming enthusiastic supporters of the terrorist organization and its ideology.[57] Jo Becker details one such case, wherein Aruna, a fifteen-year-old Tamil girl, received a written request and subsequently a follow-up visit in which the LTTE informed her family that "each house has to turn over one child. If you don't agree, we will take a child anyway."[58]

This type of coercion mirrors the experience of child soldiers, who have no choice but to join the militant group and over time may eventually become enthusiastic and ardent supporters of the cause. Our field research in the Swat Valley in Pakistan among children aged seven to sixteen who were captured by the TTP found that in 45 percent of the cases, the children had been given to the terrorist organization in lieu of extortion payments when the families could not pay the five-thousand-lek fee (about $745) demanded of them. However, more than 41 percent of the children alleged that joining the TTP was either their idea or a decision made in conjunction with a family member who was already a follower.[59] According to the children's rehabilitation organization Sabaoon,

> a significant number of the inductees became involved in the movements through friends or relatives who persuaded them to comply, although they personally did not have much interest in politics of any kind. These factors remain stimuli for re-engagement, post reintegration. At Sabaoon, factors such as the personal relationships, social networks and lack of civic awareness (that contributed to child's motivation, recruitment and radicalization) are impediments to reintegration (approximately 20%) of the [Sabaoon] population.[60]

The demographics of child soldiers follow an established template. According to the Coalition to Stop the Use of Child Soldiers, most come from children "separated from their families or with disrupted family backgrounds (orphans, unaccompanied children, children from single-parent families, or from families headed by children); economically and socially deprived children (poor, rural and urban, and those without access to education, vocational training, or a reasonable standard of living); other marginalized groups (e.g. street children, certain minorities, refugees and the internally displaced); children from the conflict zones themselves."[61] In contrast, children involved in terrorist groups vary widely, from impoverished and uneducated children in Pakistan to well-educated middle-class Westerners in IS and everything in between. In chapter 3, we discuss the correlation between education and violent extremism.

Children in Battle

In 1996, with the publication of the United Nations report *Impact of Armed Conflict on Children*, the child soldier problem became widely appreciated as a global humanitarian crisis. Known as the Machel Report, it demonstrated that

> children associated with armed forces or armed groups are exposed to tremendous violence—often forced both to witness and commit violence, while themselves being abused, exploited, injured or even killed as a result. Their condition deprives them of their rights, often with severe physical and emotional consequences.[62]

The most common cited estimate is that three hundred thousand boys and girls under the age of eighteen are under arms as "soldiers but also as spies, informants, couriers, and sex-slaves in the 30-plus conflicts around the globe; serving as combatants in 75 percent of the world's conflicts."[63] In 80 percent of the conflicts, we find child fighters under fifteen, and in 18 percent, fighters under twelve. It is no surprise, therefore, that children are increasingly involved in terrorism.[64] In many cases, they may be considered expendable or easy to replace, and are used as decoys or cannon fodder so that a more seasoned fighting force can exploit their efforts.

It is important to note that issues of data collection are complicated when studying this phenomenon. As Barry Ames has observed, much of the literature on children and conflict takes an advocacy position, and most of the statistics (including the oft-cited figure of three hundred thousand children under arms) cannot be accurately verified.[65] While we cannot authenticate the number or percentages of children involved in IS as cited by NGO and UN sources,[66] the process of involvement described by our model holds true regardless. Nevertheless, counting children who are eulogized as martyrs by terrorist groups such as IS—in other words, not how many were recruited but how many have been killed—our research demonstrates that the numbers are even greater than previously reported by official sources by a factor of five or even ten times.[67]

According to medieval Islamic jurists, the defensive jihad (unlike the offensive version of jihad practiced during periods of expansion) requires every member of the "Community of Believers" (Umma) to participate in defending the community against nonbelievers. During the defensive jihad, it becomes the personal obligation—*fard 'ayn*, or "individual duty"—of every Muslim to participate, versus the more general duty for all Muslims (*fard kifaya*).

Abdullah Azzam, the original ideologue for al-Qaeda, issued a fatwa entitled *Defense of the Muslim Lands, the First Obligation after Faith*, in which he explained the obligation for everyone to participate in jihad. In this sense, the participation of all groups in society, including women and children, is required to demonstrate the urgency of the situation.[68]

> Jihad under this condition (defensive) becomes *Fard 'Ayn* (an individual and personal religious obligation) upon all the Muslims of the land, which the *Kuffar* (infidels) have attacked and upon the Muslims close by, *where the children will march forth without the permission of the parents* [emphasis added], the wife without the permission of her husband and the debtor without the permission of the creditor. And, if the Muslims of this land cannot expel the *Kuffar* because of lack of forces, because they slacken, are indolent or simply do not act, then the *Fard 'Ayn* obligation spreads . . . [and] continues until it becomes *Fard 'Ayn* (a personal religious obligation) upon the whole world.[69]

Social Networks and Recruitment

Women often become involved in terrorist networks as a result of family ties (usually along with their husbands or brothers or fathers).[70] Beyond IS, the majority of children in terrorist groups are not recruited by members of their immediate family. It should be noted that terrorist leaders across a variety of regions and cultures tend to shield their own children from involvement, instead focusing recruitment on young people to whom they are not related.

According to the Kuwaiti newspaper *Al-Anba'a*, Osama bin Laden's last wish was that his children not become involved in al-Qaeda. Bin Laden's will's "most striking feature," the newspaper noted, "is that he . . . urges his children not to join al-Qaeda or go to 'the front,' citing the example of the seventh-century Muslim caliph Omar Bin Khattab to his son Abdullah."[71] Yet Osama's son Hamza bin Laden, after years of being sheltered from the group, has become the poster child for the new al-Qaeda. In a video released on the sixth anniversary of bin Laden's assassination, Hamza provided the voice-over for a propaganda video entreating supporters to "follow in the footsteps of martyrdom-seekers before you and pick off from where they left, for this will help you."[72] The younger bin Laden, according to *Newsweek*, advised followers to

> target nonbelievers, Jewish people, Americans, Russians and NATO members. He says to do reconnaissance, avoid arousing suspicion and be self-assured, adding that extremists should convey their messages clearly during their attacks so the media can spread it.[73]

Israeli security forces have insisted that children and teenagers between the ages of eleven and eighteen have carried out numerous suicide and other terrorist attacks. The bombers are often from the same communities, same neighborhoods, or same *shilla* (kinship or client network) group. As early as 1996, Palestinian soccer players were recruited into militant activities via their coaches. Coaches, teachers, and religious leaders are all sources of community leadership who play an influential role in how violence is perceived, valued, and "marketed" to children. The children seek support and validation from participation in these violent activities. The Palestinian Authority's Ministries of Sports and Education name tournaments after Palestinian "martyrs," including bombers from (rival) groups such as Hamas and the Palestinian Islamic Jihad.[74] What happens is that one area or even one neighborhood might generate a disproportionate number of bombers, often recruited from among groups of friends or neighbors who know each other. The Palestinian city of Nablus alone has generated half of all the teenage bombers from Palestine.[75] Hamas's suicide bombing campaign of 2003–4 involved teammates from the Masjad al-Jihad soccer team. Most of the boys originated from the same neighborhood and resided within a few hundred meters of each other, and all of them belonged to the same clan (*hamula*), the al-Qawasmeh, one of the most powerful families in Hebron. The clan's leader, Abdullah al-Qawasmeh, sent eight members of the same soccer team on suicide, shooting, and bombing operations during a two-year period from 2003 to 2004, although attacks by this group continued until 2008.[76] According to an article in *Ha'aretz*, some of the terrorists who played on the Jihad Mosque team also "studied together at the Palestine Polytechnic College, about 20 of whose students carried out suicide bombings in the al-Aqsa Intifada. Fuad al-Qawasmeh's uncle ran the education department in Hebron, and his father was a moneychanger who traveled between the villages of the Hebron Hills. Eight members of the family carried out terror attacks."[77]

According to Israeli government sources, terrorist groups exploit children for "their innocent look as children and teenagers, which do not arouse suspicion and enables them to blend into populated areas. In addition, these children and teenagers, who have not yet reached adulthood, might be more susceptible to the terrorist organizations' influence and the recruitment of suicide bombers."[78] In this case, children are not used as substitute goods (i.e., as substitutes to cover the loss of adults), but as complementary goods able to accomplish something adults could not—look innocent and not arouse the same amount of suspicion. The Taliban prized child operatives; one Pakistani fighter explained, "Children are innocent, so they are the best tools against dark forces."[79]

The Palestinian Authority officially refutes the idea that it mobilizes and exploits children militarily, claiming that it does not conscript people under the age of eighteen. Militant groups say that forcing children to become involved in such activities is prohibited, that the organizations regard this as an uncrossable "red line" and that it is "absolutely prohibited,"[80] yet the *Child Soldiers Global Report* notes that Palestinian militant groups have done so.[81] Furthermore, teenage leaders of the al-Aqsa Martyrs Brigade in Tulkarm featured in the documentary film *Making of a Martyr* fully support having twelve- and thirteen-year-olds (and those even younger) wear suicide belts and become martyrs as long as they have "conviction."[82] In 2002 the Palestinian Hamas leader Salah Shehade explained that children had to be trained prior to perpetrating terrorist attacks and recruited into a special branch within the organization's military apparatus in order to instill jihadi culture and teach them to distinguish right from wrong. Such training is one of the main elements in convincing parents to send their children to perpetrate terrorist attacks.[83] Palestinians under the age of eighteen have conducted more than thirty suicide bombings since the 2000 al-Aqsa Intifada (17 percent of the total).

A similar dynamic is evident in groups in Syria and Iraq. The Islamic State's former spokesperson, Muhammad al-Adnani (killed in September 2016), claimed that IS did not mobilize anyone under the age of sixteen, yet in documentaries produced by Vice News, children as young as nine are seen being trained to use automatic weapons, and on social media, children as young as seven pose with severed heads.[84] According to UNICEF, children as young as four years old were sent to training camps "where they would learn to fight, kill, and die for the Islamic State."[85] Furthermore, IS's own telegram channels (encrypted online chat rooms) promote child martyrs, some as young as nine.[86]

Chapters 7 and 8 explore what might happen to these children and how the experiences of child soldiers can help suggest avenues for rehabilitation and reintegration.

Push and Pull Factors Explaining Involvement

To understand why adults as well as children become involved in terrorism, one needs to first understand the push and the pull factors. The structural conditions that facilitate involvement in terrorism—poverty, occupation, and grievances—are push factors. But these conditions exist for all of the members of a specific community, and thus are necessary though insufficient preconditions to explain involvement—since, as John Horgan has written elsewhere, very few people actually become involved in terrorist activity. For Horgan, to understand this selection effect one must likewise consider the specific pull factors, the things that make involvement appear personally attractive to the individual.[87]

Seeking the respect of the community and proving their dedication to a particular cause are two explanations for how and why children are drawn to violence. By engaging in militancy they demonstrate that they are just as dedicated and committed to the cause as the adults in their community. In choosing death over life, the children might think they will have a significant impact, but as children, they might not yet have a fully developed sense of mortality. In Palestine, streets and parks are named after suicide bombers and novels are written about their exploits.[88] The walls of community centers are decorated with images of martyrs, not sports or film stars. Children do not grow up wanting to "be like Mike"—instead, they want to become like the famous jihadis after whom streets and parks are named and whose images line the walls.[89]

In chapter 5 we explore the ways in which terrorist organizations deliberately construct cultures of martyrdom in their societies. Fame and notoriety are powerful pull factors for vulnerable youth. Both tap into the desire to do something heroic with one's life—especially if the life one leads is a source of pain and constant fear. Fame may also be a powerful incentive to join a terrorist movement and helps explain the allure of becoming a suicide bomber. This is equally true for young men as it is for women. The daily realities of conflict can enhance the lure of gaining the respect of one's peers and instill a sense of greater purpose, a higher calling.[90]

There is controversy surrounding children's involvement in terrorism. Some of the conventional wisdom is not borne out by empirical investigation. Pundits have argued, for example, that "children who grow up to be Islamic terrorists are products of a misogynist fundamentalist system that segregates the family into two separate areas. . . . The children are brought up [in an environment in] which the father rarely visits."[91] This argument is based on the overly simplistic assumption that segregation of the sexes automatically generates violent children.[92] Such a broad brush fails to appreciate how a culture of martyrdom is deliberately constructed and manipulated to create a generation that subscribes to the belief that death will yield a better and worthier outcome than life.

During their recruitment into the Pakistani Taliban, Pakistani children were assigned new names (aliases) in order to develop new personalities aimed at detaching them from their past lives, including their family members, and making them a part of a greater cause. Psychologists at Sabaoon, a rehabilitation facility for child militants who were forcibly recruited by the TTP, considered this a "metaphoric murder," as the child's personality was removed or extinguished (a form of deindividualization) to make way for the new identity. This loss of self-identity in a group setting leads to conformity, apathy, and obedience to authority.[93]

Beyond inveterate poverty and few educational opportunities, the absence of a strong male figure in the family and chronic insecurity (both physical and economic) may likewise make children vulnerable to recruitment. These are some of the same conditions that facilitate the entry of child soldiers into militias and warring criminal gangs, but while the environmental conditions across all types of children involved in violence look similar, the actual processes by which children become involved differ from those by which adults do, and may even differ from one terrorist group to the next.[94] The Quaker Office at the United Nations insists, however, that "children do not go to war for economic gain or to advance their careers. They are moved by patriotism to defend their country; by their religious faith to seek martyrdom in war [or are] stirred by the idea of freedom to join the national liberation movements."[95]

Many of the countries and regions where child soldiers are present have been blighted by years of social strife and civil war. In Colombia's fifty-two-year civil war, children constituted one-quarter of the combatants in the guerrilla forces or paramilitaries. According to Jo Becker,

> the guerillas and paramilitaries recruited children as young as 8 to carry supplies or information, act as early warning guards, or carry explosives. By the time they were 13 most child soldiers were trained in the use of automatic weapons, mortars, grenades, and explosives. Children participated in battles and were often expected to torture or execute captured enemies.[96]

During civil war, governments collapse, their economies are ruined, they are unable to enforce law and order or provide basic services, and the countries are beset by poverty, disease, and broken families. There are no rules of engagement in these situations.[97]

Civil wars also cause disruption in the family, primarily by taking the men away from the family to fight. These male figures of authority (the traditional role model or father figure) are replaced by coaches, religious leaders, and community leaders, as well as by peer groups. The absence of male authority also means that young boys become responsible for providing for and protecting the women of the family at a much earlier age. They learn to use a gun at the age of six or seven, and by the time they are fourteen or fifteen, they go off to join the fight themselves. Children are also under severe peer pressure to sign up, to belong to something more organized than the streets, for a chance to attain some kind of glory or redeem their honor.

Peter Singer's assertion that using children "has been a way for even the weakest and most unpopular organizations to generate significant amounts of force with almost no investment" appears to be correct.[98] In Sri Lanka, the LTTE stepped up its use of young teenage operatives after it suffered a loss of manpower or high casualties. The baby tigers (*bakuts*) in Sri Lanka were established in 1984 after regular units suffered significant casualties during the nineteen-year civil war. According to the South Asia Terrorism Portal,

> after 1987 the LTTE integrated children with other units to offset heavy losses in combat. A study by a UK-based Sri Lankan researcher Dushy Ranatunge revealed that at least 60 per cent of the dead LTTE fighters were under 18 and were mostly girls and boys aged 10–16.[99]

In contrast to some terrorist organizations that recruit children and groom them over an extended period of time, groups that lack legitimacy or popularity will resort to trickery or use children so young that they are incapable of comprehending their actions. The use of children in Afghanistan and Pakistan is a reflection of the Taliban's weakness, especially as they often deceive the young recruits by not telling them that they have "volunteered" for a suicide mission.[100] Iraqi Defense Ministry spokesman Mohammed al-Askari said that al-Qaeda in Iraq's exploitation of children was a "sign of desperation" and added that "using children is disgusting."[101] Robert Tynes and Bryan Early argue that rebels are much more likely than governments to exploit children as combatants. They point out that within Pakistan, training camps set up by the Taliban taught "boys as young as five to be soldiers, human shields, and suicide bombers. Yet the Pakistani military abstained from employing child soldiers."[102]

In Afghanistan in May 2006, the Taliban tried to dupe a six-year-old boy, Juma Gul, into becoming a suicide bomber. They placed an improvised explosive device on him to wear, telling him it would "shower flowers and food when he pushed the plunger." They told him that as soon as he saw a group of American soldiers, he should "throw [his] body at them."[103] In Pakistan, according to our sources there, if the commanders grow tired of a boy they have been physically abusing, they will "volunteer" him for a suicide mission.[104] In Iraq, the predecessor to IS, al-Qaeda in Iraq, conscripted girls as young as thirteen and fourteen when recruitment for the group lagged in the face of the Arab Awakening. Thomas Ricks reports that when al-Qaeda in Iraq became aware that coalition soldiers at Iraqi checkpoints had been instructed to permit cars with children to pass through without inspection, the group began placing children in cars to get through checkpoints, turning them into unwitting accomplices to car and truck bombings.[105] In all of these instances, the groups were not at the height of their power but on the decline, in the process of losing territory as well as hearts and minds (and the tactic of tricking children certainly did not help remedy this loss). These were acts of desperation.

In September 2011, Reuters documented the kidnapping of dozens of Afghan boys to be trained as Taliban fighters. It appears that as groups become weaker over time and require additional manpower, they will increasingly mobilize children, by force, because they cannot locate willing adults. As the phenomenon spreads, the use of younger and younger operatives is likely to elicit fewer shocked responses; this seems to be the case in Africa, where child soldiers are used by governments and insurgent groups alike. It is crucial to address this problem now, while it is still relatively rare, before "baby bombers" or "terror tots" become routine. Since 2017, as IS has lost most of its territory, it has shifted again to using more and more child bombers in Wilayet Khorasan, its Afghan province.[106]

In 2007, the US and Iraqi militaries released captured videos of masked and armed youngsters being trained in camps for insurgent fighters. The videos showed boys as young as nine wearing balaclava masks and European football jerseys and brandishing pistols, machine guns, and rocket launchers during a series of training exercises.[107]

During the Iran-Iraq War (1980–88), Iran deployed children in "human wave offensives" in which children were utilized as cannon fodder or minesweepers, against Iraqi forces. The Khomeini regime, according to one report in 1984, "coerced legions of defenseless children to their deaths."[108] Local militias and clergy were given quotas of children to recruit, and the parents of children killed in battle were remunerated with money, additional food rations, or an identity card indicating that they were the parents of a martyr.[109] The children wore a plastic key around their necks, allegedly given to them by the ayatollah to symbolize their key to paradise. During the eight-year war with Iraq, more than 33,000 high school students were killed, 2,853 were injured, and 2,433 were taken prisoner. The boys, aged twelve to sixteen, were provided a short indoctrination into the Shiite tradition of martyrdom, and then sent weaponless into battle against Iraqi armored divisions.[110]

Mobilization of the Basij force peaked in December 1986 when some hundred thousand volunteers were sent to the Iraqi front. The disproportionate casualties and wounded among the children reflected their lack of training. Nevertheless, Iran's willingness to sacrifice children in this way struck terror in the hearts of the Iraqi forces facing them and gave the regime a psychological advantage over Iraqi troops. One Iraqi officer who faced the Basij force reported,

> They [the children] chant "Allahu Akbar" and they keep coming, and we keep shooting, sweeping our machine guns around like sickles. My men are eighteen, nineteen, just a few years older than these kids. I've seen them crying, and at times the officers have had to kick them back to their guns. Once we had Iranian kids on bikes cycling towards us, and my men all started laughing, and then these kids started lobbing their hand grenades and we stopped laughing and started shooting.[111]

Over the first three years of its existence (2014–17), IS has consistently featured children in its propaganda, as bombers, suicide bombers, foot soldiers who detonate vehicle-born improvised explosive devices (VBIEDs), and *inghemasi* (commando units composed of mixed adult/child rapid reaction teams). Joby Warrick notes that

> indeed ISIS would frequently boast about its youth camps, offering virtual tours on social media of facilities with names such as "al-Zarqawi Camp." Photographs and videos posted to Twitter showed prepubescent boys in military garb, firing weapons, and practicing maneuvers. Other images depicted young trainees being directed to execute prisoners with gunshots to the head.[112]

IS's systematic use of children is more widespread than previously imagined. There were eighty-nine known cases of children sacrificed for IS between January 2015 and January 2016, more than double the most regularly cited estimate.[113] From January 2016 until May 2017, the number doubled again; our data (December 2015 until December 2017) includes over 350 children or youth who have been eulogized on IS channels. On a month-by-month basis, the rate of young suicide deaths rose during that period, from six in January 2015 to eleven in January 2016 to forty-three in January 2017. The rate of operations involving one or more children is likewise increasing; three times as many children and youth were involved in operations in January 2016 as in January 2015.[114] In December 2016–January 2017, fifty-one children and youth were eulogized by the IS propaganda channels as suicide bombers.[115] By the end of our data collection (December 2017), the number of children had exceeded 350. Since January 2018, IS has continued to employ young children, especially in Wilayet Khorasan.

As terrorists continuously adapt to changing security environments and security targets become more difficult for adults to penetrate, the burden has shifted to children and youth (and very old men, aged sixty-five and older, as well as people with physical disabilities in wheelchairs or missing limbs) as suicide bombers—distorting the concept of usefulness.[116]

Recruitment as a Process

The mobilization of a population for political violence (and the necessary social ecology) requires years of indoctrination by the media, sources of religious authority, schoolteachers, and the larger community. This environment provides a facilitating milieu for mobilization and the resonance of the terrorists' message. From biographies, autobiographies, and interviews with journalists and even prison psychologists, we have extensive data about the recruitment of adults into terrorist groups. According to the journalist Nasra Hassan, for every suicide bomber killed, the terrorist group responsible for the attack is able to recruit a dozen more.[117] Each terror attack brings in new waves of adult volunteers, especially if it is considered "successful" (by the number of casualties) and the organization's propaganda glorifies the attack and the attacker. Some recruits may volunteer by seeking out the organization, or they might be approached by a third party after stating, sometimes quite innocently, that they aspired to become *shahids* (martyrs).

The situation is different with child recruits. The younger the person, the more likely that a third party is also young, and that intermediaries (or what we call in chapter 4 "deviant peers") negotiate between the potential recruit and the organization. Evidence from Israel suggests that a terrorist organization may approach family members of known militants or those who have already died, so they might avenge the death of their relatives. At some point in the process, a meeting might be arranged with a high-ranking official or a noted religious personality in which the recruits are told that they have been chosen for the holy mission to promote their beliefs and be inducted into the prestigious and holy fraternity as *shahids*.[118]

According to the psychologist Ariel Merari, who has interviewed dozens of failed bombers in Israeli jails, the recruitment of Palestinian suicide bombers follows a preset pattern. Senior members of a group identify specific people who have intense patriotic fervor. These individuals are then invited to discuss their love of country and hatred for Israel. Potential recruits are asked to commit to getting training (i.e., to translate their desire for revenge into action). Those admitted for training are separated into small groups of three to five people. These cohort groups may also include young people at various stages of being trained to be operatives and suicide bombers. The younger recruits are mentored by older members. The skills imparted may include making bombs, using disguises (mimicry and deceptive signaling), and selecting targets.[119]

The organizations usually require attacks to be branded in order for them to receive full credit. This development arose when multiple organizations sought to claim operations for which they were not responsible, hoping to bandwagon on the popularity of successful attacks. In the videotapes, the individuals declare themselves to be "living martyrs" for Islam and commit themselves to the love of Allah. In one hand they might hold the Qur'an, in the other, a rifle. They might wear a green or black headband emblazoned with the *shehada* (declaration of faith) "There is no God but Allah and Muhammad is his Prophet" or the name of the group to which they belong. This last-will-and-testament video binds them to the final deed, since it is sent home to the family of the recruit before he or she executes the final plan of attack. Since December 2015, IS has produced a steady stream of "about to die" images, videos, and memes that serve to fully commit the attacker, credit the organization for the operation, and recruit more bombers for the cause.[120]

The step-by-step process of getting the individual mentally prepared for an attack includes having recruits lie in empty graves, so they can see how peaceful their deaths will be, and reminding them that life and especially old age bring sickness, decrepitude, and betrayal.[121] This preparation for death is a crucial part of the process. The aim is to give death new meaning, increase suggestibility, instill tranquility and peace of mind, reduce fear, increase enthusiasm, and mobilize anger and aggression toward the target, while at the same time ensuring that the recruit keeps a clear mind in order to focus on the mission and pay attention to the smallest details.[122]

Not only will the recruits earn a place beside Allah, but their relatives will be entitled to a place in heaven because of their martyrdom. Their martyr photo is emblazoned on posters that will be placed on walls throughout the community the moment they succeed in their mission—so they will become inspirational role models to other would-be bombers. To stifle concerns about the pain from wounds inflicted by exploding nails and other bomb parts, they are told that before the first drop of their blood even touches the ground, they will already be seated at the side of Allah, feeling no pain, but only pleasure. An ultimate incentive for young males is the promise of heavenly bliss with seventy-two doe-eyed *houris*, or virgins, in the next life. The martyrs become heroes (and heroines), role models of self-sacrifice for the next cadre of young bombers.[123]

Young girls may not be promised seventy-two virgins, but they are told that in paradise they will sit by the Prophet's Muhammad's side, be more beautiful than they were in life, and find the perfect husband. Not only do they have the honor of sitting next to the prophet, but seventy of their closest relatives will join them in heaven. Thus, with one act of violence, young women can feel as if they have helped their families in a much more significant fashion than they could have in life.[124] In this setting, martyrdom is perceived as a type of sacrifice and is framed rhetorically as altruistic (through the recruit's willingness to sacrifice the self for the greater good of the community). Cindy Ness has argued that female bombers are illustrative of "the most profound form of selflessness."[125]

In 2001 the BBC aired a report about "Paradise Camps"—summer camps run by the Islamic Jihad in which young Palestinian boys are given military training and shown pictures of suicide bombers. "We are teaching the children that suicide bombing is the only thing that make[s] the Israeli people very frightened. Furthermore, we are teaching them that we have the right to do it," said camp counselor Mohammed el Hattab.[126] Rallies commonly feature children wearing bombers' belts. Fifth and sixth graders study poems commemorating the bombers.[127] According to the Israeli watchdog group Palestinian Media Watch, a summer camp for "young leaders" in Bethlehem was named after the female bomber Dalal Mughrabi:

> The Ministry of Social Affairs in Ramallah opened in Bethlehem the second Shahida (Martyr) Dalal Mughrabi camp. . . . The camp was opened in the headquarters of Light of Generations' youth association in Bethlehem. . . . [The camp] aims at training young leaders in the eastern countryside of Bethlehem . . . including 70 young girls from the Dar Salah village and neighboring villages participated.[128]

Within a few weeks, the Palestine Authority also named a town square in Ramallah after Mughrabi. At the summer camps, children are allegedly encouraged to learn how to role-play attacks and shoot guns, and are given instruction in how to blow up Israeli buses and settlements. After the BBC report aired, Palestinian officials vowed to close the Paradise Camps. Nonetheless, a culture of martyrdom transforms suicide bombers into rock stars, sports heroes, and religious idols rolled into one.

In Pakistan, religious schools deliberately target young women, in part due to the realization that by doing so, the groups will be able to influence an entire family. As young women educate their children, talk to their neighbors, and disseminate the ideology, radical interpretations flourish and grow. In Pakistan, this appears to be the first step toward militarizing women in general.[129]

Recruitment of children is not limited to regions experiencing conflict. Children are increasingly being targeted for internet-based recruitment, which uses video games and even comic books. Jonathan Evans, the former chief of MI5, has argued that at least two thousand people in Britain pose a threat to the country's security because of their support for al-Qaeda-inspired terrorism—and increasingly, these supporters include children. "As I speak," he said, "terrorists are methodically and intentionally targeting young people and children in this country. They are radicalising, indoctrinating and grooming young, vulnerable people to carry out acts of terrorism."[130]

However, critics have raised a red flag over British government policies intended to stem radicalization, as programs such as PREVENT and CHANNEL have resulted in concern regarding the long-term social and psychological impact of counter extremism policies on Muslim children.[131] This concern relates to the suppression of children's free speech, and instances when overly concerned teachers misunderstand or misrepresent student vulnerabilities. In one often-cited example, the mispronunciation of the word "terraced" led to the questioning of a ten-year-old boy in Lancashire when his teacher misunderstood him to have said "terrorist."[132] Much of the focus of these programs is on policing online engagements and trying to prevent radicalization. The deliberate targeting of youth online, especially through social media, has exploded in recent years to near-critical proportions, as terrorist groups have become increasingly savvy at using the internet to disseminate propaganda and attract new recruits.

One of the savviest jihadi recruiters, the slain al-Qaeda in the Arabian Peninsula leader Anwar al-Awlaki (killed September 30, 2011), explained how useful the internet was for broadening the global jihad. In his treatise "44 Ways to Support Jihad," al-Awlaki noted that

> the Internet has become a great medium for spreading the call of jihad and following the news of the mujahedeen. Brothers and sisters can themselves become "Internet mujahedeen" by establishing discussion forums for posting information relating to jihad, establishing email lists to share information with other interested brothers and sisters, and posting jihad literature and news.[133]

Al-Awlaki encouraged his followers to set up websites to focus on the plight of Muslims and the exploits of the mujahedeen, and to post graphic videos to YouTube and social networking sites.[134] Al-Qaeda emphasized online self-radicalization using websites, virtual magazines, and social media.[135] IS has taken this model and perfected it, changing the platforms, using targeted messages, and understanding how to resonate better with youth in the Middle East and from communities around the world.

Other new media specifically aimed at young people have increasingly been used to glamorize terror and promote global jihad. In addition to Hamas's terrorist Mickey Mouse, the media have reported the use of Twitter and Facebook to radicalize and recruit young Muslims. Other youth media have also been tapped, including music videos and internet chat rooms. In Indonesia, the infamous Bali bomber Ali Imron, one of the men who planned and carried out one of Indonesia's deadliest terrorist attacks, has been turned into a comic book hero. The 2002 bombings in Bali killed 202 people, many of them foreign tourists. Imron managed to avoid the death sentence (which was carried out against his accomplices) because he expressed remorse and cooperated with police investigators. Beginning in September 2010, the Indonesian government distributed ten thousand copies of the comic book *Ketika nurani bicara* (When the conscience speaks) to schools, universities, mosques, and libraries. The Indonesian government hoped that the graphic novel would stop impressionable teens from falling under the spell of Islamic extremism and have a deradicalizing effect on Muslim youth. However, it is equally possible that it will inspire young people to follow in Imron's footsteps in hopes of becoming a famous comic book character too.[136]

In the chapters that follow, we explore how and why terrorist groups target children and youth. While our focus is not exclusively on IS, that case study has dominated the headlines, and the terrorist organization has raised the bar for terror groups' exploitation of children. While groups in the past most certainly used children in a variety of roles, IS parades them for the camera and uses them not just to recruit other youth but to goad and shame adults into participating in the conflict. In the next chapter, we examine the areas of similarity and difference between child soldiers and those children involved in terrorist organizations.

CHILD SOLDIERS VERSUS CHILDREN IN TERRORIST GROUPS

The question . . . is whether we in the developed world believe [that] . . . a kid who has been abducted, abused, drugged up and indoctrinated under duress and fear, then armed, programmed, and trained to kill and maim—whether that child is equal to your own child? Is the child in the middle of a civil war, or genocide, [who is] ten years old, as human as your own child?

Roméo Dallaire

Terrorist groups might view children as substitute goods for adults and recruit them after battle losses to replenish their ranks. Some groups may or may not have an a priori preference for children.[1] This chapter contrasts child soldiers with children who have been recruited into terrorist organizations, both coercively and voluntarily. While many similarities exist, the processes and structural conditions (contexts) for recruiting children differ in critical ways: the role of parents, the perversion of education, the use of narcotics, the question of whether or not girls are on the front lines, and the community's degree of encouragement of children's involvement. In chapter 6 we introduce a multistage model of socialization and recruitment to better understand how children are socialized into terrorism. This chapter highlights the variation in how and why children are used by militant groups and asserts that these differences are meaningful across groups and regions.

History of Children and War

Historically, children were largely prohibited from participating directly in conflict, or, if they did, it was in a limited capacity. According to F. K. Owen,

> the chivalric code prohibited civilians from participating, and kings meted out drastic punishment to any nobleman who recruited peasants or children. The Catholic Church opposed the famous Children's Crusade in the 13th century, and the children never made it to Palestine,

let alone engaged in battle. Outside the feudal system, wealthy burghers of the time, seeking private profit and territorial gains, recruited mercenaries, sometimes including boys. But the child soldier is really a product of the later era of standing armies.[2]

The restriction against using children changed with the emergence of the nation-state, although they remained in support roles and were rarely present on the front lines. The Prussian king Frederick the Great included children among his soldiers at the battle of Zorndoff in 1758. He is quoted as saying, "Come children, die with me for the fatherland,"[3] and many of his soldiers were teenaged boys. But this was exceptional; until the 1930s, children might be drummers or standard bearers but rarely participated in combat. A shift occurred during World War II, when several thousand children became involved in the European resistance movements.[4] Furthermore, wars of national liberation were exempt from the ban on child soldiers.[5] Predictably, children took up arms during the wars of colonial liberation during the 1950s and 1960s.[6] This exemption continues until today; as many terrorist organizations define themselves as freedom fighters for national self-determination, they waive the moral principle against using children in favor of the needs of the nation and the greater good.

American military sources stress that the problem of child soldiers and children in armed groups, gangs, and guerrilla forces has reached critical proportions in Latin America, Europe, and the Middle East over the past twenty years. While there is no one template that captures the recruitment and experiences of child soldiers in Africa, Asia, and Latin America, many of the children's autobiographies describe notable similarities.[7] That said, generalizations about child soldiers fail to depict the wide variation present in the countries and the nonstate actors that use children on the front lines.[8] Data from Vera Achvarina and Simon Reich suggests significant variation in the number of children in the armed forces—from Uganda, with extremely high levels of child recruitment, to Angola, where children composed less than 4 percent of the military.[9]

Much of the literature has aggregated child soldiers along with children in terrorist groups solely based on their age. Ilene Cohn and Guy Goodwin-Gill theoretically merge anyone under the age of eighteen, regardless of the manner in which they were mobilized.[10] Peter Singer's groundbreaking study of child soldiers, *Children at War*, blurs case studies of child soldiers in Africa (e.g., Sierra Leone) with those of children in terrorist groups (Palestine and Sri Lanka).[11] But closer examination reveals notable areas of divergence. It is worth highlighting where this book converges and contrasts with Singer's. He summarizes his findings in the following way:

When children are present, conflicts tend to be easier to start, harder to end, and involve greater losses of life. They lay the foundations for future conflicts within the state and through the spread of these now-trained and experienced fighters to other areas. . . . The presence of children on the battlefield adds to the overall confusion of battle and can slow the progress of forces, as well as increasing casualty totals on both sides. And finally, conflicts where children are involved entail massive violations of the laws of war, higher casualties, compared to their adult compatriots.[12]

Singer's hypothesis that the presence of children causes higher casualties is not entirely accurate in the case of terrorist groups. Our research shows that children are more likely than adults to be preempted or caught, or to change their minds; thus, attacks involving children have higher failure rates and might not result in higher casualties. Moreover, the data on IS demonstrates that children are used for the element of surprise—not *instead* of adults, but in different roles, ranging from scouts to executioners, and often as part of mixed units in which children "serve" alongside adults.

Groups tend to mobilize children during long-standing, multigenerational conflicts. To institutionalize the process and guarantee a constant source of fresh recruits, terrorist organizations have established youth wings or movements intended to help young people transition into the group while also providing training and imparting a particular skill set. Terrorist leaders might consider these venues ideal for "talent spotting."[13] At the same time, terrorist groups may also have strict minimum ages for involvement in violence (usually sixteen),[14] although certain groups employ younger children as apprentices. With the emergence of IS, many of these established categories have unraveled. Beginning in 2014, increasingly younger operatives have engaged in a wide variety of roles within terrorist organizations—roles ordinarily reserved for adults (e.g., recruiters, propagandists, car bombers). The use of preadolescent and prepubescent suicide bombers—a previously unheard of, beyond-the-pale phenomenon—has been gaining momentum, not just within IS but in its affiliates, such as Boko Haram and Wilayet Khorasan (Afghanistan), and in comparable organizational twin groups,[15] such as the Pakistani Taliban.[16]

Based on the available data and after extensive research, we have determined that the most significant difference between child soldiers and children mobilized into terrorist organizations is the microprocesses of recruitment. The degree of co-optation versus coercion helps explain the willingness of parents and the community as a whole to allow militants to access the children. Most stories recounted by former child soldiers describe a thoroughly coercive process in which children who had lost family members were forced to join militias (often the very groups that had killed their families) at gunpoint. The child soldiers are clearly acting against their will (at least at the outset); for instance, the use of drugs was a common theme in the recruitment process.

Smaller Arms

The introduction of children into combat was supposedly precipitated by the decrease in armament size and the increase in small arms availability—making it easier and cheaper for children to operate the weapons and making them more attractive as recruits. Anthony Cordesman posits that the increase in the number of children involved was correlated to the changing nature of warfare and the shrinking size of weaponry, which made it more amenable for small fingers and hands.[17]

According to Rachel Stohl, the "availability of small arms is without question a contributing factor to the use of child soldiers."[18] The Coalition to Stop the Use of Child Soldiers corroborates this view, observing that "the widespread availability of modern lightweight weapons enables children to become efficient killers in combat."[19] Elisabeth Schauer and Thomas Elbert argue that "the development of light weapons, such as automatic guns suitable for children, was a prerequisite for the involvement of children in modern conflicts that typically . . . target civilians."[20] Weapons used in conflicts during the eighteenth and nineteenth centuries (rifles, flintlocks, muskets, long rifles, and cannons) dwarfed children in both height and weight, although there were still instances of child recruits during the American Civil War and the American Revolution. The Civil War, in many ways an outlier, was the war of "boy soldiers"; according to David Rosen, "Historical analysis suggests that between 250,000 and 420,000 boy soldiers, including many in their early teens and even younger, served in the Union and Confederate armies."[21]

Beginning in the 1990s, the introduction of small arms on the battlefield meant that the smaller-sized weapons eliminated a child's physical constraint, including getting injured from the kickback of firing weapons bigger than they were or carrying unwieldy weapons.[22] Once this constraint no longer existed, children would either be preferable (superior goods) or less desirable (inferior goods) for military combat. This varied not just by conflict, but also during specific time periods when terrorist organizations would alter their recruitment strategies.[23]

Child combatants might be preferable to adults for several reasons cited in the literature, including their being easier to control or manipulate, being more obedient to authority, not fearing for their own lives, having few (if any) family responsibilities, and, most of all, being cheaper to feed or remunerate, since most of the children are not compensated, and since children also do not understand the value of goods and money the same way that adults do.

Christopher Blattman ascertained that "armed groups [in Uganda] with few or limited resources forcibly recruit young adolescents because they offer the optimal combination of effectiveness and ease of retention"[24] The ease of manipulation and the lower cost outweigh the downsides of using children in battle—namely, their physical weakness and mental disadvantages. One factor to consider across militia groups and terrorist organizations is the age of initial recruitment versus the age of deployment. Some groups recruit very young children but spend years training, indoctrinating, and preparing them until they are ready for the fray. This is the case with the Kurdish Workers' Party (PKK) and the affiliated People's Protection Units (YPG). In our research sample of 610 "martyred" youth (eulogized on the Kurdish social networks) between 2000 and 2016, the average age of recruitment was fifteen years old, although many died at the age of twenty-two.[25] There are IS child recruitment offices in the Syrian cities of al-Mayadin and al-Bokamal, at which hundreds of children were reportedly recruited.[26] Our research shows that the number is likely much higher, given how many children and youth were eulogized as suicide or car bombers—representing only a fraction of those who have been recruited and trained overall.

The Taliban were early adopters of the tactic of deploying child bombers. Initially the recruits were as young as twelve, and eventually the Taliban lowered the age requirement even further. The children "were trained in weapons handling, preparing of suicide jackets and ambush attacks," explained one Pakistani military official, and "promised a place in heaven—a land of virgins and rivers made of milk and honey."[27]

There are strategic and tactical advantages to using children, including the element of surprise, which can throw off an enemy ill prepared to confront a child in battle. In some operations, a moment's hesitation is sufficient to provide tactical benefits on the battlefield, and if adults hesitate, even briefly, the militants have the upper hand. We know from our research that older children are more effective as front-line operatives. Therefore the age of recruitment is a good indicator of the extent to which an organization discounts the physical disadvantages of children. If a militia is recruiting sixteen-to-seventeen-year-olds (versus ten-to-fourteen-year-olds), this suggests that it values military effectiveness. Bernd Beber and Christopher Blattman have likened child soldiers to child labor during the Industrial Revolution, with important advantages and skills accruing as the children age.[28]

There are meaningful differences in how militant groups recruit and deploy children. It is important to disaggregate how children were recruited, what that recruitment entailed, and what role parents and the wider community played in the recruitment. The Tatmadaw army in Myanmar recruited children en masse,[29] because the country's military is required to satisfy minimum quotas, and recruiters (agents) are rewarded according to their meeting those quotas. The recruiters have a conflict of interest and an incentive to enlist the maximum number of children and youth. If adults are unwilling to join, children can and will be "picked up," threatened, and coerced to "volunteer." The children are instructed to lie on their application forms and claim to be eighteen. Such recruitment appears to be driven by profit rather than military expediency or the need to replace adults lost in battle. The Maoists in Nepal and insurgent and terrorist groups in Palestine recruit children into cultural associations before the age of fifteen. These youth movements function as a segue to front-line involvement at a later date. The Maoists go so far as to abduct children for a few weeks to expose them to the group's propaganda and then release them back to their families, hoping that the lessons (and ideology) took root and that they will return to officially enlist.[30]

In 2012, Child Soldiers International—an advocacy NGO closely associated with ending the recruitment, use, and exploitation of children by armed groups—published a report affirming that there was no formal recruitment of children in Syria, only instances of children being used as human shields. However, the report listed six states where children, while not technically recruited, were used informally by armed forces in conflict, as guides, spies, porters, or human shields: Afghanistan, Colombia, Israel, Libya, the Philippines, and Syria.[31] *Children and Armed Conflict*, a report by the special representative of the secretary-general of the United Nations, argues that the recruitment and use of children by groups continued (and likely increased) with the growth of IS in Syria and Iraq:[32]

> In rural Aleppo, Dayr al-Zawr and rural Raqqa UN found military training of at least 124 boys between 10 and 15 years of age. Verification of the use of child foreign fighters increased significantly, with 18 cases[33] of children as young as 7. . . . The U.N. verified the recruitment of children as young as 9 by the Free Syrian Army, and the recruitment of 11 Syrian refugee children from neighboring countries by Liwa' al-Tawhid.[34]

There are no "good guys" with clean hands in this conflict. Groups that are fighting IS and the murderous regime of Bashar al-Assad exploit children at rates occasionally greater than those of the Islamic State. The YPG, a proxy group supported (and funded) by the United States that has been the most steadfast adversary of IS, has recruited boys and girls as young as fourteen for combat,[35] with community pressure and coercion reportedly playing a role.[36] The Free Syrian Army has had significantly more children and youth die in combatant roles than all the jihadi groups combined. In 2016, Human Rights Watch accused two Kurdish groups, including the PKK, of deploying children. Human Rights Watch called on the Kurdish groups to "urgently demobilize children, investigate abuses, pledge to end child recruitment, and appropriately penalize commanders who fail to do so."[37]

According to the UN, at least 148 noncombatant (civilian) children were targeted by government air strikes, international forces supporting the government, and the international coalition. IS and Jabhat al-Nusra (Nusrah Front) continued to commit atrocities, including the execution of children. On March 5, 2016, Jabhat al-Nusra executed two children during a ground offensive on Kanafez (Hama). On August 22 of the same year, in Muh Hasan (Dayr al-Zawr), IS publicly amputated the limbs of a fifteen-year-old boy affiliated with the Free Syrian Army.[38]

The data we have collected for this book shows that all groups in Syria have recruited children for a variety of roles, including front-line activities, since the beginning of the Syrian civil war. Nevertheless, the source of the greatest violence against children in Syria remains the regime, which has killed significantly more civilians than IS, the al- Qaeda-affiliated groups, and the militias put together.

The issue of data collection is complicated by a few limitations, as the UN does not analytically break down the number of children in combat or explicitly explain the methodology it uses,[39] insisting instead that "hundreds of thousands of children are used as soldiers in armed conflicts around the world. Many children are abducted and beaten into submission, others join military groups to escape poverty, to defend their communities, out of a feeling of revenge or for other reasons."[40]

In individual country reports, the number of children recorded in 2015 reflects only a fraction of the reality. For example, according to the UN, the number of children recruited in Syria was 362, with twenty-one abductions, thirty-six detentions, and fifty-five killed. Yet the number of children eulogized by the militant groups in Syria, including IS, Jabhat al-Nusra (now called Jabhat Fatah al-Sham), Hizbullah, the PKK, and the Conquest of Syria Front, far exceeds these numbers. From January 2013 to March 2016 alone, almost one thousand children had their deaths celebrated by Syrian militants—eighteen times more than the fifty-five reported by the UN—and it is estimated that over five thousand were recruited, based on the number of camps and videos, and reports by the Syrian Observatory for Human Rights (SOHR). All sides in the conflict in

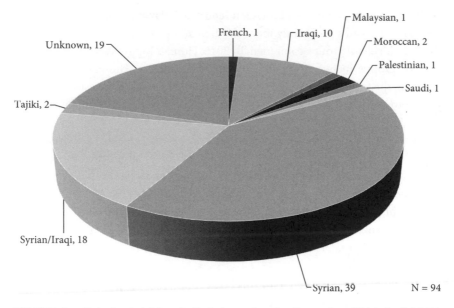

FIGURE 1.   Eulogized children in Syria by nationality, December 2014–April 2017

Syria and Iraq—including those that receive support from the West— have been exploiting children and youth, in direct violation of international treaties not to use child soldiers.[41]

During the period 1998–2008, approximately two million child soldiers died during armed conflicts, although most human rights groups use the outdated figure of three hundred thousand.[42] The UN echoes oft-cited statistics "that in more than 20 countries around the world, the number of child soldiers involved in armed conflict ranges from 200,000 to 300,000 and that more than 40 percent (80,000 to 120,000) of them are young girls."[43] Jo Becker argues that "the number of countries known to have children participating in armed conflicts dropped from thirty in the mid-1990s to seventeen in 2015."[44] These numbers have been bandied about for decades. But considering the changing nature of conflict and the difficulty of accessing conflict zones, their accuracy is highly debatable.

Human rights groups and NGOs (and the US military) estimate the number of children involved in conflict. As Barry Ames explains, the literature on children and conflict takes an advocacy position, and most of the statistics and data (including the three hundred thousand child soldiers under arms) cannot be verified with any confidence.[45] In 2016, a London-based think tank published a study about children and IS in which it reported that thirty-one thousand

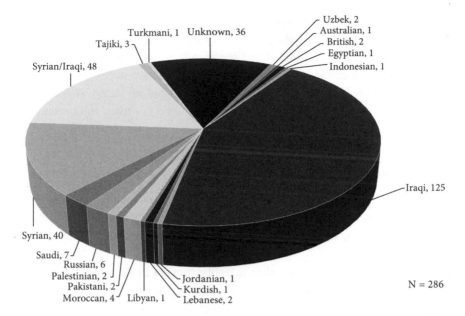

FIGURE 2.   Eulogized children in Iraq by nationality, December 2014–April 2017

women in the Islamic State were pregnant.[46] Such round numbers undoubtedly represent estimates and are not persuasive or beneficial for analysis. In fact, such estimates obscure more than they illuminate about the role of children in political violence.

For this book, the data collected on children's involvement with terrorist movements in Syria and Iraq was based on eulogies published by the groups themselves, with additional verification procedures to check the reliability of the information. To ensure that we did not depend exclusively on what terrorists disclosed or take their propaganda at face value, we supplemented this data by triangulating it with media reports in Arabic, English, and French. While it is impossible to know with absolute certainty the total number of children who have been recruited into terrorist and violent extremist groups, we are able to count the children who were killed—especially when the groups eulogize or broadcast the children as martyrs for the cause. Even if we could not authenticate the number of children recruited (e.g., through citations by UN sources or SOHR),[47] the multistage model of socialization into violent extremism proposed in chapter 6 holds true regardless of the actual number of children involved.

The six-stage socialization model was derived from case studies of children and IS; nevertheless, it can be applied to other violent extremist groups that lure children into participation. Many violent extremist organizations have extensive outreach activities, including summer camps, primary schools, educational curricula, and television shows aimed specifically at children, and institutional youth wings pull children into their movement. The six-stage model further demonstrates the ways in which children are evaluated for skills (what we call "talent spotting").[48] Children are then assigned a variety of roles, and movement from one role (task) to another is possible depending on the circumstances.

Socialization into IS

The children in IS originate from five sources: children of local fighters, children of foreign fighters, abandoned children found in local (IS-controlled) orphanages and hospitals, children coercively taken from parents, and children who volunteered.

IS thoroughly socializes the children, unlike some of its affiliated groups such as Boko Haram, which coerces and dupes children into engaging in front-line activities—often without their knowing they have volunteered for a suicide bombing operation. IS accomplishes this socialization in a number of ways, most visibly through public events aimed at raising awareness. Some of these "meet-and-greets," which might be small scale, attract children by offering them toys and candy if they show up.[49] Local children help out by waving the black IS flag, distributing sweets, or luring other children. These public events encourage local children to come out and learn more about what IS has to offer; using other children as intermediaries is an effective recruitment tool.[50]

Children are required to attend and witness public executions. At first they are exposed only to filmed executions, but eventually they are present at the live events. In the propaganda videos, children can be seen pushing through the crowds to reach prime viewing positions for the graphic violence to follow. Their visible reaction to beheadings is one of simultaneous revulsion and curiosity. But the children learn why the punishment is meted out, and thanks to the routine spectacle of such events, they soon internalize and consider normal what IS does to all those who commit infractions against the Caliphate.

According to the Syrian Observatory for Human Rights, IS targets a variety of children—both local and foreign:

> Children who want to join ISIS without the approval of their parents . . . come to the squares where the executions, whipping, crucifying and beheading, and stoning [are] carried out. The organization induces parents and guardians to send their sons to camps where the children undergo Sharia and military courses. . . . ISIS also tries to lure the

children by money, weapons, and cars in order to convince them to join its own camps. In addition, IS receives and takes care of children who suffer from congenital malformations.[51]

Thus children face a selection for desirability. Reports from Syria allege that, as in the euthanasia programs of the past (for example, Aktion T4 in Nazi Germany),[52] IS euthanized children with disabilities.[53] IS issued a fatwa authorizing the killing of all children with disabilities. Human rights reports cite the estimate that thirty-eight children have been killed by lethal injection or suffocation, although SOHR implies that IS has a found a new way to exploit children with disabilities—by using them as suicide bombers. Leading up to the battle of Mosul, this was most observable with IS's tactical innovation of using wheelchair-bound fighters who had to be lowered into vehicles to serve as car bombers. Human rights groups allege that children with disabilities are exploited in a variety of nefarious ways, not just as suicide bombers.[54]

The children of foreign fighters learn that even peripheral participation is generously rewarded. The children are carefully choreographed for the camera, for which they are posed and coached on how to respond. In some cases, the children are praised for holding a weapon or the decapitated head of a victim.[55] The children of foreign fighters are also given priority to be Cubs of the Caliphate—however, as we describe in chapter 4, they are far less likely to perish as martyrs.

Witnessing graphically violent events is consistent with the experiences of child soldiers. Child soldier autobiographies describe a uniform narrative in which the militias force children to perpetrate extreme acts of violence in order to prevent them from defecting. Jo Becker explains that child soldiers' having perpetrated acts of violence against their own families or communities means that even if they could escape, "they may be unable to return home for fear of punishment. . . . Their families and home communities may be unwilling to accept them, particularly if they committed atrocities."[56] This is one of the ways in which the militias construct a no-exit option. Examples of forcibly recruited children having to kill or rape members of their own families are likewise a common theme in biographies and autobiographies, such as Ishmael Beah's autobiography *A Long Way Gone*.[57]

Children hold a variety of roles or jobs in terrorist groups, from legal activities (in support roles) to front-line activities in which they perform the same functions as adults. In order to appreciate this variety, we have organized the kinds of roles in a way that differentiates support from front-line activity, and informal involvement with the movement from formal participation in it.

Younger or newer recruits are initially assigned to support roles. In the LTTE, new recruits were given a wooden rifle to help them become accustomed

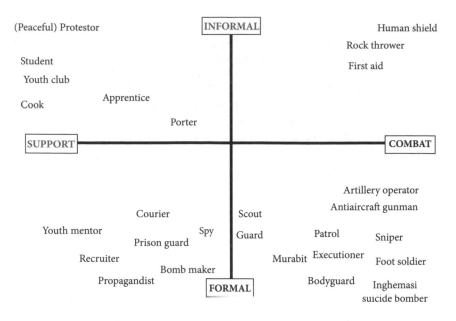

FIGURE 3.   Children's roles in violent extremist organizations

to the real thing. Children serve first as messengers and spies; around the age of ten, when they are strong enough to manage a weapon, they are trained for a minimum number of years. Older children receive a minimum of six months of physical and weapons training.[58] Among the Palestinian militant groups, the Popular Front for the Liberation of Palestine recruits children for cultural and educational activities, during which time they are evaluated. Voluntary membership is only permitted at eighteen, which is commensurate with the policy in other left-leaning revolutionary movements.[59]

One important detail to appreciate between adults and children in terrorist organizations is that adults tend to be better educated and come from families with higher-than-average incomes in their society. The reverse is often true for children. Because of their age, children recruited by terrorist groups will logically be less educated than adults, but when recruiting them, terrorist groups target children from the poorest, most vulnerable segments of society. When recruiting adults, these same groups often select from the wealthy, educated, and upper classes.

While there are similarities between child soldiers and children in terrorist movements, there are five main areas of divergence: the role played by parents and authority figures (community leaders, teachers, coaches), the use and abuse of drugs, access to education, children's roles in the movement, and whether females (or young girls) are active members of the group in combat roles.

Role of Parents and Guardians

Ease of access to children appears to be a more plausible explanation for the proliferation of child soldiers since the 1990s than the "shrinking weapons" theory. Whether militias exploit orphans, street children, or refugees living in camps, including camps for internally displaced persons (IDPs), a common theme is that these children lack adult protection and supervision, most often because their parents have been killed. Vera Achvarina and Simon Reich explain the ease with which militia groups are able to access refugee and IDP camps in search of child recruits,[60] and Alfred Zack-Williams demonstrates how militias transition street children effortlessly from gangs into military units.[61] In Colombia, militarized gangs loitered outside transit centers in hopes of recruiting or re-recruiting youth into their organizations.

In civil wars such as the one in Sierra Leone, many children are orphans, because their parents have been killed. Stories abound of Revolutionary United Front (RUF) abductees being forced to kill their own parents or other family members to create distance from their former civilian selves and construct new identities as RUF soldiers. In his book *In Sierra Leone*, Michael D. Jackson observes that

> the abduction of children by the RUF, and their adoption by rebel leaders—who were regarded as fathers, and [were] called Pappy or Pa—recalls the initiatory seizure of children, whose ties with their parents are symbolically severed so that they can be reborn, in the bush, as men. This idea that war like initiation, or play, or an adventure—is a moment out of time, spatially separated from the moral world, may also explain why many combatants anticipate a remorse-free return to civilian life.[62]

When parents are alive, their willingness to provide violent extremist groups with access to their children is different from isolated children being forcibly conscripted as child soldiers. Parental "consent" is complicated by the exigencies of war and the coercive environments in which many families live. Some parents may be enthusiastic supporters of a movement, encouraging and lauding their children's involvement, while others allow violent extremists access, not necessarily because they subscribe to a radical ideology, but because they might not have a choice if they are to survive.[63] Such coercion was apparent in the Swat Valley in Pakistan, where the TTP went door to door demanding exorbitant financial payments from residents. Those unable to pay—which in such a poor region were the majority—were then required to provide one of their children as a recruit. The average family size was seven children. In these cases, families faced a terrible dilemma: pay an extortionate tax (double most families' annual income) or surrender a child to the movement. The parents we spoke to implied that if they had not surrendered one child, the terrorists could (and likely would) take all of their children, and so they made an impossible choice and handed over a child.[64]

Alternatively, the terrorist group may portray itself in a positive light, conveying to the community and to parents that involvement would be beneficial for the child. Deception and manipulation came to define the TTP's child induction practices.[65] Targeting children at risk provided the group with the perfect opportunity to reach out to parents to help "save" their children. The militants promised to foster an environment marked by discipline, belonging, purpose, and meaning.[66] As a result of these promises, some families willingly agreed to their child's involvement.

In essence, the Pakistani Taliban promoted itself as a solution to family problems ranging from antisocial behavior to substance abuse. In one case, a mother we met disclosed that her son had suffered from alcohol and drug problems during his preteens, and she had mistakenly assumed that the TTP could and would "clean him up."[67] In fact, membership in the militant movement did not resolve the boy's problems, but created new ones. After capture by the Pakistani military, he was sent to the Sabaoon rehabilitation facility; upon release, he resumed his drug abuse, adding dried scorpions to hashish (to increase potency or as a homeopathic remedy for erectile dysfunction). The practice, in which scorpions are dried by the sun or burnt by coal, and the poisonous tail mixed with narcotics to create a powerful hallucinogen, is common to the region. According to one news report, "The high lasts for almost ten hours. The first six hours are more painful, as the body adjusts to the high."[68] Privately his mother shared her greatest fear—that the Taliban had sexually abused the boy.[69]

Doctors and therapists have explained that young boys might have been sexually abused by commanders (along the lines of the child soldiers portrayed in the film *Beasts of No Nation*) prior to a suicide operation, which left them with no way out and no way to refuse their mission.[70] In other cases, children were abused with electric shocks to or burning of the genitals, raped (mostly boys but some girls), sexually humiliated, or threatened with the rape of other family members. Some girls were abducted by government forces at checkpoints or during home invasions and then raped or gang-raped, occasionally in front of family members.[71]

There are similarities between IS Cubs, children in the TTP, and the Moro Islamic Liberation Front. In each of these cases, parents are involved in the recruitment process. Thousands of foreign fighters have flocked to the areas under IS's control and have brought their families with them. In contrast, the vast majority of children forcibly conscripted as child soldiers by African militias had little to no contact with their parents and tended to be indoctrinated in more coercive ways. In Lucinda Woodward and Peter Galvin's study of ten former child soldiers, only four "indicated that recruitment took the form of gradual indoctrination through friendship or peer pressure."[72] In the literature on child soldiers in Africa, most of the children have been orphaned or abandoned, and are either abducted or have completely left their families behind.[73] The children are socialized to form close bonds with the armed group, which acts as a replacement for their real family.

The biographies and autobiographies written by and about former child soldiers tend to (inadvertently) echo a Westernized and utopian view of childhood, which is seen as comprising a dozen years of idyllic innocence—a normative approach that some anthropologists challenge as being culturally dissonant. It is important to balance what *should be* childhood with what has historically *been* childhood in non-Western societies, notably the historical continuities and cultural practices and meanings surrounding children that make their participation in conflict somehow legible. There are palpable differences between childhood in less-developed countries and childhood in first-world countries. By some measures the former is considerably worse (because of lack of access to food, water, education, or jobs). Child poverty, according to a UNICEF report, "can be measured in an absolute sense—the lack of some fixed minimum package of goods and services. Or it can be measured in a relative sense—falling behind, by more than a certain degree from the average standard"[74] But in other areas—for example, happiness or depression—variation cannot be correlated directly to wealth or the country's GDP.

Susan Shepler writes that the presence of children on the battlefield impacts the civilian population and shapes how power is structured in society: "Their specific distress can only be understood through their own notions of youth, and has to do with the inversion of age hierarchies, the breakdown of extended family ties, the effects of improper training and initiation, and the future of the nation."[75] Stohl contends that militarized children have a long-term impact, as children will transition into criminality or seek opportunities for reengagement—fostering an endless cycle of violence:

> After a conflict, small arms may become instruments for other forms of violence such as crime and banditry. In some areas, these surplus weapons may create a culture of violence that traps whole societies in an endless cycle of war. When children have no experience with or exposure to non-violent conflict resolution, small arms become the tools for conflict resolution.[76]

For some trauma specialists, the mere fact of being raised by people other than one's immediate family can be positively correlated with children's trauma.

Shepler problematizes the concept of an innocent, stress-free childhood, which she claims does not exist in most parts of Africa, where patronage, large families, and a tradition of fosterage—children going to live with extended family to access school or pay off parental debt—prevail. This translates into children routinely being raised by people other than their parents, but also into a context in which mentorship, apprenticeship, and labor are not viewed in the same pejorative ways as child labor is viewed in the West. Thus for Shepler, the transition from parents to other adults raising children is less jarring than one would expect.[77]

Access to and Use of Drugs

The biographies and autobiographies of child soldiers, and hundreds of interviews conducted by Tanya Zayed (formerly of the Roméo Dallaire Child Soldiers Initiative), with child soldiers and UNICEF staff, describe the use of drugs and other intoxicants to alternately prepare or reward children for combat. In some instances, reports describe children receiving intoxicants after a military operation, as a form of reward or to calm them down after an especially high-risk mission. "Fighting with a gun is not easy because it puts so much pressure on the mind. So we needed to free the mind by taking drugs, and it worked."[78] It is important to note that drug use among child soldiers was not universal, and reports from Rwanda and the Philippines demonstrate that it was not prevalent among child soldiers there.

Analyzing all armed conflicts in Africa from 1960 to 2006, Robert Tynes found that drugs were used in less than 50 percent of the cases where children were part of the fight. "Rather than encompassing the entire continent," Tynes observes, "drug use tended to parallel illicit drug trade routes."[79] But in many contexts where child soldiers are used, they are coerced and manipulated with alcohol and drugs. According to Zayed, boys involved in various militia groups in the Democratic Republic of the Congo (DRC) told interviewers that their first day's lessons included how to roll a joint (marijuana cigarette). They would sit in a circle and learn how to smoke.[80] Subsequent lessons included putting naked boys who had been drugged in huts, with a constant stream of naked girls entering and exiting. Having never been with a woman before, the boys were taught what they were supposed to do with the girls. In essence, the girls sometimes had to instruct the boys in how to rape.[81]

The main purpose of drug use was to dull the child's senses or induce a kind of euphoria and make the child feel as if he or she were invincible. This supplemented the messages given to child combatants in the Lord's Resistance Army (LRA) in Uganda, who were told that Joseph Kony's "magical powers" would

TABLE 1 Drug use by conflict

DRUG	CONFLICT
Alcohol	Central African Republic
	Congo
	Liberia
	Sierra Leone
Cannabis	Central African Republic
	DRC
	DRC (hashish)
	Liberia (hashish and marijuana)
	Sierra Leone
	Somalia (khat)
Cigarettes	Colombia
	Congo Brazzaville
	Nepal
Cocaine	Colombia
	Liberia
	Sierra Leone
Coffee, herbs, papaya, gunpowder	Congo Brazzaville
	Sierra Leone
Gunpowder mixed with cocaine	DRC
	Liberia
	Sierra Leone
Hallucinatory pills (uppers)	Liberia (bubbles = amphetamines)
	Sierra Leone
	Somalia (amphetamines)
	Uganda
Heroin	Burma
	Mozambique
	Sierra Leone
Palm wine	Sierra Leone
Shi-Congo	DRC

Sources: Phil Ashby, "Child Combatants: A Soldiers Perspective," *Lancet* 360 (December 2002), https://www.thelancet.com/pdfs/journals/lancet/PIIS0140673602118009.pdf; Richard Maclure and Myriam Denov, "I Didn't Want to Die So I Joined Them": Structuration and the Process of Becoming Boy Soldiers in Sierra Leone," *Terrorism and Political Violence* 18 (2006): pp. 119–135; ILO (International Labour Office), "*Wounded Childhood: The Use of Children in Armed Conflict in Central Africa*," ILO report, April 2003, Geneva, Switzerland; Jill Trenholm, Pia Olsson, Martha Blomqvist, and Beth Maina Ahlberg, "Constructing Soldiers from Boys in Eastern Democratic Republic of Congo," *Men and Masculinities* 16, no. 2 (June 2013): 203–27. doi:10.1177/1097184X12470113.

protect them from harm. Intoxicants might be mixed with gunpowder, which was also treated as a drug, and for females used as a means of contraception, or to abort a fetus in the case of unwanted pregnancies.

There was variation in the types of drugs used by different militias and in different conflicts. In Iran, some reports of "martyr's syrup" being distributed to the children before they were sent to the front raised questions regarding whether the Iranian government drugged its child soldiers. This is hard to imagine given Islam's prohibition against using drugs.[82]

In Sierra Leone, there were reports of marijuana, cocaine (sometimes purchased with the proceeds of RUF sales of blood diamonds), palm wine, alcohol, and gunpowder use, as well as mixing together coffee, gunpowder, herbs, and papaya leaves to make a potent drink. In the DRC, hashish was the drug of choice; it was used in shi-congo as well, along with a marijuana-like substance.

Unlike in Mozambique, Sierra Leone, and Uganda—where drugs were used to recruit, reward, and exploit child soldiers—in Rwanda, child soldiers reported that they used neither alcohol nor drugs. "The consumption of narcotics was strictly prohibited in the ranks of the FPR [Patriotic Rwandan Front] and the children in the rebel groups did not have the means to procure them."[83] This prohibition against drugs might have encouraged parents to permit their children to be involved with militant groups. Thus in terror organizations that strictly prohibited the use of narcotics and alcohol, parents did not object to children's involvement because it was a guarantee that their children would not use drugs. According to the International Labour Office report on the Philippines, parents are happy to have their children involved with Moro National Liberation Front so that they won't be influenced by drug or alcohol use. In our interviews at the Sabaoon rehabilitation facility in Pakistan, membership in the TTP was perceived to be a solution to addiction. In fact, the use of drugs in Pakistan varied from one unit of the TTP to another: the children in one facility (Sabaoon) saw no drug use, whereas children in the Quetta school were all addicted to drugs provided by the terrorist group.

Schooling

One area of important divergence between child soldiers and children recruited into terrorist groups is whether or not the group educates children. Education is especially important in the developing world because, according to Jo Becker, evidence shows that "children who stay in school enjoy better health, better job prospects, higher earnings as adults, and are less likely to end up in child labor, child marriage, or as child soldiers."[84] Displacement during civil wars has caused the percentage of children out of school to reach historic proportions.

It is also via schooling that some children take their first steps toward terrorist recruitment. The role that education (which some might consider brainwashing) plays in convincing youth to adopt radical views or absorb a group's ideology varies substantially from one militant group to another. It is worth noting that many terrorist organizations consider ideological training necessary to guarantee their continuity and longevity, and they expend significant resources to ensure that the next generation knows the creed and vernacular of the group. An important caveat to this observation is that not all education is considered equal. One of the core issues for Boko Haram (a name that loosely translates as "Western education [*karatun boko*] is Islamically prohibited [*haram*]") was that secular education was not permitted but Islamic education was. There were widespread feelings of mistrust or disapproval about Western education, insofar as it was perceived to be a form of Westernization or the imposition of Western values.[85]

In 2009, after the first leader's death, acting leader Mallam Sanni Umanai explained,

> Boko Haram does not in any way mean, "Western education is a sin" as the infidel media continue to portray us. Boko Haram actually means "Western civilization" is forbidden. The difference is that while the first gives the impression that we are opposed to formal education coming from the West, which is not true, the second affirms our belief in the supremacy of Islamic culture.[86]

This antipathy toward Western culture and education is comparable to that of the Taliban (named after the teenaged schoolboys, Talibs, who led the movement), who also only permitted religious education, and only for boys—destroying schools that educated girls or preventing girls' education altogether. Schools have been the target of militant attacks as well as their ideal venue for recruitment. Those schools whose teaching and curricula the terrorists cannot control, they simply destroy. Between 2009 and 2012, the Taliban conducted 838 attacks against schools. Between 2009 and 2015, Boko Haram destroyed over 900 schools and forced 1,500 more to close. During their assaults against Western education, Boko Haram burned down buildings, slaughtered teachers and students, and over time increasingly abducted young boys and girls to be coerced into joining the militants.[87] In Syria, more than 6,000 schools were closed, destroyed, or damaged between 2011 and 2016, and in Afghanistan there have been 1,100 attacks on schools, according to the UN.[88]

Children who have been conscripted into military units, however, tend to be uneducated—the militias do not run schools to ideologically groom youth. This is in part because war decimates the education system and may make it too dangerous for children to attend school. Within the militias, children are most often portrayed as low-skilled members of the military, valuable exclusively because of their youth and availability to fill the ranks. In most cases, they receive little training, and they are frequently massacred.[89] If anything, such children are seen as expendable, mere cannon fodder for the military unit. Little to no effort is made to ensure that they share the same worldview, although propaganda is disseminated.

In August 2016, a fifteen-year-old boy wearing a suicide belt with an improvised explosive device (IED) was preempted in Kirkuk before he could reach his civilian target, a Shia school.[90] The boy, who had been recruited by IS, had been in an IDP camp for one week before he set out on his mission. Like other terrorist groups, IS aggressively recruits from orphanages and refugee camps. Our research asserts that IS has emptied the orphanages in the areas under its control, creating their special Ashbal units, the Cubs of the Caliphate. As Joby Warrick explains,

> Meanwhile, the city's hundreds of orphaned children and teens were moved to military camps to learn to shoot rifles and drive suicide trucks. [One] would sometimes see the young ISIS recruits in military convoys, carrying guns, and wearing oversized uniforms. Some of the boys were younger than sixteen; when the schools were closed there was nothing for them to do.[91]

In Sri Lanka, the LTTE recruited children from schools in the North and East. During the course of Mia Bloom's field research in 2002, Tamil mothers in the areas under LTTE control confided that they had started to homeschool their children for fear that they would be recruited (i.e., kidnapped) during the day by the LTTE.[92] Schools are on the front lines of many wars, including the 2004 Chechen separatist siege of a grade school in Beslan, Ossetia;[93] the Pakistani Taliban's Peshawar school massacre, which killed more than 130 children;[94] Boko Haram's abduction of 219 schoolgirls in Chibok, Nigeria, in April 2014; and the thousands of schools destroyed or occupied in Syria since the beginning of the civil war.[95] Less well publicized are the Aboke girls kidnapped from their boarding school in Uganda by the LRA, much in the same manner as the Chibok girls taken by Boko Haram.[96]

The LTTE in Sri Lanka used propaganda in schools to attract young recruits. Families of soldiers were accorded special status in the community, which served to encourage children from other families to join. The Maoists enacted similar policies in Nepal to educate young recruits.[97]

In Syria and Iraq, the IS curriculum is little more than indoctrination; the real use of school is to foment unity, create the impression of a band of brothers, and bring children to the attention of IS personnel. While it is highly unlikely that children will share the radical views of the adults from the get-go, they are manipulated, brainwashed, and coerced. According to Richard Gilbert,

> conscience is a learned and not an inherited characteristic, a child's beliefs and attitudes are imprinted on its brain by its parents, guardians, and teachers, both secular and religious. With a short memory and an embryonic intellect, a child cannot form a developed, rational judgment. Deprived of conscience, a child is easily led to accept, and exercise, brutality as normal.[98]

IS began this trend in 2014 and has since increased it exponentially through 2018. Our experiences in the Swat Valley, Pakistan, demonstrate that children barely understand the radical jihadi ideology, and at most simply parrot what they have heard from adults, without being radicalized in any real sense. There are differences between educating children and training them for militant activities. IS has combined the two tracks for the Cubs of the Caliphate by simultaneously training the children physically and indoctrinating them in the study of religion and the ideology of the group. While IS has educated many Syrian and Iraqi children following its capture of expanses of Syrian and Iraqi territory, only a select few have been chosen to become Cubs. At Cubs training, children face a grueling physical and mental regimen lasting anywhere from thirty to fifty days. A crisis, such as a battle, may result in some children being pushed through training faster than others, to report to the front lines for any number of duties. The children mimic the style of their adult role models, wear similar uniforms, and learn the vernacular of the group. They learn who their enemies are and why they must be eradicated.

Cub recruits witness crucifixions, stonings, and beheadings. Being present for such acts doesn't just represent (de)sensitization to the new "normal" it also demonstrates loyalty and commitment to the group. Violence becomes part of a daily ritual, and soon commitment spirals. The socialization process intensifies, and the children's commitment deepens. Beginning in December 2015, IS initiated a sustained campaign of child suicide bombers.

Accounts given by children to local NGOs paint a bleak picture of daily life in the IS camps. The children are mentally and physically exhausted and sleep on flea-infested mattresses. Yet these shared experiences build camaraderie. The children form close bonds with each other and eventually feel deep pride in what they are doing.

A final, extreme test of loyalty awaits the Cubs. There have been several videos in which it is the children who execute prisoners, and these graphic images have been preserved in IS's propaganda magazines *Da'biq* and *Rumiyah* as well as on videos produced by al-Hayat Media Center and circulated on their encrypted Telegram channels and networks. The videos have increased in scope and number over the past three years, as has the extent of the graphic violence they depict.[99]

There is another difference between the Cubs and child soldiers. Children's involvement in IS appears to be more gradual, whereas child soldiers are forced to pull the trigger immediately. One twelve-year-old explained, "The village is not safe; it is better to go to war. If I go to war and I am killed, it is finished for me. If I kill my enemy, it is finished for him. I won't wait in the village to die."[100]

In many conflicts in Africa, children were part of dedicated units made up of children and led by slightly older children. The RUF instituted a Small Boys Unit, in which child commanders (slightly older) were considered "ruthless . . . or in the jargon of the RUF *wild boys & hard boys*."[101] In contrast, IS uses a mixture of different arrangements. In some cases, the children are put into units with adults; in an innovation introduced in December 2015 called *inghemasi*, two to three children or youth are placed in high-risk commando units alongside three or four adults.

Role of Children

The children of IS have multiple, and occasionally overlapping, roles. However, there is also evidence of a clear specialization for those identified as having distinct skills. Some Cubs are assigned to checkpoint or bodyguard duty, which, although mostly a support function, may involve donning a suicide vest—even if they are not intended to be suicide bombers. Children who display aptitude for disseminating ideological content might be deployed as recruiters on mobile Dawa caravans or, eventually, as recruiters from the pulpit.

These gifted children embrace their public-speaking role and may be more articulate and persuasive than their adult counterparts. The main role of child recruiters is not only to incite adults to take action, but also to lure more children with the promise of status, purpose, and admiration from the militants and the public alike. IS is essentially using children to recruit more children. Having children helm propaganda is part of the group's psychological impact on adults, as it shames men to witness children being more "manly" than they are. This also explains IS's motivation in deploying children as part of *inghemasi* operations since December 2015. If a child penetrates the target in the first wave, it becomes highly unlikely that the adults will defect or change their minds at the last minute, lest the youth appear braver or manlier than the adults.

Recently graduated Cubs are publicly paraded in full uniform, carrying weapons, to signal strength and discipline to onlookers. The children are instructed to stand rigid while being beaten with sticks by their adult commanders, to demonstrate resolve and toughness. In the background, dozens of younger (still civilian) children admire the masked recruits. The cycle repeats itself, with each wave of graduates acting as a beacon for other children. Terrorist organizations have as their first priority survival, so ensuring the continuity and longevity of the group requires thinking about the future. IS is far more than a simple terrorist organization, but there can be no doubt that it has embraced the need to groom the next generation.

Parents report that isolation from the family occurs at this stage. The children are not allowed to receive visitors, and some family members have been threatened with violence when they have pleaded with IS commanders to let them see their children. Like the separation of child soldiers, being split from the family unit appears a necessary prerequisite to breaking down resistance. As with the child soldiers in Africa, by far the most important mechanism preventing desertion is the threat of corporal punishment. Child deserters were publicly beaten, and in previous conflicts, they were killed in front of other combatants in order to deter potential desertions, as was the case in the DRC and Colombia.[102]

One of the main reasons to recruit child soldiers is that they do not have exit options and can be kept in the force through the threat of violence or for small rations, rather than salaries. There is evidence to suggest that child soldiers are often not paid, unlike children in terrorist organizations, who receive some remuneration. According to the *Washington Post*, in Yemen, the children are paid about three dollars a day, whereas according to Al Jazeera, compensation is closer to two dollars.[103] Other media reports with interviewees contradict these claims and insist that they are not paid at all but receive food and a bag of *khat*, a narcotic plant common in Yemen.[104] There is varying information as to whether children in IS are actually paid. According to Mahmoud, one child who escaped, "They promised us cars, guns, and money then they promised that we would go to heaven."[105] In some cases, parents benefit financially from their children's participation. The variation is based on the type of child recruit. For example, local residents are under pressure to supply children in exchange for protection (from predation from IS) and to guarantee their supply of food, shelter, and provision of salaries from IS. In Pakistan, the children were a substitute for the TTP's extortion demands.

Some scholars have argued that joining an armed group might be a good option for children as a form of protection[106]—that in some contexts, it is safer to be part of an armed group than to be attacked by one. Participation in an armed group can also allow a child to loot and have something to eat. These are luxuries not available to noncombatants.[107]

Child soldiers might also be separated from their extended family. They are isolated by being moved away from their traditional villages or forced to kill family members in order to destroy the option of returning home;[108] the LRA moved abductees far away from home to discourage escape.[109] Often there are no family members left alive to visit the children, and extended family members may not want any contact with them after they have been forcibly recruited. For some child soldiers, the groups would mark the children permanently, as a form of social control; in some cases this marking was literal, sustained through tattooing to establish in- and out-groups. Children in some cases are also branded. Some analysts view tattooing as developing an esprit de corps, whereas branding is a more coercive way of conveying ownership and control.

Among child soldiers there was an explicit promotion through the ranks, and one form of reward was the permission and privilege to lead one's own unit if the conflict persisted. Beyond status, the group provided child soldiers with more privileges, including access to sex.[110] The allocation of rewards and promotions was yet another method of strengthening solidarity and collective pride among RUF boy soldiers in Sierra Leone. As a general rule, the more aggressive the child soldiers were seen to be, the greater the degree of property destruction and looting that resulted, and the more children were abducted. The more children were abducted, the more that youth rose through the ranks of the RUF. Promotion to the rank of commander was deemed to be the pinnacle of success. A source of privilege as well as pride, being a commander meant being allowed to lead units of other child combatants—called "Small Boys Units" according to Zayed—and having sexual license with women and girls.[111] Sexual violence and gratification may be their own reward. Jill Trenholm and her coauthors suggest that feelings of powerlessness and emasculation might lead a child soldier to commit sexual violence, and different groups permitted this to varying degrees (there was significant variation from one group to the next with regard to the pervasiveness of sexual violence).[112] Gang rape may also be used as a bonding tool within armed groups.[113]

Child soldiers in Africa are not recruited for the future, but for the present. Most die in battle and only a handful ever progress through the ranks to become adult leaders (sometimes because the conflicts don't last very long). The assumption appears to be that a group can always recruit more children. Those children who refuse to follow orders or try to escape are killed.[114] Some limited exceptions to this generalization exist. Some child captives reported being educated in RUF camps in Sierra Leone, where makeshift schools used fragments and scraps of revolutionary texts. Indoctrination into Joseph Kony's LRA in Uganda included spiritual training, misinformation, and a combination of fear and violence. Christopher Blattman observes that

> spiritual practices appear central to motivating recruits and can be seen as an attempt to create new social bonds based on a shared cosmology (as well as fear). Kony created a cult of mystery and spiritual power, which few abductees or civilians disbelieve even now.[115]

As a result of indoctrination, the children in the LRA were so brutal that, according to Anthony Vinci, they inflicted fear "due to their own fearlessness in combat and complete disregard for human life."[116] In addition to ideological training, the children reported receiving some basic training in the art of "bush warfare." Captive children adapt quickly and exult in their newfound skills and the chance, perhaps for the first time in their lives, to show off what they are capable of. "Boy soldiers in Liberia," notes Paul Richards, "have spoken longingly of their guns not as weapons of destruction but as being the first piece of modern *kit* they have ever known how to handle."[117]

Girls in Combat Roles

There has been widespread interest in women and gender-based violence perpetrated by the Islamic State. The issue is especially salient given the increasing number of children involved in violent extremist organizations. The Islamic Caliphate has taken to targeting young girls for recruitment, wherein the group marries the young women off to foreign fighters. Additionally the media has been fascinated by the "Jihadi Bride"[118] phenomenon in which women voluntarily sought to emigrate and join the Caliphate. During 2014–2017 IS punctuated its violent territorial campaign with the systematic abuse of women. It occasionally boasted about its activities. In its heyday IS revived the practice of sexual slavery, war booty and concubinage using an antiquated interpretation of the Islamic distribution of the spoils of war as expounded in Surat al-Anfal (8:41).[119]

Gender-based violence and the exploitation of women were used as incentives for male fighters to join the fray and remain. To this end, women in the Caliphate were fully commoditized and used to recruit, reward, retain male fighters (whether local or foreign),[120] and reproduce. ISIS capitalized on access to women to lure men to the caliphate: they were potential wives, ranked according to a variety of criteria—skin and hair color, country of origin, and breast size—and allocated to men based on a patriarchal system of hierarchy and status.[121] In so doing, women were systematically exploited as a means of staving off its declining rate of recruitment and presenting a bulwark against defection, an issue that could, in the medium term, rend the organization apart if not effectively stemmed. Having a wife, a child, and a house were strong incentives not to leave ISIS territory.[122]

In the next chapter we explore how children are taught to hate. While we touched on the crucial role of schooling in this chapter to distinguish terrorist groups from most cases of child soldiers, it is important to ascertain the types of material children are taught in order to appreciate the social ecology of terrorism, and how an environment that is conducive to violence is constructed.

LEARNING TO HATE
Socialization and Cultural Influences

No one is born hating another person because of the color of his skin, or his background, or his religion. People must learn to hate, and if they can learn to hate, they can be taught to love, for love comes more naturally to the human heart than its opposite.

Nelson Mandela, *Long Walk to Freedom*

Children are not "born" into terrorism but learn to want to be a part of a terrorist movement. According to a 2016 report by the United Nations High Commissioners for Refugees (UNHCR), more than 3.7 million Syrian refugee children are out of school on any given day. One in three schools (over six thousand) in Syria have been destroyed or damaged.[1] In Iraq, the situation is equally dire, if not more so. The UN estimates that around 10 percent of Iraqi children—more than 1.5 million—have been forced to flee their homes since 2014. UNICEF estimates that one in five Iraqi schools is closed because of the war, and with 35 percent of the Iraqi population under eighteen, Save the Children estimates that 1,050,000 children in IS-held areas either are not in school or attend schools controlled by the terrorists.[2] Schools that remain open during the conflict can provide militias or terrorists with easy access to abduct or recruit youth as soldiers, as sex slaves, or for ransom.[3]

Nigeria has the highest number of children not attending school. In 2010, 10.5 million children—one in three—were roaming the streets, mostly concentrated in the northern regions, which suffered from a 70 percent illiteracy rate. Islamist-leaning politicians in northern Nigeria introduced Islamic boarding schools, known as *almajirai*, which are comparable to South Asian *madrassas* and Southeast Asian *pesantrens* and are, according to Virginia Comoli, "aimed at [educating] boys from families too poor to properly support them."[4] The children studying at the *almajirai* (some as young as four or five) do not learn English or Hausa, nor do they acquire any skills conducive to future employment; they only memorize the Qur'an. The *almajirai* serve as recruitment centers for local politicians in need of muscle to intimidate their rivals, and the children become easy recruits for Boko Haram. Oluwole "Wole" Soyinka, the winner of the 1986 Nobel Prize in Literature, contends that the schools are the breeding grounds for the *almajiri* students to be unleashed on society by Boko Haram as foot soldiers:

> They were bred in *madrassas* and are generally known as the *almajiris*. From knives and machetes, bows, and poisoned arrows they have gradu- ated to AK-47s, homemade bombs, and explosive-packed vehicles. Only the mechanism of inflicting death has changed, nothing else.[5]

Although this is difficult to confirm, Soyinka claims that the *almajiri* consti- tuted the bulk of Boko Haram car bombers and suicide bombers.[6] Terrorist orga- nizations (in contrast to militias recruiting child soldiers) prioritize ideologically grooming the next generation. In this chapter we explore how education and the intentional biases depicted in children's textbooks play a role in children's recruitment into terrorist groups and create fertile ground for possible future radicalization. In essence, we explore how children learn to hate.

Education is crucial to childhood development by creating opportunities, but some types of education can distort how young people view their world. In recent years the relationship between education and terrorism has been shown to be an inverse one—that is, many terrorists are the by-products of a Western education or are better educated and better off financially than the average person in their community. Existing research has argued that most terrorists are disproportion- ately well educated and financially better off than their peers.[7] Marc Sageman contends that poverty is not directly correlated with involvement in terrorism.[8] Claude Berrebi found that "both higher education and standard of living are pos- itively associated with participation in Hamas or PIJ [Palestinian Islamic Jihad] and with becoming a suicide bomber."[9]

While this certainly holds true for adults across many terrorist groups (though some exceptions apply where the ethnic group might have been denied access to education as part of the state's counterterrorism policies), it is not true of youth involved in militant organizations. The majority of terrorists in Alan Kruger and Jitka Maleckova's research were in their twenties or thirties, and were overwhelm- ingly college educated.[10] All of the studies to date have focused on adult members of terrorist groups and have tracked adult operatives, but never children. Child recruits by definition and by their age will be less educated and less wealthy; nev- ertheless, the poverty of their families and communities may play a role, which is not the case with adults.

Afghan and Pakistani youth recruited into the Taliban pose an intellectual challenge to the conventional wisdom that poverty and lack of education are inversely related to terrorism. The research collected by Sabaoon shows that the social ecology and structural conditions for adults are not the same as they are for children. Darcy Noricks's data posits a negative correlation between wealth and involvement in terrorism for adults, and Sabaoon's data substantiates these findings. Its report says that for the practitioners treating children recruited by the Taliban (both coercively and those who joined "voluntarily"), "recruitment of children and adolescents is significantly correlated with economic deprivation in Pakistan, particularly in Swat, and we have similar findings from the Quetta population as well."[11] Within the geographic areas of Malakand and the Federally Administered Tribal Areas, the lower economic echelons are particularly vulnerable to recruitment because the population is "desperately poor," such that the therapists at Sabaoon concluded, "Life after death and the narrative of the terrorist commanders becomes a potent stimulus for joining the group."[12]

Ilene Cohn and Guy Goodwin-Gill offer a possible explanation: wealthier children may be absent from the locations from which militias ordinarily recruit. For example, we know that many militant organizations opportunistically recruit from orphanages, public transportation, and IDP camps. This has been as true of child soldiers in Liberia and Rwanda as it was for LTTE,[13] and for IS when it emptied out Syrian orphanages. Cohn and Goodwin-Gill further hypothesize that during conflicts, schools might be closed or destroyed, leaving youth without education or hopes for the future. Wealthy parents may be able to "buy back" their children's freedom in exchange for a fine, levy, or tax. Alternatively, wealthy children are often sent abroad for school, especially in conflict zones, and are not present during recruitment.[14]

Poverty may likewise play a role in establishing children's beliefs. In her documentary *Children of Terror*, the filmmaker Sharmeen Obeid-Chinoy documented Pakistani schools that were producing young suicide bombers. In an interview, she explained that the causal connection between structural conditions of poverty and violent outcomes seemed clear:

> Those with education or financial means flee and those who remain try to live amid the violence and downward economic spiral. . . . This is how terrorists ensure having a steady supply of recruits—they create an unworkable society, and then offer an alternative one—one that they, of course, control with violence, intimidation, and manipulation. They make use of disasters, both natural and those they created, by offering aid to those in need, but with very tangled strings attached.[15]

Because of the financial hardship facing families in Pakistan, Afghanistan, Nigeria, Syria, and Iraq, children are forced to find food and money anywhere they can. In Pakistan or Afghanistan, boys might be offered a place in a madrassa (religious school), where they will be fed and taught and provided with free room and board. However, the content of the instruction comprises a radical ideology that is intolerant, including of other Muslims, and that views the West as an enemy.[16] This is not to say that poverty is the only cause of children's involvement in violent extremism, but like other structural conditions, it provides a context that enables terrorist organizations to exploit children. In southern Afghanistan, families are allegedly proud of the fact that their young sons—many under fifteen—are glorifying the name of Islam by "attacking the enemy" and becoming martyrs (i.e., suicide bombers). The Taliban reportedly pays as much as $12,000 per child to the children's families.[17] According to Obeid-Chinoy,

> These boys belonged to large families; some had up to ten siblings. Their parents were poor and could not take care of them, so they had been sent off to remote Islamic schools in Pakistan. The children, many of whom were residents of refugee camps in Karachi, have been greatly affected by the violence around them, and this environment influences the type of adults they become.[18]

Other children might have to choose from among a variety of bad options; if they do not join the militant group they will be forced onto the street. Like child soldiers, children might join a group out of desperation—they lack food or shelter, they are orphans, or they are generally at risk. Once the children are mobilized into terrorist organizations and have experienced front-line action, some might even enjoy the experience of empowerment or belonging—much as adults do when part of a terrorist group that provides benefits, opportunities, and a feeling of belonging to something bigger than oneself.[19]

In the data of 192 boys, aged eight to sixteen, from the Sabaoon rehabilitation facility in Pakistan,[20] and studies conducted by Palestinian psychologists of children who had joined militant groups, ideology was secondary to other factors that influenced the children's "decision" to join. However, the emotional bonds made at the Paradise summer camps or at the madrassas are not easily severed. One individual who graduated from Sabaoon became an informant and handed over his uncle to security forces, and his family has been divided over this decision ever since. According to the school's director, Feriha Peracha, Sabaoon has not had any cases of recidivism.[21]

The presence or absence of schooling distinguishes extremist groups' attitudes vis-à-vis children from each other and from those of African militias. One of the major differences between child soldiers and those in terrorist movements that we explored in chapter 2 emphasized the importance of education. Within the African militias, children were portrayed as low-skilled members—valuable exclusively because of their youth and availability to fill the ranks. Militias rarely educated young recruits, seeing them instead as expendable.[22] However, in terrorist organizations, there appears to be a desire and a need to educate as well as train the next generation. Many terrorist organizations want to ensure the ideological consistency and purity of the next generation and expend significant resources on the children's education. In explaining the shift away from forced recruitment of children and the need for an educated generation, one guerrilla leader from El Salvador's Farabundo Martí National Liberation Front said, "We don't need cannon fodder, we need consciousness and without that it's better that they stay home."[23]

Children who have been forcibly conscripted tend to be uneducated—most militias do not run schools to train their youth. Terrorist groups take their first steps toward recruitment at school. Education plays a role in convincing youth to adopt radical views or absorb and parrot a group's ideology. This brainwashing varies from one militant group to another.

Jacob Olidort, formally of the Washington Institute, explored children's education and textbooks in areas under IS's control.[24] IS schools represent one aspect of the group's enterprise to transform children from peripheral bystanders to fully committed insiders. Aymenn al-Tamimi explains that education has been used to ensure that the children subscribe to the same ideology as their parents.[25] After IS took over Mosul in 2014, studies of law, political science, and fine arts at the University of Mosul were terminated, and Islamic studies and other aspects of the university's curriculum radically changed. Mixed-sex education or coeducation ended, and males and females attended the university separately—alternating between days so that not only were women in different classrooms, but they were absent from campus altogether on the days that men were present.[26] In primary and secondary education, IS began using the same textbooks and curricula as those used in Saudi Arabia, which promote Wahhabi Islam, comprising hatred toward the Shia sect and antagonism toward other faiths.[27] Within two years of the establishment of the caliphate, IS issued a fatwa (religious ruling) to create original course materials.[28]

This task fell to IS's "department of education," Khaled al-Afari (a.k.a. Dhul-Qarnayn, "the man with two horns"), a thirty-year-old Turkmen (occasionally described as Egyptian) from Tal Afar, who holds a degree in Islamic science. With Syria's fragmentation, IS assumed de facto control over schools and mosques. In October 2014 al-Afari's ministry issued a new set of guidelines for teachers working in areas controlled by the Islamic State.[29] The new guidelines called on teachers to emphasize creationism, reject Darwinism, eliminate music and the arts, teach history from a Sunni Muslim perspective, discard all vestiges of modernity, and segregate the sexes.[30] In K–12 schools, according to one report, "art, music, philosophy and social studies classes were cancelled and geography, history and literature lessons as well as any teaching about Christianity became forbidden subjects."[31] These were replaced with religious topics such as Qur'an memorization, *tawheed* (monotheism), *salat* (prayer), and *aqeedah* (creed), among others.[32] The curriculum changed significantly: specific secular subjects were removed entirely from study, and others were heavily redacted to ensure ideological uniformity. In order to maintain some scientific standards, classes in physics, chemistry, mathematics, Arabic, and English remained, but this reflected a need for these skills for governing the caliphate and for fighting. Anything in the curriculum that implied charging financial interest, establishing democracy, or calling for elections was removed.[33] Physical education was rebranded as "jihadi training" and included shooting, swimming, and horseback riding.[34]

Though many of the original (male) Syrian schoolteachers remained on the job, they had to teach the IS-approved curriculum to gender-segregated pupils. Attendance at schools did not appear to be forced, and parents willingly sent their children there, although a few reports surfaced of some parents choosing to homeschool in order to avoid the IS schools (as was the case in Sri Lanka when the LTTE recruited youth from K–12 schools).

Refugees interviewed by Save the Children at the Jad'ah camp (close to Qayyarah) in Nineveh, Iraq, explained that "the extremist content of the [IS] curriculum is aimed at brainwashing children and turning them into fighters."[35] The terror group's curriculum infuses each subject with military images and vocabulary, and, at the more advanced levels, "trains students how to make suicide bombs and techniques for carrying out a successful beheading," according to the Fox News reporter John Huddy.[36] One father interviewed by Save the Children recalled, "They would teach children how to make bombs. When children came out from school there was a big TV in the garden where they were showing propaganda: how to kill and how to make suicide bombs and how to cut heads off."[37]

The school curriculum is blatant indoctrination, and governments (e.g., in Iraq) reject IS-controlled education. Iraq's Ministry of Education won't accept IS certificates or qualifications in the areas under its control.[38] But education is only part of the modus operandi for these "schools," as the lectures, discussions, and curriculum bring the children closer to each other—and to the attention of IS personnel, who "talent scout" for children exhibiting early potential for Cub status in IS's dedicated training camps. According to one child who escaped, training lasted for forty-five days, and the "camp included children from Turkey, Iraq, and even the United States, who were put through the boot camp which included weapons training and target practice."[39]

Through this process of socialization and selection, IS makes entry into the Cubs unit a rare commodity that every child desires. By limiting access, IS fosters competition among the children for membership. Younger students might be groomed first as spies, encouraged to inform on family members or neighbors who violate the rules or criticize IS, but they are promised the future prospect of Cub training if they complete these tasks successfully.[40]

In one of the group's propaganda videos, IS presented the "Farouq Institute for Cubs," in which fifteen Yezidi children were trained in the three essentials: teaching Qur'an, specifically as related to (the lesser) jihad (holy war); weapons training; and managing prisoners.[41] In another highly choreographed video released by Nineveh Provincial Media, Cubs were taught martial arts and self-defense, and put through rigorous physical training while their instructors punched them, kicked them, or hit them with wooden sticks.[42] Interviewed by Iraqi news, one recruit who escaped from IS recounted that "IS takes children from mosques brainwashes them and trains them which involves breaking sticks on their stomachs and tiles on their heads before sending them to execute missions," ostensibly to toughen the children up.[43]

Militarized Classrooms and Textbooks

The former special representative for the UN secretary-general Zainab Zerrougui posited a direct connection between child recruitment and a lack of access to education. One reason for this correlation is the increasing degree to which schools have been seized by militias or government forces, making them inhospitable environments for learning (especially for girls, who face harassment or sexual predation if military units inhabit school buildings).[44] The UNHCR acknowledges that education functions as a protection tool in two ways. First, when schools are secure, they provide children with a safe place to gather. Second, providing refugees with an education affords them more choices for their future and hopefully reduces the allure of military recruitment.[45]

Schools are an early (and easy) target during conflict. Human Rights Watch (HRW) has documented their systematic takeover by militaries, militias, and extremists. Schools have also become a locus for recruitment. The LTTE broadcasts *Rambo*-like TV movies of live combat training (and actual combat), parades units of young soldiers before schoolchildren as they emerge from class, conducts military training on school grounds, and gives talks at schools about the need for soldiers. At least one school in the LTTE zone had a combination memorial hall and playground replete with photos of young martyrs (*tiyakiyakku*) and a play area in which guns were mounted next to the seesaws. Tamil children spend several hours a day digging bunkers (militarized civic duty) and are asked to join the LTTE formally.[46] Field research in Sri Lanka (in Vavunya and Killanochi) revealed parents who routinely prevented their children from attending school for fear of the possible recruitment that might occur there, when they were not around to protect them.[47]

"We see everything from troops using schools as their bases, barracks and training grounds to classrooms being converted into weapons depots, detention centers and even places where torture is carried out—in some cases with children witnessing or hearing it," says Zama Coursen-Neff, pointing to HRW research on the occupation of schools in Somalia, Yemen, the Philippines, Thailand, Iraq, and India. Violent extremist groups use buildings, infrastructure, and access to students. Coursen-Neff's report highlights the extent to which classrooms have joined the front lines as both militias and government troops take them over and repurpose them for their benefit.[48] For example, in Bihar in 2009, "the soldiers had moved into the school after a group of Maoist rebels attacked and destroyed the police station where the troops were based. On any given day, from 25 to 40 armed men were deployed at the school. They had added brick sentry boxes on the school roof and other fortifications, including sandbags, around the main gate."[49] The report examines multiple cases in which students no longer had access to classrooms, and many girls refused to go to school for fear of harassment or worse:

> When troops move in, children are either displaced entirely, denying them education, or forced to try to study alongside armed men. Worse, the military use of schools can turn schools into legitimate military objectives under the laws of war. Children and teachers have been killed or wounded when opposing forces have attacked occupied schools.[50]

There has been little awareness of how pervasive the military use of schools is during war—it has been a feature of the majority of recent conflicts—and how badly it harms children.[51] UN Security Council resolution 2143, issued on March 7, 2014, expressed "deep concern at the military use of schools in contravention of applicable international law . . . [and urged] all parties to armed conflict to respect the civilian character of schools."[52]

Schools taken over by militants and/or government troops can provide a child's first exposure to ideology, expectations of political involvement, and peer pressure to join their friends in protests, demonstrations, and other youth movements. Children may genuinely develop an ideological commitment to a cause; participation in extremist groups may be its own reward. Rommel Banlaoi explains the ideological inducements used to recruit children into terrorist organizations in the LTTE and some Palestinian groups that target children with intense propaganda.[53] Children's experiences in school are dictated by the content of instruction, the degree to which teachers impart their own political views, and the content of the textbooks that they use.

The Israel-Palestine conflict has produced a comprehensive literature highlighting the biases present in children's textbooks, which shape the views and ideologies of youth on both sides. Both Israeli and Palestinian textbooks have been extensively criticized as sources of radicalization (and xenophobia) and function as an impediment to peaceful coexistence between the two communities. The major complaint is the degree to which, as Daniel Bar Tal and Sami Adwan put it, "textbooks misrepresent the conflict by omitting, marginalizing or magnifying certain events or processes in order to present them in line with the society's own national narrative."[54] This critique is accurate for the textbooks of both sides, which have promoted a selective history in which the experiences of the other have not received the same attention as each side's own (real or perceived) grievances. Absent from most textbooks is a dehumanization of the other, although negative portrayals of the other are consistent across both communities' textbooks.[55] As Bar Tal, Adwan, and Wexler report,

> both Israeli and Palestinian books present unilateral national narratives that present the other as enemy and chronicle negative actions by the other. Historical events, while not false or fabricated, are selectively presented to reinforce each community's national narrative.[56]

One might expect Israel, as a democracy, to produce textbooks featuring a more evenhanded presentation of the facts, but this is not the case. Furthermore, Israel receives more US foreign aid than any other country in the world,[57] and according to Israeli sources, since 1950, the United States has provided in excess of $3.2 billion in assistance to the United Nations Relief and Works Agency to operate schools in Palestinian refugee camps.[58] The Palestinian Authority undertook a reform of its textbooks in 1994 and again in 2004; however, the new editions, albeit improved, still fail to foster peaceful attitudes toward Israel. The books include references to the anti-Semitic document known as the *Protocols of the Elders of Zion* (fabricated by the Russian secret police), and they fail to recognize the existence of the State of Israel or discuss religious tolerance of Jewish people.[59] Defining Israel's founding as a "catastrophe unprecedented in history" and "a theft perpetrated by Zionist gangs," describing Israel as both "colonial imperialist" and "racist," and presenting the conflict as a religious war leaves little latitude for students to have neutral attitudes toward Israel.

During the same period, the right-wing Knesset member Geula Cohen, originally a member of the Irgun Underground who had parted ways with Menachem Begin to join the Stern Gang because she found the Irgun too moderate,[60] blocked the publication of updated Israeli high school textbooks that acknowledged the 1948 Naqba (Disaster), as Palestinians, echoing their textbooks,[61] refer to the May 1948 creation of the State of Israel.[62] Cohen was a member of the Knesset's

Education and Culture Committee on and off from 1974 to 1992 and was a vocal critic of the revisionist Israeli history movement sparked by the declassification of official government documents in 1987.[63] Also prohibited was any mention that Palestinians had been expelled en masse from Israeli-controlled territory in 1947–48 as part of Operation Dalet, which sought to hold control of strategic areas through ethnic cleansing, using deception, terrorizing civilians, and threatening to allow right-wing extremist groups (such as the Stern Gang or Lehi) access to villages to repeat their massacre at Deir Yassin.[64] In 2015, the Education Ministry released its new high school civics textbook, *To Be Israeli Citizens*, which had been in the works for five years. The book did not recognize the Palestinian right to statehood, and also implied that Palestinian incitement had played a role in the assassination of Yitzhak Rabin.[65] Bar Tal, Adwan, and Wexler write that

> both Israeli and Palestinian books present exclusive unilateral national narratives that present a wealth of information about the other as enemy and a dearth of information about the other in positive or human light. Historical events, while not false or fabricated, are selectively presented to reinforce each national narrative.[66]

Palestinian children are exposed to violence on a daily basis, through their experiences participating in nonviolent resistance as well as their exposure to media and television programs aimed specifically at them in order to foster an environment conducive to martyrdom. This manipulation of children's media is explored in greater detail in chapter 5.

The early indoctrination of children using militarized textbooks or children's books is a common feature in virtually every long-standing conflict. This is not unique to the Middle East, although many of the examples in this book are from that region. While conducting field research in Northern Ireland, we found children's baby bibs emblazoned with the logos of terrorist organizations such as the Red Hand of Ulster or ethnic or political identifiers ("baby Prod" for a supporter of Ulster/Loyalist/Protestant Nationalism), and, archived at Linen Hall, a children's book for the Catholic supporters of the Provisional IRA: "A is for Armalite that sends them all running" (Armalite being the American-made small firearm, roughly the equivalent of an AR-10, used by the IRA in the 1970s and 1980s during the Troubles).[67]

From Where Did the Radical Education Rhetoric in the Region Originate?

Within the Middle East, education was traditionally divided between secular education—reserved for the elites and the wealthiest members of society—and religious education, available in both the public and the private sectors. The Islamic curriculum and religious studies taught by madrassas, while giving a sense of identity and providing students with the fundamentals of Islamic culture and tradition, tended not to include secular and scientific subjects required for the modern world; madrassas were the leftover remnants of formal Islamic learning from previous centuries. However, as most central governments in the region were weak, the development of "modern" schooling was slow, marked by repeated contests and tensions between entrenched and powerful religious forces. Madrassas and state officials vied to build the institutions and capacities of the modern nation-state by drawing on scientific and technological know-how.[68]

Shockingly, a lot of the most extreme rhetoric in the region's textbooks comes from an unlikely source: the US Agency for International Development (USAID).[69] During the Cold War, and especially during the Russian occupation of Afghanistan, the United States funded educational products designed to instill a hatred of Russian foreigners (occupiers) and incite an Islamic resistance. They did not anticipate that the books would eventually see the US and the West as the foreign interlopers. It was a case of the best intentions paving the road to hell.

The educational development programs undertaken by the United States in Afghanistan were consistent with US strategy vis-à-vis countries in danger of falling into the Soviet sphere of influence: provide development aid and technical assistance in sufficient quantity to win over the population's "hearts and minds" against the Soviet menace, and simultaneously incentivize national leadership to cooperate with US objectives. This was the principal idea behind the establishment of USAID.

Following the colonial era, Pakistan (created in 1947) and Afghanistan (founded in 1709) benefited from the Cold War strategy of providing development aid to countries teetering on the edge of Communist threats from the Soviet sphere. According to Roozbeh Shirazi, "Beginning in the 1950s, American educational consultants—including Teachers College at Columbia University (TCCU) and the University of Wyoming (UW)—helped design and implement a secular educational system in Afghanistan that emphasized the compatibility of Islam with 'Western' philosophies[70] and challenged Soviet influence."[71]

US financial assistance drastically increased during the Russian invasion and the war in Afghanistan, from $30 million in 1980 to $600 million per year from 1986 to 1989, matched dollar for dollar by Saudi Arabia. The Pakistani Inter-Service Intelligence distributed the funds to the mujahideen to wage a guerrilla campaign against the Soviet occupation force. As part of this effort, US education assistance took a sharp ideological turn, using textbooks distributed to both secular schools and madrassas on the Pakistani side of the border, where millions of Afghan refugees had fled, to promote an Islamic justification for an insurgency. US and Saudi funds were also used to build and maintain madrassas and schools in the Afghan refugee camps.[72] A collaboration between USAID and the Center for Afghanistan Studies at the University of Nebraska, Omaha (with funding in excess of $51 million), produced textbooks for the madrassas specifically written to give what Christopher Candland calls "religious sanction to armed struggle in defense of Islam."[73]

During this period, there was an increase in Saudi Arabia's educational and religious outreach (*dawah*) to places such as Pakistan and Afghanistan. The initial export of Wahhabism began in response to the popularity of Pan-Arabism and Arab Socialism. The ruling Saud family founded the Muslim World League to promote religious solidarity. However, it was the threat of the Islamic Revolution in Iran, especially after the temporary seizure of the Grand Mosque in Mecca in 1979, that prompted the Saudis to promote their own interpretation of Islamic values through education. In 1982, King Fahd issued a directive declaring that "no limits be put on expenditures for the propagation of Islam."[74]

Shirazi describes the Afghan textbooks, even those written for children in elementary school, as "explicitly violent."[75] The first-grade textbook taught children the alphabet with the pneumonic, "*Alef* is for Allah, *jim* is for jihad, and *shin* is for Shakir, who conducts jihad with his sword. God becomes happy with the defeat of the Russians."[76] Subsequent primary school textbooks reinforced these themes. Third- and fifth-grade textbooks depicted Kalashnikov rifles, rocket-propelled grenades, and tanks. A fourth-grade math textbook stated that the speed of a round fired from a Kalashnikov rifle was eight hundred meters per second, and then asked, "If a Russian is at a distance of 3200 meters from a mujahid, and that mujahid aims at the Russian's head, calculate how many seconds it will take for the bullet to strike the Russian in the forehead."[77]

This use of school textbooks to indoctrinate children has parallels with the books created by IS. In the Afghan textbooks created in Nebraska in the 1980s, children were taught the alphabet with violent or military imagery. John Huddy reports that in these books' alphabet lessons, "the letter 'S' is for sniper, with a picture of, presumably, an ISIS fighter aiming his rifle. The letter 'W,' or woman, shows an indiscernible black figure—presumably a burqa-clad female."[78] This is also true of the textbooks used by the Islamic State, in which every subject from grammar to mathematics uses violent or warfare-related frames of reference (*B* is for bomb and *D* is for dagger). According to the BBC, as soon as children turn five, they "are introduced to a vocabulary of strife and gore, in their school curriculum books . . . as teachers are encouraged to 'inject zeal through fervent rhymes that terrorize the enemies of Islam.'"[79]

When IS took over Syrian and Iraqi schools, it initially used highly censored Syrian books; then it switched to Saudi religious textbooks that shared IS's view of the world, identifying their common enemies as the Shia, Jews, and nonbelievers. But eventually IS rebranded the textbooks to reflect its own specific ideology (which is overtly anti-Saudi). The IS flag and logo were incorporated into the pages of the books, constituting a form of branding.[80] The BBC reports that

> the IS curriculum was finally rolled out for the 2015–2016 school year. Children would enroll at the age of five and graduate at 15, shaving four full years off the traditional school life. They would be educated in 12 various disciplines, but these would be steeped in Islamic State's doctrine and its world vision. Jihad became institutionalised, the enemy was everyone beyond the borders of the caliphate.[81]

An English-language primary school textbook teaches children how to tell time by using a clock, which is fastened to bundled sticks of dynamite (i.e., bombs).

In a book for first-grade students discovered in the al-Muthana district of Eastern Mosul, students are asked to solve "arithmetic problems and equations featuring Kalashnikov rifles, IS flags, tanks and military aircraft rather than

FIGURE 4. IS tanks and weapons

FIGURE 5. Math with guns

apples and oranges presenting instruments of violence as a normal part of every day life."[82] Another mathematics textbook asks students to solve equations such as, "If the Islamic State has 275,220 heroes in a battle and the unbelievers have 356,230, who has more soldiers?"[83]

FIGURE 6. IS textbook showing children training for combat

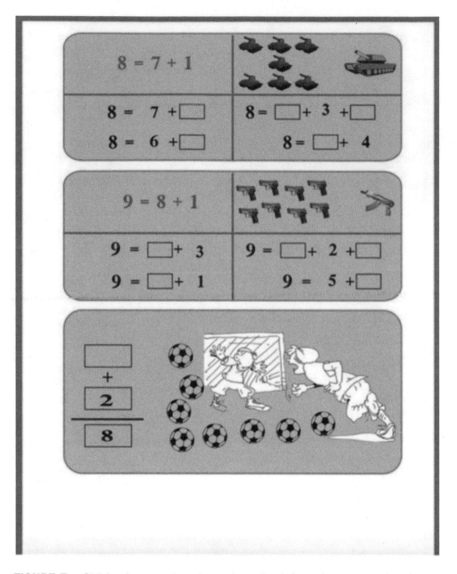

FIGURE 7. Children's second-grade math textbook featuring guns and tanks

In interviews, former teachers no longer living under IS control admit that they were forced to teach children IS propaganda and that their students became increasingly aggressive and full of hatred as they learned the IS curriculum. One former teacher interviewed by NBC News said that after IS launched its nation-wide education system in May 2015, "I was teaching them to become a young terrorist. I was simply brainwashing them."[84]

The long-term effect of brainwashing is clear from Pakistan three decades on, and the experiences in Pakistan and Afghanistan yield important lessons about how to deal with this problem in the future. Thirteen million textbooks were produced and distributed in Pakistan between 1984 and 1994. A total of fifteen million copies eventually made it to Afghanistan.[85] The books were used long after the war in Afghanistan ended. In some remote areas, the textbooks are still used today—reflecting the lingering ideology, but also likely indicating the shortage of textbooks because of extreme poverty.

The strategy of manipulating educational curricula for the purposes of insurgency initially appeared to work, although as Candland points out, USAID never expected that the same textbooks would be used against the West.[86] Shirazi explains,

> In restructuring the curriculum, the US desire to combat Islamic extremism is evident in defining education in a deeply religious society as a "predominantly secular activity." Recalibrating the goals of education in this way allows for the reduction or omission of references to Islam or Islamic symbols in educational materials.[87]

The secular character of education reform has made it easier for Islamic insurgents to frame the American presence as "anti-Islamic," and to target education development efforts, just as Islamists and the mujahideen targeted Afghan schools during the Soviet occupation. Indeed, education policy and reconstruction have proven a favorite focus of Taliban insurgents. In 2006 alone, insurgents burned down 187 schools and killed eighty-five students and more than forty teachers.[88] There have been over 1,100 attacks against schools in Afghanistan, and according to Jo Becker, "The attacks included the use of IEDs, land mines, suicide bombings, grenades thrown into school buildings or playgrounds, rocket attacks, and setting schools on fire."[89] Throughout the Pashtun Belt, an average of more than one girls' school a day was burned down or bombed in 2007, a rate faster than the schools could be built, replaced, or repaired. In Afghanistan, where USAID built hundreds of schools after 2001, the Taliban burned down 1,089 between 2005 and 2007 alone.[90]

The former Harvard University president Larry Summers, no proponent of women's education[91], once concluded that girls' education might yield the highest rate of return of any investment in the developing world. "Educated women have fewer children; provide better nutrition, health, and education to their families; experience significantly lower child mortality; and generate more income than women with little or no schooling. Investing to educate them thus creates a virtuous cycle for their community. . . . Similarly, children benefit more from an increase in their mother's education than from the equivalent increase in their father's."[92]

Girls' education lowers birth rates, which, by extension, helps developing countries improve per capita income. Better-educated women bear fewer children because they marry later and have fewer years for childbearing. They also are better able to make informed, confident decisions about reproduction. In fact, increasing the average education level of women by three years can lower their individual birth rate by one child. Female education also boosts productivity. World Bank studies indicate that, in areas where women have very little schooling, providing them with at least another year of primary education is a better way to raise farm yields than increasing access to and or fertilizer usage. As men increasingly seek jobs away from farms, women become more responsible for managing the land. Because women tend to cultivate different crops than their husbands do, they cannot rely on men for training and need their own access to relevant information. As land grows scarcer and fertilizers yield diminishing returns, the next revolution in agricultural productivity may well be driven by women's education.[93]

The Soviet experience in Afghanistan, and later the US experience, provides some important insights about what not to do. Forced secularization of education does not generate comparable successes, and the challenge of reeducating Syrian and Iraqi students will be to find the best middle road between all religious studies and none.

Across the border in Pakistan, a similar story can be told of the Federally Administered Tribal Areas, and even Peshawar, the capital of the North-West Frontier Province.

Education in Pakistan

Madrassas, the predominant Islamic educational institution from the eleventh century onward, were sponsored by wealthy patrons who could use the madrassa for their own political ends.[94] During the colonial era, madrassas became a mechanism whereby colonized Islamic society could maintain its Muslim identity. If the colonizing powers themselves did not directly impose an alternative educational system on their Muslim possessions (a costly and not obviously economically advantageous enterprise), they at least opened the door to alternative forms of education. Wadad Kadi notes that "it was during this period . . . that new government bureaucratic structures were erected, and that Christian missionary schools and colleges were founded, using foreign languages and teaching foreign literatures."[95] The secularization of education—a process advanced by newly formed Middle Eastern states during the postcolonial era—also gained ground during the colonial era. The madrassa system operated antithetically to these influences throughout the colonial period.

According to Francis Robinson, following the 1857 Indian mutiny at the hands of Muslim Sepoys, "Islamic knowledge" in the hands of the madrassas was "uncoupled from [British] power."[96] The madrassas became focal points for Muslim elites in the context of British-administered colonial India. Reactions among these elites varied. They used the madrassa system alternatively for the expansion of modern academic subject matter, in particular the natural sciences, among Muslims (the Aligarh school), and for the propagation of politicized and fundamentalist Islam (based on the Deobandi school), in an effort to preserve their status as minority elites under the British system.[97] The madrassa became an instrument of radical, political Islam. Even in the absence of British colonial rule, the teaching propagated in the Pakistani madrassas perpetuated a deep-seated suspicion of all things Western, including any elements of postcolonial local or national government deemed un-Islamic.

In this context of extreme poverty and lack of educational opportunity, the madrassa has historically filled the void where the state has been derelict in its duty to provide citizens with access to education. According to Ranjit Sau, "One can find a common pattern in several major Muslim countries—countries that have over seven-tenths of their population professing Islam: the ruling elite derives legitimacy, not by popular mandate, but from the benediction of clerics, in exchange for a sector of society, namely, education, donated to the latter. Saudi Arabia, Egypt and Pakistan fit this description quite well."[98]

Pakistan has 68.4 million people between the ages of five and nineteen, though less than thirty million of them are in any kind of school. "When you look at consequences of these kids not going to school," according to USAID's Mosharraf Zaidi, interviewed by Frontline, "let's set aside the fear mongering and the scare-mongering of 'what if all these kids become terrorists.' But setting this aside, the real problem is that if you aren't capable of participating in the global economy, you will be very, very poor. And desperate and extreme poverty has some diabolical consequences for society and for individuals."[99] In contrast to this poverty and the absence of a serious national effort to provide public education, Pakistan's madrassas offer free tuition and a hot meal every day. According to the headmaster of one madrassa in Lahore, "Parents who are educated don't send their kids to madrassa, they send them to private schools, universities."[100]

Literacy in the tribal territories is estimated to be 11 percent for men and less than 1 percent for women.[101] Peter Singer notes that

> the reason for the madrassas' new centrality stems from the weakening of the Pakistani state. . . . The madrassas became immensely popular by targeting the lower class and refugee populations, whom the Pakistani state has failed to provide proper access to education.[102]

In more modern times, it was the madrassa system of Pakistan—especially along the border with Afghanistan—that gave rise to the Taliban ("the Students") movement. According to the *9/11 Commission Report*,

> Pakistan's endemic poverty, widespread corruption, and often-ineffective government create opportunities for Islamist recruitment. Poor education is a particular concern. Millions of families, especially those with little money, send their children to religious schools, or madrassas. Many of these schools are the only opportunity available for an education, but some have been used as incubators for violent extremism.[103]

Nevertheless, for all the attention that madrassas receive, madrassa enrollment accounts for less than 1 percent of enrollment overall, and less than 7.5 percent of enrollment in the border region with Afghanistan, where madrassa enrollment is highest.[104]

Christopher Candland observes that the most obvious reason parents send their children to madrassas is that madrassa enrollment provides children with protection from Pakistan's harsh vagrancy law, for which thousands of Pakistani children are jailed each year.[105] "Many *madaris* [a synonym of madrassah] are free," he points out. "*Madaris* provide children with a place to sleep and meals as well as books and instruction. . . . *Madaris* often serve as care-providing institutions for parents who cannot take care of their children."[106]

According to Paul Watson, the education curriculum approved by Pakistan's government is difficult to discern from the rhetoric of radical religious madrassas. The current social studies curriculum guidelines for sixth and seventh grades instruct textbook writers and teachers to "develop aspiration for jihad" and "develop a sense of respect for the struggle of [the] Muslim population for achieving independence. . . . In North-West Frontier Province, which is governed by supporters of the ousted Taliban regime in neighboring Afghanistan, the federally approved Islamic studies textbook for eighth grade teaches students they must be prepared 'to sacrifice every precious thing, including life, for jihad.'" The chapter continues, "At present, jihad is continuing in different parts of the world. Numerous mujahideen of Islam are involved in defending their religion, and independence, and to help their oppressed brothers across the world."[107] Efforts to secularize the curriculum were blamed on the West. Large protests marked the announcement of the US aid package, the Kerry-Lugar bill, which earmarked hundreds of millions of dollars for education reform.[108]

Reports of young boys abducted by militants and forced to take up arms or become suicide bombers are increasingly common. A school in Pirano, Pakistan, in the Swat Valley (the location of many of these abductions), developed a curriculum emphasizing the compatibility of Islam with democracy and human rights, together with individual counseling, to rehabilitate child fighters captured by the Pakistani military. Some ninety boys, ages twelve to eighteen, were initially enrolled in the pilot program.[109]

In sum, education can play a positive or negative role in fostering attitudes that will leave an imprint on children well into adulthood. In countries in which children's textbooks are manipulated to discreetly convey a message or bias against any particular ethnic, religious, or other group, there can be untold unintended negative consequences in the long term. At the same time, education is the best possible means of reintegrating youth who have been exposed to violence or radicalization. If Sabaoon is any indication of what is required, it is very time-consuming and expensive to undo negative programming of children. Feriha Peracha, Sabaoon's director, explains,

> It can take six months to four years to reintegrate a young militant, depending on the factors that pushed them into militancy. Teenagers take longer than pre-teens. Each student costs approximately $200 to $350 per month.[110]

With what looks like the inevitable defeat of IS on the battlefield, the United States, Europe, and the Middle East face the prospect of what to do with the children and youth who have been exposed to or participated in horrific acts of violence. In chapter 7, we will explore what best practices can be inferred from disarmament, demobilization, and reintegration (DDR) programs in Africa and Latin America, and what possible measures we can suggest to break the cycle of violence. In the next chapters, we explore how children are coerced and occasionally seduced into terrorist violence and highlight the ways in which groups manipulate youth and their parents.

PATHWAYS TO INVOLVEMENT
Coercion

> Violence is a slippery concept—nonlinear, destructive, *and*
> reproductive. . . . Violence can never be understood solely in terms
> of its physicality—force, assault, or the infliction of pain—alone.
> Violence also includes assaults on the person, dignity, sense of worth
> or value of the victim. The social and cultural dimensions of violence
> are what gives violence its power and meaning.
>
> Nancy Scheper-Hughes and Philippe I. Bourgois, *Violence in War and Peace*

In January 2014, Spozhmai, the eight-year-old sister of an Afghan Taliban commander, claimed that her brother had forced her to wear a suicide belt to attack a border police checkpoint in Khan Nasheen near Kandahar.[1] Seven years before Spozhmai's preempted attack, in June 2007, seven-year-old Juma Gul approached the Afghan National Army and claimed that the Taliban had cornered him in Ghazni and "put something on him." The Taliban tricked Juma into wearing a vest they claimed would spray flowers when he pressed a button (not cause him to explode). According to the boy's account, the Taliban instructed him to "throw your body at any American soldiers" he saw. In an interview with the Associated Press, Juma further explained, "When they first put the vest on my body I didn't know what to think, but then I felt it [the bomb]. . . . After I figured out it was a bomb, I went to the Afghan soldiers for help."[2]

The exploitation of Juma, who was described in the Western media as "a dirt-caked child who collected scrap metal for money,"[3] shocked Afghan soldiers. How could someone so young be sent on a suicide mission? While the Afghan troops lionized Juma for not carrying out his orders, treating him and his brother to a lavish meal with then president Hamid Karzai,[4] the Jirga (community elders) in Ghazni were less impressed that the Taliban had tried to trick a child into martyrdom. Moreover, the elders turned against Taliban commanders and began cooperating with coalition troops.[5]

This example further demonstrates the variety of ways in which children can be coerced into terrorism, from outright force to subtle trickery. These methods range from compellence (kill or be killed) and explicit threats (kill or we kill someone you love) to subtle forms of coercion (such as trickery) and/or community and peer pressure.[6] Terrorist groups use a variety of tricks, such that children may be too young to understand, or even to realize, that they have "volunteered" for a mission. Such coercion contrasts sharply with instances described in this book in which youth are gradually socialized, trained from an early age, and prepared for front-line activity in the course of an extended socialization process.

In this chapter we explain the areas of convergence between terrorists and pedophiles. The similarities predominantly regard how children and parents are both groomed to get access to the children and normalize aberrant behavior. There are two processes that lead to children's involvement in terrorist violence: (1) targeted recruitment initiated by adults, or (2) facilitated engagement, in which a child, responding to personal, social, and/or cultural factors, seeks out engagement with the group. Not every terrorist group uses coercion to compel operatives, but in recent years, several groups have used a litany of coercive and manipulative tactics to target youth (and women) for mobilization. Furthermore, many of these tactics mirror those used by pedophiles to recruit victims for sexual exploitation.

The Question of Motivation

John Horgan argues that it "might be better to consider ways in which our knowledge of psychological processes inform our understanding of terrorism,"[7] and that it is necessary to think of engagement in terms of "dimensions, processes, and pathways."[8] This "arc" of terrorism comprises the process of involvement, engagement, and disengagement—emphasizing antecedent behavior, consequences, and outcomes. The process also varies from group to group and person to person. The psychiatrist Jeff Victoroff has concluded that terrorists are "psychologically extremely heterogeneous. Whatever his stated goals and group of identity, every terrorist, like every person, is motivated by his own complex of psycho-social experiences and traits."[9]

However, existing models describing the motivation to join a terrorist group do not consider coercion as part of the process; instead, like models of terrorist behavior, they are composed of both push and pull factors rather than brute force. A United Nations Report emphasized that "IS prioritizes children as a vehicle for ensuring long-term loyalty, adherence to their ideology and a cadre of devoted fighters that will see violence as a way of life."[10] Given the group's need to survive, it routinely engages in "talent spotting"; children with physical and mental aptitude and potential are highly prized, and they progress through its ranks swiftly. Because one of the most important priorities for violent extremist groups is to guarantee their survival, such groups emphasize the need for new recruits.[11] Audrey Kurth Cronin identified the "failure to evolve" as the primary factor explaining the "death" of so many terrorist groups (it is often alleged that as many as 90 percent fail within the first two years),[12] including well-established European groups in the 1960s, such as the Red Brigades in Italy and the Aryan Republican Army in the US.[13] According to Seth Jones and Martin Libicki, who reviewed 648 cases, terrorist groups end in one of four ways: policing (40 percent), military force (7 percent), politics (e.g., splintering or transitioning by giving up arms and participating in the political process) (43 percent), or victory (10 percent), most within the first few years of their existence.[14] To survive and thrive in such a competitive environment where the likelihood of failure is high, groups must ensure continuity and plan for succession.[15] To do this, they prepare the "next generation" through youth groups, youth wings, and various mechanisms to engage children.

In Afghanistan, children might be duped or tricked into terrorism—as was the case with Juma Gul. The ways in which children are subtly and not-so-subtly coerced vary from luring to the outright coercion used by Nigeria's Boko Haram (IS's West African affiliate), which kidnaps children and trains them to be suicide bombers. In Iraq and Syria, IS engages youth on a spectrum of coercion. While the group actively recruits using a variety of lures with a gradual process of involvement, there are also reported cases of brute force, kidnapping, and unqualified coercion. For example, IS kidnapped hundreds of Yazidi children in August 2014, and the UN alleges that it also kidnapped four hundred children from Anbar Province (who would not be Yazidi).[16] Many of the male Yazidi children were successfully brainwashed, and, to date, two of them, the brothers Abu Khattab al-Sinjari and Abu Yussuf al-Sinjari (kidnapped in 2014 and featured in propaganda videos in 2015), have been deployed as suicide bombers. Abu Khattab's suicide mission occurred on December 12, 2016, after which IS "eulogized" him on its official propaganda channels. His older brother was shown detonating a vehicle-based improvised explosive device (VBIED) in an IS video released on February 14, 2017. A "last will and testament" video featuring the brothers demonstrated the extent of the boys' brainwashing, as they testified that before joining the Cubs, they had worshiped the devil and were going to hell. "When we were in Sinjar," they said, "we worshiped the devil and we were without God. . . . We were ignorant and not aware of concepts such as Halal and Haram."[17] Becoming martyrs for the Islamic State would be their salvation. After the release of the video, the boys were identified as eleven- and twelve-year-old Amjad and Asaad-Alyas Mahjo.[18]

Abduction is one of the most prevalent modes of recruitment for the Pakistani and Afghan Taliban, who have relied heavily on kidnapping children and/or extorting their parents to hand over the children to the groups. According to Pakistani general Asim Bajwa, teenage bombers have been responsible for the deaths of four hundred Pakistani soldiers, making these young bombers a serious threat. General Bajwa nevertheless contends that many of the children were forced to join the terrorists.[19] "When Talibans [sic] gained control of some of the areas," he says, "they asked families to give away one child along with some cattle and some money contributing to their cause and the parents had no option but they did it out of fear."[20]

In several cases of jihadi groups in Afghanistan, Pakistan, Syria, and Iraq, we can observe that terrorist groups employ three types of conscription: outright coercion, engagement in which families consent (to a degree of involvement), and a hybrid in which the community supports children's involvement in violence and limited coercion is used to force families to comply. All of these vary in their degree of coercion. In the case of children forcibly recruited by the Pakistani Taliban, we see outright coercion; alternatively, in Pakistan and Afghanistan, families who are already members of the organization will encourage or consent to their children's engagement. In the case of IS Cubs, foreign fighters take their children to Mosul or Raqqa with the conscious intention to involve them in IS activities. Children's involvement in terrorist groups implies family consent. Finally, there are instances in which the community expects children to become involved, especially in conflict areas under occupation; in such cases, initial participation revolves around support roles, and subsequently children become more and more involved. In examples of children's involvement in Lebanon, Palestine, and Sri Lanka, the community largely supports children's recruitment and there exists real peer pressure for children to step up and help their community. While al-Shabaab (also known as Harakat al-Shabaab al-Mujahideen, a jihadist fundamentalist group based in East Africa) employed some limited online recruitment of young adults (most of whom were over sixteen), the Islamic State has distinguished itself in the online space in the extent of their recruitment, which can occur at very long distances with a modem and high-speed connection. Like pedophiles grooming young victims on the internet, IS has approached children using online and offline recruitment. Also like pedophiles, the group uses a gradual desensitization process that exposes children to extreme violence in order to normalize aberrant behavior.[21] IS has used the internet in a more focused way than previous terrorist groups and has particularly exploited social media platforms as they have emerged. Like pedophiles, IS lures youth on social media and chat rooms in order to exploit them. Social media is used to disseminate propaganda, to expose young people to violent images, and eventually for targeted recruitment.

In 2009, the Homeland Security Institute explained how online recruitment had become relevant:

> The Internet has become an important resource for disseminating terrorist propaganda and instructions to young persons that might not otherwise have direct contact with group recruiters or supporters. The Internet is accessible, cheap, and anonymous. It offers terrorists a variety of mediums to disseminate messages and provides connections to recruiters and recruits that might not otherwise be possible. Some groups have established websites designed specifically for youth audiences, disseminating propaganda through colorful cartoons and games.[22]

We have suggested that the mechanisms of IS socialization form a process, whereby children are exposed to violence as spectators and eventually become (enthusiastic) participants, by which time violence has been routinized and the children are permanently impacted psychologically. This is all the more salient given the role played by the children's sources of authority, notably parents and extended families. The terrorists' shift toward using younger and younger operatives and parental collusion violates the basic assumption that parents will protect their children at all costs (barring cases of infanticide).[23]

How and why families willingly allow access to their children has been explored in the literature on child protection and pedophilia. In this literature, "institutional grooming," which caregivers and/or others with a guardianship role engage in for the purpose of gaining access to children,[24] closely relates to the development of an environment conducive to recruitment, one in which abusers inoculate bystanders around the child. Furthermore, these violent extremist organizations require community support to mobilize youth and develop relationships with caregivers, guardians, and the broader community. By developing and exploiting a trust relationship with individuals around the child (who might be considered the target), the recruiter reduces the family members' and the community's vigilance and suspicion, and also creates an environment in which it is less likely that targets will be able to disclose the details of their recruitment.

"Child grooming," the process by which pedophiles "entrap" victims, is analogous to a kind of courtship.[25] Throughout the literature on pedophilia, experts have identified different stages of child grooming: identifying a victim, gaining his or her trust and establishing rapport, fulfilling the child's needs, isolating the child, shifting the child's moral (normative) views, and using blackmail or coercion to maintain control over the child.[26] In this chapter we identify how the stages of grooming for sexual exploitation correspond with analogous processes that terrorist groups use to lure children both offline (in real life) and online.

Like pedophiles, terrorists exploit new technologies, shifting the traditional recruitment of the past to a mixture of online and offline platforms. The techniques used by pedophile groomers to manipulate youth (e.g., flattery, bribes, threats), and the ways that young people engage in risk-taking behavior on the internet (e.g., communicating and sharing personal information with strangers), further support this comparison.[27] Whereas terrorist groups previously relied primarily on in-person, face-to-face recruitment, often in the form of extended engagement with the organization and at training camps, over the past ten years, most terrorist recruitment has shifted to the online space, where it occurs virtually. Groups have used this space to radicalize youth.[28]

The goal of sexual grooming is to gain access to the target. This process may be gradual, as the recruiter needs to desensitize bystanders and conceal his or her interest in the child, thus creating and maintaining an environment in which increasing interest in children is normalized. Any successful reduction in levels of instinctive parental vigilance and suspicion also allows the recruiter to isolate the child from potential sources of prosocial norms and information that might conflict with the recruiter's extremist narrative (e.g., from parents, teachers, or from more moderate influences). One of the key tactics terrorist recruiters employ, cited in works by Marc Sageman, Edwin Bakker, and Mia Bloom,[29] is isolating an operative from friends and family prior to a suicide mission. Isolating youth from alternative narratives and positive influences becomes key to preparing them for violence. Some terrorist groups need not conceal their motives in order to recruit youth but do conceal what training entails and the extent to which children are abused (physically, emotionally, and in some cases, like the Taliban, sexually).

Parents and teachers inoculate youth from extremism, but these same sources of authority within the child's family or community (coaches, teachers, religious leaders) can also play a damaging role by allowing or facilitating terrorist recruiters' access. As we have discussed, in most cases of terrorism, parents encourage or possibly coerce their children to become involved and join the group.

IS has provided many examples of parents who took their very young children to Raqqa or Mosul when they made *hijra* (emigrated) to the so-called caliphate. These children could not possibly have consented to involvement, since they were too young and had no say in the family's move. The children of foreign fighters are a key source of recruitment and have been especially prominent in the group's propaganda efforts. One early and especially blatant example was the Australian jihadi Khaled Sharrouf, who posed his then seven-year-old son, Abdullah, holding a severed head, and posted the photo to social media on August 11, 2014.[30]

Sharrouf had a history of violence; five years before he went to Syria, he served a four-year jail sentence for planning terrorist attacks in Sydney and Melbourne. Even though the Australian government had confiscated his passport and prohibited him from leaving the country, he used his brother's documents to travel to Syria—taking with him his wife, Tara Nettleton, and their five children: Zaynab, Hoda, Abdullah, Zarqawi, and Humzeh.[31] Sharrouf was reportedly killed in a drone strike in June 2015,[32] and Tara died from complications associated with appendicitis that September. Tara's mother, Karen, has since been petitioning the Australian government to permit her grandchildren to return home, and she even tried to rescue them in a failed extraction in 2016.[33]

Khadijah (neé Grace) Dare, a formerly devout Christian who converted to Islam in 2010, involved her child with IS at a very young age. After marrying Deniz Yoncaci as a teenager in Lewisham, United Kingdom, she gave birth to a son, Isa.[34] A few months later, the couple divorced.[35] Grace, now calling herself Khadijah, took the baby to Syria in 2012 to marry a Swedish foreign fighter. Dare has since become a much-touted propagandist, especially after being widowed. After the death of the journalist James Foley, Dare expressed her desire to be the first IS woman to execute a Western journalist.[36] Writing under the nom de guerre "Muhajirah fi Sham" (immigrant in Syria), she posted the following typo-laden message: "Any links 4 da execution of da journalist plz. Allahu Akbar. UK must b shaking up ha ha. I wna b da 1st UK woman 2 kill a UK or US terorrist!"[37]

Dare featured Isa (a toddler) in jihadi propaganda images and videos, and even posed him with an AK-47. In 2016, IS's main propaganda machine, al-Hayat Media Center, released a video in which four-year-old Isa, audibly encouraged by Khadijah in the background, pressed a remote control that set off an improvised device in a car, killing the three people inside.[38]

As we have explained, there are cases in which families foster children's involvement. This is usually more common in cases where children live with their extended families, such as uncles and aunts, rather than with their biological parents. In conflict areas where the terrorists impose a "tax" on the population to provide conscripts, families are more likely to surrender nieces or nephews to save their own children.[39] As described in chapter 1, the Tamil Tigers required every family to provide at least one recruit for the cause.[40]

In interviews we conducted in Mingora in Pakistan's Swat Valley,[41] we encountered children forcibly recruited by the Pakistani Taliban (TTP) and trained to carry out suicide attacks against civilians. The trajectory of involvement for most of these children involved varying degrees of coercion. The typical story told by many of the children in the Sabaoon rehabilitation center was that recruitment involved using force against their families in addition to pressuring them personally. As described in chapter 1, TTP terrorists would approach families and demand exorbitant financial donations to the cause (five thousand lek—a slang term for rupees—equaling around $745), which would be an annual wage for most of the residents of this poor region. Families living below the poverty line could not come up with this "contribution," so the terrorist group took a child instead. In this way, parents were coerced into handing their children over. Once in the group, many of the children were also sexually abused.[42]

The children at Sabaoon exemplify the challenges of classifying children's involvement in violent extremism in a binary fashion as either coerced or voluntary. According to Sabaoon's statistics, 58 percent of the children in its care were forcibly recruited or physically kidnapped by the TTP; another 41 percent joined the TTP after having run away from home. Such classifications are especially challenging given the age of some of the children (one boy, "Yusuf" (not his real name), "volunteered" to be a suicide bomber at eight), and very young children making life-and-death decisions are controversial to say the least. The Sabaoon children provide insight into the correlation between the nature of children's mobilization into terrorist activities and the types of roles assigned to the children once in the group. The doctors and social workers at Sabaoon discovered that children who were coerced (kidnapped or forced) to join were less likely to be given roles that involved meaningful responsibilities. Surprisingly, those who volunteered were eligible and thus more likely to become martyrs or suicide bombers. Our discussions revealed that children who were coerced into the group could and did deliberately get caught or make some other mistake in order to purposely fail in their suicide mission.[43]

The application of criminological models of child exploitation to our study shows how terrorist groups employ many of the same tactics and strategies as pedophiles, both online and offline. David Finkelhor's process model of child grooming for sexual abuse can also be a means of understanding how adults target and recruit children for militancy.[44] Tony Ward and Stephen Hudson found that different offenders vary in their offense style and the degree to which they utilize violence or grooming strategies.[45] These include dangerous situations of abuse in which children's boundaries are violated with unwanted touching and contact, and other ways in which offenders groom or desensitize their victims.[46]

While Finkelhor's model specifies sexual abuse, Ian Elliott and Mia Bloom adapted it to explain how groups and recruiters target and lure children to perpetrate violence.[47] Finkelhor's model describes four of the common preconditions to child sexual exploitation:

1. Motivation (wanting to abuse or exploit children)
2. Overcoming internal inhibitions (against acting on that motivation)

3. Overcoming external inhibitors (to committing the exploitation or abuse)
4. Undermining or overcoming the child's resistance to engaging in sexual activity—or, in our model, to perpetrating violence

Elliott and Bloom refined Finkelhor's grooming model to match identifiable processes for the specific contexts of children's involvement in terrorism. The primary area of overlap is Finkelhor's third phase—overcoming external impediments to committing abuse (or, in the case of terrorists, violence), which includes gaining access to the child, creating situations conducive to the occurrence of violence (and abuse), and finally, having children groom their acquaintances and friends.

According to Zsuzsanna Rutai, grooming is a "process by which a person prepares a child and the environment for the abuse of this child. Specific goals include gaining access to the child, gaining the child's compliance and maintaining the child's secrecy to avoid disclosure."[48] The key difference, as Finkelhor himself has observed, is that unlike pedophiles, terrorist groups make no effort to conceal their behavior[49]—in fact, they herald the exploitation of children in their propaganda and use this to recruit other children (and goad or guilt adults into participating). On its online encrypted platform, Telegram, IS has generated dozens of propaganda videos and memes using children. The group routinely uses the same child in multiple propaganda productions year in and year out.

Like abusers targeting children for sexual predation, violent extremist organizations expend a great deal of effort selecting, isolating, training, and preparing children for engagement. In essence, grooming can explain how an individual manipulates a young person to engage in behaviors that the child would not have otherwise engaged in. While, it does not explain all recruitment of children to terrorism. Human goals tend to be "nested": to achieve one, we need to first achieve others, which in turn have other subordinate related goals.[50] These subordinate goals require the target to be desensitized to extremism and violence. These grooming and desensitization processes may occur simultaneously and, given that each child will present with unique social ecology, can be regulated (i.e., emphasized or minimized).

Grooming for Terrorism

According to Elliott and Bloom, the first phase of the grooming model is a potentiality phase. This is a process in which an adult recruiter develops a relationship with a child through four mechanisms: rapport building, incentivization, disinhibition, and security management.[51] Rapport building fosters and regulates the relationship between a recruiter and a child. Individuals, notes Linda Tickle-Degnen, demonstrate rapport "through a stream of interlinked signals and responses that are shaped by their personal physical and psychological properties, the parameters of the task in which they are engaged, and the physical and social environment of their actions."[52]

Children are recruited via social networks, as well as through community-centered activities.[53] At the age of puberty in the Middle East, boys form play and membership peer groups called *shillas*. The *shilla* is a lifetime membership group that protects the neighborhood. Those children who graduate from high school, college, or a military academy have an additional kinship network, called a *dufa'a* network, based on the year of their graduation. Friends radicalize and mobilize each other as a cohort, which may explain why they are often involved in terrorist movements (or operations) together and simultaneously. This was equally the case with youth involved in leftist terrorist movements in Europe in the 1960s and 1970s. These *dufa'a* networks are especially strong and can result in lifelong friendships, akin to those of fraternity brothers. For Marc Sageman, this constitutes the "group of guys" he describes in his work *Leaderless Jihad*.[54]

> The group acts as an echo chamber, amplifying grievances, intensifying bonds to each other, and breeding [certain] values. . . . The natural group dynamics result in a spiral of mutual encouragement and escalation, transforming a few young Muslims into dedicated terrorists willing to follow the model of their heroes and sacrifice themselves for comrades and cause.[55]

Scott Atran clarifies how group dynamics coalesce to steer children toward extremism:

> Heroic action for a great cause is the ultimate end. The path to violent extremism is mostly a matter of individual motivations and small group dynamics in a specific historical context. Those who go on to violence generally do so by way of family and friends within specific "scenes": neighborhoods, schools (classes, dorms), workplaces, common leisure activities (soccer, barbershop, café), and, increasingly, online chat rooms.[56]

For violent extremist groups in multiethnic conflicts, sectarianism may be a powerful bonding factor, creating and exploiting a sense of belonging based on identity, religious belief, or ideology. The ability to build rapport and establish trust requires a degree of cultural affinity: the same references that might work in a British context would not resonate nearly as well with American or European youth. Thus, the recruiter identifies and operates within a frame of reference that reflects the distinctive background of the target. Shared characteristics and interests, coupled with an atmosphere of care and concern, will engender confidence and comfort. According to a Homeland Security Institute paper, the internet plays a vital role in fostering the "social bonds necessary for radicalization and recruitment," and provides a venue to "perpetuate radicalization among like-minded individuals (whether they are peers in similar situations or recruiters, online or offline), [after which] their radicalization may then progress inside these groups." The internet, it continues, also "can intensify a sense of identity" through "group polarization," in which members perpetuate their own radicalization through discussion, with the facilitation of a terrorist recruiter.[57] Both the Afghan Taliban and IS employ recruiters of similar age, location, and shared interests to enlist like-minded individuals.[58]

One of the ways in which recruiters establish rapport is through their choice of platform and the content of their message. Anthony Faiola and Souad Mekhennet, detailing IS's methods of luring lonely young people from Europe, report that "they are employing propaganda tailor-made for youths, including several recent graphic videos showing grammar-school-age children executing prisoners and a newly released computer game, inspired by 'Grand Theft Auto,' in which users kill enemies under the Islamic State flag."[59]

Ariel Merrari's seminal analysis of suicide terrorism provides many examples of the tactics used by terrorist recruiters, highlighting processes of friendliness and flattery, the "reverential" aura of the recruiter, the long periods during which the targets are "coaxed," and the one-on-one, dyadic nature of recruitment.[60] Terrorist organizations also use young intermediaries, who are often members of the target's own peer group. Over the course of our research, we have observed older youths recruiting younger children, as well as older children recruiting their younger siblings, into terrorist movements. In the literature on child protection, the term "deviant peer" describes older children who recruit younger children (often younger siblings) for abuse. The older children may do this to sustain the abuser's interest or because they seek to "please" the abuser.[61] We see this form of deviant peer dynamics in terrorist recruitment tactics.

IS has its foreign fighters recruit individuals from their native countries as a form of deviant peer recruitment. The recruiter speaks the same language as the target, and his or her ability to develop rapport is predicated on the two of them understanding each other and having similar frames of reference. Thus IS women are successful recruiters of young teenage girls, as they share common interests, likes, and dislikes to foster rapport and deepen their bond. A British-born IS emigrant to the caliphate can discuss celebrities, snack foods, and sports teams that resonate with a British teenager more effectively than someone from a different country with different points of reference. IS matches recruiters to their targets, having French women recruit young French girls, American women recruit American girls, and British women recruit British and Scottish teens. Shukri Amin, a seventeen-year-old Virginia resident, was found guilty in 2015 of encouraging American teenagers and having provided financial support to travel to Syria. Aqsa Mahmood (Umm Layth), a Scottish radiology student who disappeared from Glasgow in 2014, targets girls in the UK and Scotland, including three teenage girls from Bethnal Green Academy. Hoda Muthana (Umm Jihad) fled Alabama in 2014 and now recruits other girls from the United States, such as Jaelyn Young, a student at Mississippi State University.[62]

Under various social media accounts, Hoda Muthana has fostered online radicalization and encouraged action within the United States. In her social media posts, she has advocated killing President Barack Obama, and at other times has sought to inspire domestic attacks:

> You have much to do while you live under our greatest enemy, enough of your sleeping! Go on drive-bys truck and drive all over them. Veterans, Patriot, Memorial etc. Day parades . . . go on drive by's + spill all of their blood or rent a big truck n drive all over them. Kill them.[63]

Incentivization is how a recruiter gets the child to engage in specific ("goal-oriented") activities. Sexual predators lure children with gifts, bribes, and other monetary incentives. In the context of violent extremism, these incentives entice children to join the group, adopt its radical ideology, and engage in acts of violence.

The most basic form of incentive is remunerative, in which the child receives material rewards in exchange for action. Some incentives provide a material "pull." After taking over the schools in Syria and Iraq, IS lured children by offering them toys and candy to turn up at small-scale social gatherings or work the crowd, helping to recruit other children. Some Syrian and Iraqi children report joining the movement to guarantee their families' survival, as a form of transactional exchange; by joining the Cubs of the Caliphate, the children ensure the physical survival of their parents.[64] Whether and how much the Cubs were paid remains an issue of contention within published reports. Some reports insist that Cubs made $200 per month (half the amount of what the adults reportedly made), whereas others dispute the idea that children are remunerated at all, stating instead that payments are made directly to the parents for the children's participation.[65]

Other incentives provide an economic "push" to engagement. In Nigeria, a recent United States Institute of Peace (USIP) report identified unemployment and poverty as the second-most significant reason (after radicalization) for children to engage in violence.[66] Another report says that for Nigeria's Boko Haram, because of "the combination of bad governance, centralization of power and wealth, political intrigue, crumbling infrastructure, [and] regional disparities . . . it is no wonder that many observers have argued that Nigeria offers the kinds of conditions in which revolutionaries and extremists have found fertile ground for recruiting and launching violent movements."[67] In Somalia, reports describe former al-Shabaab members, recruited as children, explaining that they had joined because it "paid well" ($50–$150 per month) and required little effort.[68]

The financial incentives for youth might be more relevant than they are for adults; studies have shown that most adults who join terrorist movements are often better educated and have a higher-than-average income. The perpetrators of both the Lashkar-e-Taiba massacre in Mumbai in 2008 and the 9/11 attacks were wealthy and educated,[69] as were the attackers in 2016 in Dhaka, Bangladesh. As we have shown, this is not the case with children, so financial inducements might play a more pronounced role with them.

However, targeting children in areas with very low levels of literacy might be counterproductive, as the organization needs to recruit for roles requiring a variety of technical skills.[70] The organizations "talent scout" for natural aptitude, and most groups recruit high- and low-skilled individuals for different tasks. Financial incentives do not always have their intended effect, especially when monetary gains conflict with established religious or moral beliefs.[71] The remunerative incentives for children are often a low-risk/high-reward option for violent extremist groups, since children typically require less reward for their commitment, and because their dependence on the organization is higher than it is for adults.[72] The authors of the Boko Haram USIP report cautioned that there was no simple cause-and-effect link between economic factors and child radicalization; "rather, privation and other frustrating conditions of life render children highly vulnerable to manipulation by extremist ideologues."[73]

A second form of incentive can be classified as moral. Such incentives include appeals to the child's self-esteem; the framing of activities or beliefs as "right," "worthy," or "admirable"; and the suggestion that noncompliance will have overtly negative consequences for the target's (child's) reputation or character. Muhsin Hassan quotes a young al-Shabaab member as saying, "Walking the city with a gun as a member of al-Shabaab ensured everybody feared and respected you. Girls also liked you."[74] Children involved in terrorist groups may be treated as heroes by their peers, and their families are often provided with material assistance.[75] Such peer (as well as adult) role models offer an authoritarian legitimacy to moral incentives.[76]

There is also evidence of religious incentives in children's recruitment.[77] Former child al-Shabaab members have described a process of "mental manipulation," in which religion is used to justify the violent ideology and recruiters seek to "convince you that joining . . . was your religious duty."[78] In Nigeria, "ignorance of [Islamic] religious teaching" and the distortion of the faith are key factors in children's adoption of extreme religious views and their vulnerability to recruitment by Boko Haram. Not all moral incentives are sectarian. By emphasizing a stereotyped view of the adversary, group insulation, unanimity, shared morality and cultural characteristics, a "sacred" unquestionable authority and sense of invulnerability, and a hard-line approach to dissent, the recruiters can create a sense of groupthink and concurrence seeking in the recruits.[79] Similarly, empowering a group that ordinarily has no influence might prove a powerful lure.

UNICEF's Aasmund Lok identifies another moral incentive: "Breadwinners could have been killed or went missing. So some of the young ones had to step up and find ways to support themselves and their families."[80] Finally, offering young people a new identity, a sense of belonging, and a highly structured set of beliefs and values contributes to their self-esteem. A former Cub named Yasir explained how being part of the group made him feel "proud, strong and filled with a sense of purpose" even though the violence perpetrated by the group made him feel ill.[81]

The third form of incentives is coercive, where the motivation to participate results from the expectation of negative consequences for noncompliance (at the most extreme level, violence against the child or the child's immediate family). For example, in 2014, Russian television reported that "10-year old Abdullah *voluntarily* [emphasis added] joined IS, following in his father's and brother's footsteps," and added, "There are boys who are taken away from their families and forced to be in the group."[82]

One child who escaped from IS explained why he had joined Daesh: because, he said, "IS had killed 12 members of my family. They killed my brother-in-law and arrested my sister and her child. My other brother-in-law fled. That means we were a wanted family. If I hadn't joined, I would have been killed."[83]

Occasionally, children are forced on threat of death to join; this was the case with Usaid Barho, a 14-year-old Syrian boy recruited by IS to blow up the Shiite al-Bayah mosque in Baghdad. As Barho approached the mosque a policeman, Sayid Ali, began to search him. Barho confessed, "I'm a suicide bomber. I'm a Muslim and don't have any intention to kill Muslims. I want to go back home to see my mother. Can you help me?" Barho's subsequent testimony intimated that recruits were given the option to either become a fighter or a suicide bomber. He calculated that he had a better chance of survival as a suicide bomber because "I'd be able to hand myself in to the authorities without having to face the risk of being killed. As a fighter, I wouldn't get such a chance."[84]

Another example of coercion was Mohammed (not his real name), discussed below. As Ali Hashem explained, Barho had changed his mind at the last minute.

Just before he entered the mosque, he approached the guards and asked for their assistance. Removing his jacket, he explained, "I'm wearing a [suicide] vest, but I don't want to blow myself up."[85] Barho described his experience as brainwashing and what he termed IS's "seduction." The *New York Times* reported that IS had convinced Barho that Shiites were infidels who had to be killed, and, furthermore, that "if he did not fight, Shiites would come and rape his mother."[86] Another boy, Mohammed, interviewed by CNN, explained that while studying at the mosque, IS "taught us we should enroll in Jihad with them. . . . I wanted to go but my father did not allow me to." IS told Mohammed's father, "If you prevent Mohammed from coming to the camp, we will cut off your head."[87] Mohammed's father, according to the CNN report, "tried to visit him several times, but was turned back by guards who told him that the boy wasn't there, or on patrol."[88]

Children who are coerced (physically or as a result of threats to their parents) will be more likely to deliberately make mistakes, allow themselves to get caught, or purposely fail in their mission. Examples from Afghanistan, Syria, and Pakistan suggest that coercive threats, particularly against family members, are *less* likely to lead to a cooperative and successful combatant.[89] In 2016, another Iraqi bomber, aged 13, allowed himself to get caught in Kirkuk rather than carry out his mission against civilian targets.[90] This "weapon of the weak" occurs often when children need to show that they made a good-faith attempt to save face and their loved ones, but ultimately prefer to fail in their mission.

The fourth form of incentives is a natural, internal psychological device that intrinsically motivates people to action. Making membership in a terrorist group rare and valuable, by not targeting all children equally for recruitment, fosters the innate competitiveness of children. Terrorist groups make involvement appear desirable, a commodity that children are encouraged to aspire to and compete for. IS deliberately instills competition or jealousy among the Cubs, such that Cubs wearing brand-new uniforms are pictured in their propaganda posted on Telegram next to children in civilian dress. The new clothes, new weapons, and preferential treatment make the other children want to be involved themselves. The terrorist groups go to great lengths to portray engagement as exciting and worthy. There are emotional or sensational effects associated with violent and destructive acts, including the desire for ultimate meaning, a sense of identity, and the thirst for glory and esteem.[91] Excitement, friendship, group identity, and respect—these motivations are just as appealing and important to children as they are to adults. Young members of violent gangs express the same motivations: peer friendship, pride, identity development, enhancement of self-esteem, excitement, and acquisition of resources.[92]

Disinhibition reduces the child's ability to respond to information—typically via the use of intoxicants. According to the Roméo Dallaire Child Soldiers

Initiative, drugs and alcohol are used to disinhibit and reward child soldiers.[93] Elliott argues that the internet can also function as a disinhibitor, as users are more likely to engage in risky behavior online, away from guardians and the constraints of the offline world, that they may not have engaged in in person.[94] There are some concerns that older children might be susceptible to and capable of "self-radicalizing" by accessing, online, jihadi materials produced by extremist organizations.[95]

IS's multifaceted communications strategy and online social media have been effective in disseminating its projection of statehood, military success, and religious legitimacy in order to recruit and mobilize foreign fighters. As Mia Bloom has explained elsewhere, militant and terrorist groups use the internet to streamline the recruitment, radicalization, and training processes, using websites, chat rooms, video messaging, and popular social media services such as Twitter and Facebook (and increasingly Telegram) to contact and communicate with recruits. Anwar al-Awlaki, one of al-Qaeda's savviest jihadi recruiters, is quoted as admitting that "[the] Internet has become a great medium for spreading the call of jihad."[96]

IS is hardly unique in deliberately targeting children—especially young males—for indoctrination. Kumar Ramakrishna notes that "its ideological parent al-Qaeda sought to radicalize youth into its virulent varieties of Islamist extremism as well. The British MI5 warned in 2007 that al-Qaeda and its affiliates were seeking to radicalize children as young as 15 into mounting terror attacks in the United Kingdom."[97]

Protagonists seek the best possible environment in which to achieve their goals. Parallels can be drawn here between Hegghammer's "screening frameworks," based on the behavior he observed of al-Qaeda in the Arabian Peninsula (AQAP) recruiters, and the ways in which IS screened potential recruits.[98] The development of trust is crucial, both to make someone amenable to manipulation and because of the security concerns of the recruiter. "No terrorist," write Clark McCauley and Sophia Moskalenko, "wants to try to recruit someone who might betray [him] to the authorities."[99] Interestingly, those same processes of rapport building among peers apply across a variety of terrorist organizations in which the groups are fostering an environment of trust. AQAP recruiters screened people and chose those who demonstrated signs of similar ethnicity (the extent of their "Saudiness"), similar levels of personal piety, commensurate ideological commitment (e.g., jihadi or prison experience, attendance at training camps), relevant knowledge (people/places/events, expertise), cultural familiarity, vouching for or from others, and so on. The recruiter manipulates conversational topics to establish integrity and identify potential risks of detection. Although Hegghammer's framework was originally developed for adults, it is applicable to children. The material signs of commitment the recruiter looks for would simply change in terms of form (e.g., Cub training rather than adult military training) and importance (e.g., since children are often recruited to spy, local knowledge may be of greater importance).

In the literature on child protection, desensitization is maladaptive exposure and counterconditioning, beginning with exposure to low levels of violence and progressing to increasingly more extreme acts. In the context of terrorism, this is a process in which the group alters the child's belief systems, as the child is slowly desensitized to extreme violence, making participation less arduous. It can be a controlled process, as the individual moves from a peripheral support role to more focused, violent, and unambiguously terrorist-related activities. McCauley and Moskalenko consider this a "slippery slope" in the recruitment process, which they describe as "slow and gradual, with several smaller tests before being trusted for more important missions, and with many non-violent tasks before being asked to use gun or bomb."[100] We have explored the gradual nature of the socialization process, which describes *behavioral* radicalization as compared to the radicalization of *belief*. There remain enduring questions about whether young children can be genuinely radicalized in their belief systems, or whether they simply parrot what adults have taught them.[101] Horgan suggests that most terrorists may have limited beliefs before they are "fine-tuned" by extremist peers.[102] For children, the family environment might provide these initial seeds of extremism.

As with pedophilia, maintaining secrecy at the outset can be imperative (whereas after the child has been martyred, the terrorist organization exploits the death for its advantage). The mechanism for evaluating the individual's trustworthiness uses a process of costly induction, whereby new recruits are asked to engage in a dangerous or incriminating task and their willingness and enthusiasm are used as evidence of commitment.[103] Depending on the group, children will be given low-level support tasks such as gathering intelligence, ferrying messages, or delivering packages before being entrusted with greater responsibility. The children are occasionally instructed to keep information from their families as the group fosters an exclusive relationship with them. In so doing, the group and the child form a unique bond in which secrecy is used to further the group's goals. In almost all interviews with recruited children, the children say they were separated from their families, friends, and community during the recruitment and training process. Mohammed's father was not permitted to visit his son, and the reporter who profiled Yasir explained how "for a month the [children] were kept isolated from all that they knew and loved, and not allowed even to see or speak to their families."[104]

IS video propaganda shows children watching videos of extreme violence such as stonings and public executions, including beheadings at which other children are present. Subsequent propaganda shows children taking part in executions and moving from the background to the foreground in the films. "Kids," we have noted previously, "are being subjected to a systematic process of indoctrination as they're trained by the group to be fully fledged militants."[105]

Role Succession

Organizations concerned about their longevity typically engage in mentorship, early talent spotting, and development of diversity, leadership, potential, and initiative.[106] Terrorist groups must systematically prepare goal-oriented recruits for role succession.[107]

Violent extremist groups are required to prioritize talent spotting and the development of skills. Many groups recruit for specific technical skills. A Taliban commander in Helmand told the CBS reporter Lara Logan that "it takes four, six, seven months of training. Everyone knows who is fit for what kind of work. You can easily understand their abilities for different tasks, like to be a fighter, a watchman or a suicide bomber."[108] Migration occurs between and within roles, along a spectrum from illegal (violent) and potentially illegal (aiding/abetting) roles to legal roles (intelligence gathering or message dissemination).[109] Terror groups gradually introduce young recruits to different tasks to prepare them for the demands of violent extremism. Younger recruits are initially trained to be spies. As part of the gradual process of escalating involvement, they are later encouraged to inform on family members or neighbors, which functions as a test of their loyalty. Children in IS progress "from Cub to Lion" (*Ashbal* to *Asad*), training that mirrors that of the adults, and they wear similar uniforms and learn the vernacular of the group.

Our research revealed that IS selects certain children to appear repeatedly in their video propaganda. These tend to be the children of foreign fighters, who are diverse, multicultural, multiracial, attractive, and elite—the terrorist equivalent of pageant children. Contrary to the expectation that youth appearing in IS videos are planning their martyrdom, these children are not sacrificed for the cause. Our research uncovered several examples of children who appear repeatedly in the propaganda but are not sent to their deaths (although over 350 children have died as "martyrs"). One such video, "Sang pour Sang" (Blood for blood), released in 2016, featured ethnically diverse, clean-cut children who are fully outfitted in spotless battle fatigues. These very same children appeared the following August in another IS propaganda video, executing Kurdish prisoners. The August 26, 2016, execution video featured children from Britain, Turkey, Egypt, Tunisia, and Uzbekistan, including JoJo Jones, a.k.a. Abu Abdullah al-Britani,[110] the son of Sally Jones, the British ex–punk rocker who immigrated to Syria with her young son and was on the FBI's most wanted list. A CIA reaper drone killed Sally Jones in June 2017 near the border town of Mayadin, but JoJo, then twelve, was at a Cub training camp and survived the bombardment.[111]

Propaganda videos featuring the children of foreign fighters are released regularly. On December 29, 2016, IS released a video entitled "My Father Told Me," in which a different group of ethnically diverse youth are shown in a "kill house," executing Syrian prisoners (called apostates, or *murtadd* by IS). These children appear over and over and never see battle, even though, in the video, the children are coached to say that they aspire to martyrdom. In our analysis of IS last-will-and-testament videos and the "about to die" images eulogized by the group, children in mixed *inghemasi* (suicide) units are more often Syrian and Iraqi, and not the children of foreign fighters who have appeared in propaganda. Children who repeatedly appear in the group's magazines, videos, and recruiting posters become internet superstars and appear in other iconic imagery (as avatars) on the group's encrypted social media platforms, such as Telegram. In another example, Abdullah, a young Kazakh boy, has been featured in three different videos over three years (2013, 2014, 2015), including one entitled "Race for Good," which shows several Kazakh children learning Arabic and how to handle weapons at a training camp. In the video, Abdullah is shown fieldstripping and rebuilding an AK-47 assault rifle. All of the children wear matching camouflage uniforms.[112]

During the video montage of sharia lessons and military training exercises, Abdullah is "interviewed" for the camera. The *Daily Mail* reported, "When quizzed about what he will do in the future, Abdullah declares: 'I will be the one who slaughters you, O *kuffar* [nonbeliever]. I will be a *mujahid*, inshallah [God willing].'"[113] IS released "Race for Good" through al-Hayat Media Center, and it was aired throughout the Middle East by news outlets, including Kyrgyzstan's Kloop.kg.[114] In reality, Abdullah was never selected for the battlefield; instead he appeared a few months later, in January 2015, in yet another al-Hayat Media Center production. In this video, Abdullah is shown executing two Russian prisoners forced to confess to being Federal Security Service (FSB) spies.

Implications for Psychological Practice

In sum, the recruitment of children into violent extremist groups can involve a process consistent with grooming for sexual predation, evident in the child protection literature. It is notable that the term "grooming" has been increasingly invoked in research on violent extremism, typically in a nebulous fashion, to refer to a vague process of manipulation during recruitment. Ian Elliott developed a model of a precisely defined grooming process—generalizable beyond sexual predation—based on motivation and behavior.[115] The tactics recruiters use to create an environment of trust, motivation, openness to ideas, and organizational security, before leveraging that environment for the systematic and gradual introduction of extremist and violent themes, is common between the two. One potential criticism of the analogy is that the application of a model developed in a different context and based on the behaviors of a different population is tenuous. That criticism is a valid one; the similarities between the two processes require further validation.

However, the comparison has powerful explanatory value in the context of terrorist recruitment. J. M. Berger developed a framework of "tailored" online recruitment by IS that he explicitly likens to a process of grooming. Berger's framework consists of four stages: (1) first contact, in which IS approaches a target online or responds to a target approaching the group; (2) the creation of a microcommunity, where a group of recruiters make themselves a virtually constant contact and begin to both radicalize and isolate the target from outside influences; (3) a shift to private communications and "deeper radicalization"; and (4) the identification of pro-IS actions suitable for the target. The strength of Berger's approach is that it provides an exemplary contextual framework for the way grooming manifests online in violent extremism—or the "social media ecosystem," as Berger describes it.[116]

The shift to private—preferably encrypted—online communication is an example of security management that child predators employ. There are also elements of Berger's model that allude to self-regulatory processes, such as the suggestion that the action is dependent on the level of "radicalization" at the outset, and the whole process appears to be one of gradual desensitization. Berger introduces the idea that what begins as a general goal of "extremism" in the target develops into one of a "discrete task" (e.g., public support, emigration [hijra], or violence). This process requires the recruiter to "identify the most likely action a target is willing to undertake and encourage it,"[117] a decision that is likely to be the result of a feedback process based on the recruiter's perception of adequate levels of rapport, radicalization, and security.

There are three practical implications to be derived from this analysis. First, by emphasizing process over etiology, we can understand the behavior without having to make assumptions about the psychological characteristics of either the recruiter or the target. Second, the process is dyadic and dynamic—both the recruiter and the target have personal needs, behavioral strategies, and their own idiosyncrasies. Third, because children present a lower baseline level of radicalization, their recruitment has different needs than that of adults—possibly requiring additional grooming tactics.

For child soldiers, the issues of agency and volition are routinely overlooked, as is the possibility that in many cases joining an extremist group is a rational choice (possibly the only choice) for self-preservation from harm; as such, the resilience of children should be accounted for.[118] Because each child presents recruiters with a variety of individual and situational vulnerabilities, recruiters must tailor their grooming tactics to the specific "push" and "pull" factors. This approach acknowledges the *agency* of the child—that is, that children are active, complex, resilient, and purposeful agents, who may be able (and willing) to respond positively to information even when this does not seem to be in their interest and may even place them at personal risk.[119]

Based on our research of the five hundred groups considered to be "terrorist organizations," over half employ children in some capacity, and around 30 percent have created formal pathways for children's involvement.[120] Terrorist organizations create separate units for children in order to involve them at a young age, and they occasionally use their youth movements as a testing ground to spot talent. The permissive environment for political violence depends heavily on whether there exists a culture in which death and sacrifice are considered to be the highest form of service to one's community—whether a national or religious community, since there are cultures of martyrdom evident in secular nationalist conflicts (for example, in Sri Lanka).

At the height of the LTTE's popularity, children enthusiastically joined the Bakuts (Tamil Tiger youth wing) and competed for the opportunity to enter into the elite Black Tiger suicide bomber units.[121] This also appears to have been the case with several of the Pakistani children who joined the TTP militants "voluntarily," but who reported (to their therapists and social workers at Sabaoon) the horrors of their involvement, which included severe beatings, periods of isolation, and witnessing beheadings. Other children we encountered in Pakistan described their positive experiences with the militants: they felt respected, were given important tasks, and were made to feel special and valuable, making their rehabilitation all the more challenging since they had positive memories of and associations with involvement.

Horgan has argued elsewhere that many individuals who become involved in violent extremist groups are already on that path when they are recruited. Conversely, children and young adults come to the process during a period of cognitive and social development, with open and malleable minds. They rarely possess the knowledge and experience (or cynicism) required for self-radicalization—although the economic imbalance and political instability in many at-risk communities could result in an indiscriminate sense of grievance in children.[122] For recruiters, children represent an attractive target, due to both the malleability and plasticity of their young minds and their innate neurobiological tendencies toward sensation seeking and risky behavior, particularly during adolescence, which the terrorist group can harness.[123]

Important lessons can be learned from the popularity of cognitive behavioral therapy in the treatment of sex offenders.[124] Horgan distinguishes between radicalization and violent radicalization, where the latter represents the conflation of the cognitive (radicalization) and behavioral (engagement) elements of violent extremism.[125] In an operationally useful way, radicalization becomes a cognitive behavioral process: the linking of cognitive motivations to engage with behavioral methods to participate in violent acts. Deradicalization efforts, which we explore in greater detail in chapter 7, match those seen in other forms of criminal behavior, in which pro-offending cognitions (be they religious, cultural, political, socioeconomic, etc., in their nature) are identified and challenged, the development of those cognitions is explained, and the link between them and the behaviors that have led the individual to his or her current circumstances is established and communicated.

Prevention

Ordinarily sexual grooming is notoriously difficult to detect. Many of the behaviors involved—particularly in the initial phase—may be legal and seemingly legitimate. This makes it difficult for bystanders to identify and respond to these behaviors with certainty. They are likely to have difficulties (1) identifying that there is a problem needing intervention, (2) finding the confidence to assess ambiguous behaviors as problematic (particularly given the ambiguity in many phase-one behaviors), and (3) applying the practical skills to effectively deal with the situation.

The first area for prevention is to focus on the interpersonal mechanisms (rapport, incentivization, and disinhibition), the education of the general public about the nature of the relationships between recruiters and children, and the promotion of widespread societal and community awareness of and vigilance for grooming behaviors. The second approach is to focus on the desensitization process, educating youth about appropriate physical and emotional boundaries and promoting personal safety and resilience. This could include bystander intervention—seeking to educate, equip, and empower adults (families, peers, community members) around a potential target of recruitment to intervene in instances where there is evidence of potential grooming. The third element of prevention comprises techniques to increase recruiters' effort, difficulty, risk, and likelihood of detection, thus increasing the costs of engagement while decreasing the benefit.[126] The issue of re-recruitment and recidivism also exists, and any intervention with children should provide resilience building and tangible skills for identifying and appropriately responding to (and rebuffing) the mechanisms of grooming.

In conclusion, models of pedophilia and the literature on child protection provide insight into the psychological mechanisms involved in the recruitment of children into terrorist groups. Such recruitment presents a unique challenge to child protection, and only by better understanding the processes of exploitation can we suggest some effective safeguards. It is important to understand the many ways in which children are coerced. In some instances there is an expectation that children become involved, follow in their father's (or brother's or uncle's) footsteps, or make a contribution to the community by fighting an occupation or a foreign or ethnic rival. In other cases, the children have no choice.

Children's recruitment differs from that of adults in the extent to which trickery and coercion play a crucial role, although the degree to which they are used varies from group to group. This chapter has argued that the Islamic State has relied more heavily on youth than previous groups. In these other cases, children might be groomed for eventual involvement but don't play as visible a role until they are older. In some groups no one under eighteen is permitted to join, and even if youth are recruited, they cannot play a front-line role until they are "old enough" to do so. According to Vivian Karam and Zeina Salama, no other terrorist group comes close to IS's use of children "in such a systematic and organized way."[127] The difference between IS or the Taliban and the Provisional IRA, the Basque separatist movement, or the Red Brigades is the physical control of territory, which has allowed IS and the Taliban to recruit minors. Control of territory has translated into a control of hospitals, orphanages, schools, and curricula, and has provided a steady stream of recruits. When the terrorists control territory and institutions in which children are present, they can use their leadership position to inculcate children with radical and violent political interpretations.

Abu Anas al Iraqi "media man" posing with a gun in Badiyah

Shedding light on Cubs' military and physical training in Damascus

Showing part of the "activities of caring for the weak," distributing gifts among orphans in Afghanistan

Children having executed Afghan Army spies in Nanjahar, Khorosan (Afghanistan)

John Horgan with Sabaoon therapists and social workers in Pakistan

IS's youngest executioner after killing a Kurdish prisoner in a ball pit

JoJo Jones (second from right) and other foreign-fighter children executing Kurds, from the August 26, 2016, execution video

Children in Malakand

KHAYR   محرم 1439م

الأخ أبو محي الدين الخابوري –تقبّله الله

The brother Abu Muhia al-Din al-Khabouri

Two young Balkan boys used in IS propaganda

Two young martyrs, Abu Jalebeeb al-Korasani and Abu Talha al-Balkhi, who perpetrated the attack in Kabul

Yazidi brothers—Amjad (Abu Yusuf) and Asaad (Abu Khattab) al-Sinjari (neé Alyas-Mahjo), the two boys on the far right

"Abdullah" from bystander to committed insider. Captions under figures: (left) "The Furqan Foundation in the company of a Migrant Family," The Furqan Foundation, October 14, 2013; (center) "Race Towards Good," Al-Hayat Media Center, November 22, 2014; (right) "Uncovering an Enemy Within," Al-Hayat Media Center, January 13, 2015.

PATHWAYS TO INVOLVEMENT
Consensus and Cultures of Martyrdom

The tyrant dies and his rule is over; the martyr dies and his rule begins.
Søren Kierkegaard

In the previous chapters we have explored how children grow up in extreme conditions of poverty, violence, and institutionalized harassment during prolonged periods of conflict. As they mature, the children commence involvement with violent political movements in mostly supportive roles: throwing stones at demonstrations, acting as lookouts, ferrying messages for members of a terrorist group (to whose members they might be related), or smuggling weapons.

Under these conditions, youth are repeatedly exposed to a "culture of martyrdom." While the concept of a culture of martyrdom is routinely credited for the proliferation of children wanting to join terrorist organizations, the elements that make up this culture are rarely defined, delineated, or explained. How were they constructed, and by whom?

This chapter sets out to explain the traditions of martyrdom and self-sacrifice across time and space, and how different groups have embraced the folklore of "the martyr." Our purpose in this chapter is to demonstrate that a culture of martyrdom can play a crucial role in fostering environments and creating a social ecology in which children grow up feeling that they can accomplish more with their death than with their life, while at the same time making parents enthusiastic supporters of children's participation. The chapter also compares martyrdom in several different contexts to show how this is not something unique to jihadi groups.

Studies of children living in violent communities have concluded that, as one such study puts it,

> Children who witness and are otherwise exposed to violence are deeply affected by the events, often showing symptoms of post-traumatic stress disorder.... Classic PTSD symptoms include: re-experiencing the event in play, dreams, or intrusive images and sounds associated with the event; psychic numbing characterized by subdued behavior and inactivity. In addition, the children are frequently plagued by fears of recurrence of the violence. and a pessimistic future orientation. These latter symptoms can manifest in a sense of futurelessness characterized by children's belief that they will not reach adulthood.[1]

Starting from a very early age, children in conflict areas are regularly exposed to violence (often from both sides). Exposure to violence alters the child's perceptions of right and wrong. Early trauma and adversity place a child at risk for a variety of negative outcomes, including greater likelihood of engaging in violence, as well as symptoms of posttraumatic stress disorder (intrusion, avoidance, and hypervigilance).[2] Exposure to violence might also impact children's willingness to participate in violent activities themselves, even leading them to "volunteer" to be martyrs for the cause.

The word "martyr" derives from the ancient Greek *martus* or *martys*, meaning one who bears witness. It encompasses those willing to make great sacrifices for the sake of a principle, as well as those who suffer willingly, or are persecuted, for refusing to renounce their beliefs.[3] Martyrs defend a principle or a truth for which they cannot surrender. In some instances, the martyr can be a symbol not just of faith, but of the nation. Such individuals are willing to self-sacrifice for a religious or a secular cause.

In essence, martyrdom is the process of making one's death meaningful. The martyr exchanges life for something greater and long-lasting in the afterlife.[4] Understanding the martyr as a *witness* cuts across virtually every religious tradition. David Cook, in his book *Martyrdom in Islam*, refers to the witness as the most powerful form of advertisement—communicating personal credibility and dedication.[5] The martyr's death is heroic and serves a compelling cause. Whereas "suicide is selfish ... ," Karin Fierke observes, "martyrdom is selfless."[6] For Diego Gambetta, the notion of the martyr's death implies that there exists a community that will benefit from his or her act of self-sacrifice in some way, and so the act is for the greater good.[7]

The context in which a culture of martyrdom develops is meaningful. The structural conditions that foster an environment conducive to appreciating violence can be the result of the shared experiences of a people in a conflict zone.

Ethnic groups in conflict cohere in unique ways, and the experiences of the few will be felt by the many, especially with modern technology and the global media (and increasingly social media). There are related psychological sequelae that can result from exposure to these conditions. In particular we can observe that in cases where a dominant group utilizes population control tactics, checkpoints, patrols, searches, and seizures, people suffer from feelings of intense humiliation. Terrorist organizations can (and do) exploit these feelings to intensify the individual's anger and his or her desire for significance through engagement in militant violence.[8] According to Fierke,

> When ongoing suffering or humiliation is the shared experience of the people, expressions of this pain may come to occupy a central place in the language, narrative, and practice of its culture.[9]

Humiliation may be an impetus for resistance. In situations marked by past humiliation, there is a further dynamic between emotional experiences and those expressions that are permitted. Peter Stearns and Carol Stearns discuss "emotionology," or how norms of different societies shape emotional expression and spatially limit the locations where this can be expressed. "Such emotionology," they note, "influences the individual experience of emotion through processes of socialization."[10] It is under these circumstances that a culture of martyrdom thrives and captures the imagination.

Elizabeth Castelli argues that memorializing the lives and deaths of martyrs produces a culture of its own.[11] Although over the years the concept of culture has been defined in more than 164 ways, the generally accepted understanding comprises two dimensions: a pattern of human knowledge, belief, and behavior based on social learning and symbols; and a set of shared attitudes, values, goals, and practices that characterizes an institution, organization, or group.[12] The act of martyrdom fixes identity and makes cultural practices static and absolute.[13] Moreover, it is not simply an act of self-sacrifice, but one that requires an audience (real or fictive) to recount it, interpret it, and make it meaningful.[14] Martyrdom and culture are an attempt to overcome struggle, and both are motivated by the urge to mitigate conflicts over identity.[15]

There are both offensive and defensive forms of martyrdom. Defensive martyrdom can be traced back to Christianity during the early Roman Empire; offensive martyrdom encompasses bearing witness and sacrificing the self in battle against injustice.[16] Martyrs sacrifice themselves on behalf of their community, which politicizes suffering (or death) and (re)generates national resistance. Mark Jurgensmeyer considers acts of self-sacrifice to be highly performative. In essence, martyrdom is "an act of speech" in which the suffering body communicates the injustice experienced by a community to a larger audience.[17] To create a culture of martyrdom, one needs the involvement of state (or protostate) institutions to support its creation and sustain the message. Cultures of martyrdom are constructed via children's education, the media, and especially programming directed at youth, as well as the larger supportive community. The media play a necessary role to communicate with "the enemy" and to a larger domestic constituency.[18]

The development of a culture of martyrdom explains the underlying altruistic instinct of self-sacrifice and desire to help members of one's community. This perverse "altruism" has been observed from Northern Ireland to the Middle East and South Asia. In addition to the psychological push factor of doing something for one's community, there are rewards for the individual willing to make the ultimate sacrifice: fame is a powerful pull factor for vulnerable youth. The desire to do something important with one's life and to achieve fame is seen equally among both young men and young women across a variety of cultures.

The daily realities of the conflict settings in which cultures of martyrdom develop can enhance the lure of gaining the respect of one's peers and instill a sense of greater purpose. Stanley Tambiah's analysis of martyrdom among Tamils in Sri Lanka asserts that acts of sacrifice or martyrdom conform to established Tamil social conventions—subject to assessment of legitimacy—and impact reality. "Rituals," Tambiah observes, "appeal to custom and their repetition of historical precedents."[19] In all of the cultural settings in which one finds political martyrdom and self-sacrifice, there are identifiable rituals, traditions, and steps involved in the process, whether among Catholic hunger strikers in Northern Ireland or self-immolating Buddhist monks and nuns protesting the Vietnam War. The preparation phase in the process of becoming a martyr involves self-abnegation, fasting, praying, and being separated from loved ones so that the individual does not change his or her mind at the last minute. Early cases of Palestinian suicide bombers described the would-be bomber's being instructed to lie down in an empty grave, to demystify the experience of death and eliminate any possible fear at the prospect of dying. As a culture of martyrdom takes root, the need for an extended period of preparation may decrease, as individuals require less convincing of the benefits of martyrdom. They will already be familiar with them, from symbolism and the not-so-subtle messages present all around them.

There is a tendency to erroneously assume that martyrdom represents one region, one culture, or one religion. After the attacks on September 11, many Americans came to assume that jihadi culture had a greater propensity for violence than other religions or traditions.[20] This assumption fails to recognize the extent to which other religious traditions have justified or given meaning to their own forms of political self-sacrifice.[21] Such generalizations fail to appreciate how a culture of martyrdom is constructed and manipulated to create a generation that subscribes to the belief that their death is more valuable than life. This perverse assumption likewise exists in other religions.

The recent focus on jihadi martyrdom likewise fails to appreciate martyrdom's long history of playing a significant role in other faiths. It is erroneous to attach this construct to a particular ideology. "Violence is self-perpetuating; like a drug. It sparks excitement, and an adrenaline rush, and so demands a repeat performance, in the same way that a drug becomes addictive."[22]

Constructing a culture of martyrdom transcends religious movements. Fierke highlights, for example, the Polish Solidarity movement, which developed a range of symbols, from postcards to stamps to statues, displaying images of historical martyrs, and also utilized powerful cultural symbols (e.g., the Black Madonna). Such symbols play an important role in harking back to an earlier time, which allows people to relate their individual self-sacrifice to the long history of great men and women who came before them.

In some religions the willingness to sacrifice oneself for the greater good or for the community is considered a positive.[23] Sacrificing oneself on behalf of "one's religion, political ideals, or community, is originally hardwired in the collective consciousness of Western Culture as one of the central legacies of the Christian tradition."[24] For the early Christian martyrs (Pionius and Polycarp) facing Roman torture and certain immolation, death was not the ultimate threat or what Chris Huebner calls a "final frontier to be overcome and tamed," though neither was actively desired.[25] In his work on suicide missions, Diego Gambetta highlights Buddhist monks and nuns who sacrificed their lives in protest, as well as Northern Irish hunger strikers who protested their treatment and classification as common criminals by refusing food and drink.[26] We assume that a culture of martyrdom is correlated to the concept of jihad, yet in fact there are many examples of people's willingness to endure great suffering for a cause they believe in.

In Tamil ideology, *thatkodai*, or "gift of the self," is the equivalent of Islamic and Christian martyrdom. Sharika Thiranagama establishes that *thatkodai* valorized death as the ultimate sacrifice.[27] It is worth noting that Tamils deliberately use the term *thatkodai* rather than *thatkolai*, the word for suicide,[28] much in the same way that Salafi jihadis talk of a *shahid* (witness, martyr) while avoiding the actual word for suicide—*intihar*—as suicide is strictly forbidden in Islam. The success of suicide bombing campaigns by the LTTE is highly correlated with the presence of *thatkodai* ideology. According to the former head of the LTTE's political wing, S. P. Thamilchelvam, Tamil enthusiasm for the tactic of suicide terrorism reflected the ideology of *thatkodai* (gift of the self), in which the person gives himself or herself in full.[29] The benefit of the sacrifice extends not just to the individual but also in some instances to the person's extended family. In the Tamil case, Paul Gill explains, "Those who have given themselves to the cause are *mahaveera*, 'brave ones,' and their mother is *veeravati* or 'brave mother.'"[30] This has parallels with Islamic martyrs, who can intercede for seventy of their relatives in the afterlife, guaranteeing them access to heaven and the Garden of Eden. In Islam, the mother of a martyr receives an additional *kunya* (nickname); Umm Shahid, "Mother of a Martyr," is equally esteemed in Islamic culture as it is in Tamil culture.

Hunger strikes in Ireland can be traced back to the ancient tradition of self-sacrifice in the face of economic injustice, known as *cealachan*, and are an integral part of Irish history and mythology. The legal code enshrined in the Brehon (Anglicisation of Gaelic breitheamh, or *brithem*) laws provided a means for seeking redress, including the willingness to die by self-starvation on the doorstep of the source of offense.[31] In the medieval code *Senchus Mor*, fasting (Gaelic *troscad*) was done against someone who had offended, and in the tradition of *cealachan*, one achieved justice by starving oneself. The mythology of this historical precedent inspired the patriotism of the 1916 Easter Rising. During this initial phase of Irish nationalism, the Irish Republican Army hunger strikes were political weapons and not motivated by economic reasons. In the period between 1913 and 1923, there were more than fifty hunger strikes.[32] In 1923, more than eight thousand political prisoners opposed to the Anglo-Irish Treaty went on a hunger strike, and two died before the protest was called off.[33]

The better-known Irish hunger strikes occurred decades later, in 1980–81, when members of the Provisional IRA—a radical splinter of the original—incarcerated at Long Kesh prison held a strike led by Bobby Sands. Sands, along with nine other men and three women, intended to force the British Crown to recognize them as political prisoners, subject to the Geneva Conventions, and not as common criminals. Ten died in the process, including Sands, a recently elected member of Parliament. In interviews with former hunger strikers from Armagh Gaol, they made clear that although the hunger strike was intended to send a clear message of their willingness to die, death was never their goal.[34] For people who went on strike, opposition to the injustice of the criminalization was first and foremost. Their willingness to sacrifice themselves to improve their countrymen's conditions rendered their acts altruistic in a way that jihadi martyrdom is not.

The hunger strikers were, according to Fierke, martyrs "whose acts of self sacrifice were proof that they were acting not out of self interest but political conviction for a just cause, and with undeniable support, both at home and abroad."[35] The reaction among the Irish Republican community was to virtually deify Bobby Sands and the other hunger strikers. Their images were painted along the Falls Road in Belfast and became iconic symbols of British injustice (and especially Margaret Thatcher's unwillingness to compromise and her willingness to let a democratically elected member of Parliament die), and parks and streets were named after Sands in countries around the world. Sands's sister Bernadette eventually became the leader of a dissident offshoot organization—one that organizes youth groups and camps to prepare the next generation.

The Buddhist tradition likewise prohibits suicide but allows for self-sacrifice under specific circumstances. In certain strains of Buddhism, notably Mahayana Buddhism, predominant in Southeast Asia, the faith is concerned with social justice and emphasizes active compassion (*karuna*) and benevolence. "While suicide is prohibited in Buddhism," writes Fierke, "self-immolation, if undertaken with proper intention, is in the exceptional case of Bodhisattva, understood as offering a sacrifice to the Buddha that transcends moral precepts."[36]

The self-immolation by a seventy-three-year-old Buddhist monk, Thich Quang Duc, on June 11, 1964, had its roots in the Lotus Sutra. During the 1960s, self-immolation became a form of political protest against foreign occupation, a response to government coercion against the Buddhist faith (and monasteries) and the injustices perpetrated by immoral rulers such as Ngô Đình Diệm. In the Lotus Sutra, self-immolation comprises two meanings; the first is an act of offering, which places it within the framework of self-sacrifice. The second places *gan* within a context of the persecution and destruction of the people, the individual sacrifices the self to Buddha in the hope of bringing all living things closer to liberation. The *gan* offering is an act of communication.[37] Not only did hundreds of monks and nuns make this sacrifice, but so did nine Americans, including a Quaker from Pennsylvania named Norman Morrison, who died outside the Pentagon on November 3, 1965—in full view of Secretary of Defense Robert McNamara.[38]

Self-immolation or self-sacrifice, continued to punctuate peace movements. It even sparked the Arab Spring, when on December 17, 2010, a lone Tunisian fruit peddler, Muhammed Bouazizi, sparked outrage with one act "igniting weeks of demonstrations that spread across the country and unseated Zine al-Abidine Ben Ali after 23 years of repressive rule," according to a Reuters account.[39] This act was soon followed and emulated by other people in the region. James Verini reports that

> in January [2012], five young Moroccan men auto-cremated (the more accurate term; "self-immolation" technically means any form of self-destruction) following a fifty-two-year-old pensioner in Jordan and an elderly woman in Bahrain. The young men belonged to a group called Unemployed Graduates that had been occupying the Ministry of Higher Education building. They followed upon the action of Mohammed Bouazizi, the Tunisian street vendor, whose self-immolation—inspired by the chronic poverty and corruption of his country—helped incite the Arab Spring.[40]

The spread of these acts of reflected a sense of helplessness, and the repressive government reactions fueled the contagion. Many Arab governments accused the protesters of being controlled by terrorist factions. The Arab Federation of Psychiatrists did not believe that Bouazizi's self-immolation (and the other copycat protests) had anything to do with "martyrdom fantasies"; rather, their suicides were cries for help against the powerlessness, desperation, and frustration of poverty and humiliation.

Bouazizi's act was one of protest.[41] Like the Irish tradition of the Brehon laws and the self-immolation of Buddhist monks and nuns, it was an act of suicide committed in full public view. Bouazizi's mother, along with activists and many commentators in the Arab press, considered him a martyr, whereas the lack of any religious motivation made it simply a suicide for the religious authorities at al-Azhar University, such as Mohammed Rifa al-Tahtawi. Further, suicide is frowned on by Islamic religious sources of authority, whereas the sheikhs rarely condemn acts of "self-sacrifice" by suicide bombers in Israel or in Iraq against US soldiers.

Gambetta makes the distinction between people who kill themselves and others and those who kill only themselves. In essence, both are acts intended to make a public statement about injustice and to influence an audience, yet the difference between killing oneself for a cause (martyrdom) and having one's success depend on killing others in the process makes one an act of protest and the other an act of terror.[42]

Michael Hardt and Antonio Negri classify two contrasting images of martyrdom:

> The one form, which is exemplified by the suicide bomber, poses martyrdom as a response of destruction, including self-destruction, to an act of injustice. The other form of martyrdom, however, is completely different. In this form, the martyr does not seek destruction but is struck down by the violence of the powerful. Martyrdom of this type is a testimony. . . . This martyrdom is an act of love.[43]

Like its origin in Greek, the Arabic term for martyr, *shahid*, means witness, and the *shahada* ("There is no god but God and Muhammed is his Prophet") constitutes the primary testimony of faith and an assertion about the unity of God. In the Sunni Muslim tradition, martyrdom is linked to jihad as the noblest act of testifying for one's faith. As an example, David Cook relates the story of the Ethiopian slave Bilal, who was persecuted for his beliefs as a follower of the Prophet Muhammed. Bilal became a powerful symbol on account of his willingness to suffer for Islam.[44] For Shia Islam, martyrdom is more closely linked to rituals of suffering, mourning, and redemption.[45] While martyrdom can trace its lineage back to both Sunni and Shia traditions, those traditions evolved different understandings of the concept of martyrdom until the modern era, when the traditions associated with offensive martyrdom merged the Sunni and Shia interpretations. "In the twentieth century," Fierke explains, "Sunni revivalists once again highlighted the importance of physical jihad and armed struggle, and it became the duty of the individual Muslim to participate in Jihad to liberate the land in the case of Muslim territory being occupied by an enemy invader."[46]

In the Islamic tradition, suicide and martyrdom are distinct from each other. Suicide (*intihar*) is strictly prohibited in the Qur'an, as it is for all the Abrahamic faiths. There is no greater taboo in Islam than committing suicide. The Qur'an emphatically states, "Do not kill yourselves, for God is merciful to you. If any of you does these things out of hostility and injustice, we shall make him suffer Fire: that is easy for God" (4:29). Babak Rahimi adds, "As noble as it is to die in battle, to die at the enemy's hands is a just cause—so has it been considered shameful to willfully take one's own life."[47] In contrast, Sahih al-Bukhari explained that martyrdom is an act of devotion to God: "Whoever asks Allah sincerely for martyrdom [Allahumma inni as'aluk ash-shahadah], Allah will cause him to reach the status of the martyrs even if he dies in his bed."[48] Martyrdom by Salafi jihadi militants makes a connection between earthly and divine objectives: the martyr gives up his or her earthly life with the promise of continuing life in paradise.[49]

One of the earliest Islamic martyrs was a woman named Sumayyah bint Khayyat, killed in AD 615 by the Meccan tribal chief Abu Jahl for espousing Islamic beliefs five years after the Prophet began to spread the faith.[50] Ziaud din Sardar dates the origins of a modern culture of martyrdom in the region to the 1979 Iranian Revolution.[51] Martyrdom went from being associated with select historical figures in classical Shia history (the fourth caliph, Ali, and his son Imam Hussein) to something contemporary, commonplace, and achievable by ordinary people willing to do something extraordinary.

A wave of extremist ideologies swept through the Middle East in the revolution's aftermath, shifting the conception of martyrdom from the classical one (a willingness to die in battle against impossible odds) to a more active one (seeking martyrdom on purpose). In the original conception, martyrdom epitomized an exemplary ethical model of moral action in the struggle (jihad) for the sacred, manifested in the ultimate sacrifice of the self. The process of giving up one's life for the cause or for higher existence was a noble act: "It was not merely the death that identified martyrdom," Rahimi says, "but the very fulfillment of the duty of obedience to the will of God that brought one to the level of the sacred."[52] Fighting against immeasurable odds, or volunteering for high-risk missions, demonstrated bravery, and not the desire for death. Within the Shia faith, martyrdom involves women and children, because Imam Hussein's son was killed at Karbala. The passion plays that occur annually during the feast of Ashura include the participation of women and children.[53] Not until the first Iran-Iraq War, when people volunteered for suicide missions, did the meaning metamorphose into what we understand as martyrdom today. For Ali Shariati, the chief ideologue of the Iranian Revolution, "Martyrdom is the expression of the value, the ideal in which the martyr sacrifices himself for something greater and more lasting, leaving behind a permanent and valuable legacy."[54] For jihadi Salafi (Sunni) groups, "to die a martyr's death is to protect and honor the faith and the integrity of Islam," which have been polluted by impure nonbelievers.[55]

According to Ziauddin Sardar, when Iran employed teenage conscripts in its eight-year war with Iraq (1980–88), "a whole generation of young people was sacrificed on the battlefield. All of them became martyrs. And fountains of 'blood'—actually colored water—gushed forth in Martyrs' Squares throughout Iran."[56] During the war, battalions of women voluntarily cleared minefields, and the first child suicide bomber, Mohammed Hossein Fahmideh, aged thirteen,[57] threw himself at an Iraqi tank after hiding a hand grenade under his shirt.[58] Not only was Fahmideh technically the very first suicide bomber to die in 1980 (he was also one of the youngest, until the Islamic State began weaponizing eight- and ten-year-olds) but in the aftermath of his martyrdom he became a kind of cult figure representing the best of Shia Islam. "Streets throughout the country," notes Joyce Davis, "were named in his honor, as were hospitals, schools, and sports stadiums."[59] His death was likened to the martyrdom of the Prophet Muhammed's grandson Hussein (killed at Karbala) and was celebrated by the Ayatollah Khomeini, who called him "our leader" and encouraged other teens to follow in his footsteps. According to Davis, Fahmideh was one of thousands of boys who were martyred during the Iran-Iraq War.[60] In transforming Fahmideh into a teen idol, the Iranian regime produced scores of promotional goods bearing his image, including lunchboxes. He was also featured on posters along major roads, on a giant mural near Tehran University,[61] and on Iranian currency, and in 1986, Iran celebrated the anniversary of his martyrdom by issuing a commemorative stamp.[62] "On the mural," notes Steve Inskeep, "the child [Fahmideh] is watched over by the late Ayatollah Khomeini, who proclaimed that the martyred child was the revolution's true leader. Murals with similar themes cover walls all over the city."[63]

The ayatollah decreed that the anniversary of Fahmideh's death, October 30, would become "Student Basij Day"—an official holiday. The ayatollah had made Fahmideh into a source of emulation for all Iranian teens. A monument was erected on the outskirts of Tehran, and the cemetery where he is buried became a place of pilgrimage for young Iranians. Decades later, Fahmideh's "heroic exploits" are retold each year during Ashura celebrations.

Reflecting back on their youth, members of the Basij force, now adults, regard themselves as having missed out on their childhood, and many suffer from long-term posttraumatic stress. According to one former child soldier, "We were fascinated with becoming heroes. Now, 31 years after I first went to the frontline, I am still tortured by bodies without heads, by bodies torn apart and by horrifying sounds of explosions. I see all of them in my nightmares."[64]

All of the different interpretations of martyrdom across religious traditions view suicide as sacred, with the ultimate end state of producing a more lasting life—one that is transcendent and immortal. "The distinctive characteristic of a martyr is that he charges the atmosphere with courage and zeal. He revives the spirit of valor and fortitude . . . among the people who have lost it. That is why Islam is always in need of martyrs."[65]

The Iranian Revolution exported this new interpretation of "everyday martyrdom" to other parts of the Middle East. First the tactic spread to other Shia enclaves in Lebanon and Kuwait, and eventually it also spread among the Palestinians, Iraqis, and Afghans. Ultimately it metastasized into the almost daily occurrence we see today, in France, Mali, Turkey, Iraq, Nigeria, and Syria.[66] In 1983, when the US stationed marines in Beirut, the leaders of the Islamic Resistance movement, Hizbullah, coupled Shia religious traditions of martyrdom with the innovation of truck and car bombs. It is precisely this culture of glorification that has infected a generation of children with the belief that death trumps any possible accomplishments one will achieve during one's life. Suicide bombing became the tactic of choice, one notably used by Salafi jihadis (Sunnis) against other Muslims more often than against symbols of foreign occupation.

From years of studying suicide bombers in a variety of contexts, it becomes clear that the groups utilize a calculated process, though the rituals and traditions vary from place to place. In some circumstances there is an official ceremony, where the group celebrates the bomber by throwing him or her a wedding. In other cases, the leader of the movement may prepare the bomber a final meal, and the group will capture the moment for posterity, to be used in propaganda and for commemoration. The time required to prepare a bomber varies from several weeks to several months. According to David Brooks, would-be suicide bombers undergo an intense psychological indoctrination process, similar to those used by the Jim Jones and Solar Temple cults. The bombers, Brooks writes, are

> given countless hours of intense and intimate spiritual training. They are instructed in the details of *jihad*, reminded of the need for revenge, and

reassured about the rewards they can expect in the afterlife. They are told that their families will be guaranteed a place with God, and that there are also considerable rewards for their families in this life, including cash bonuses of several thousand dollars donated by the government of Iraq, some individual Saudis, and various groups sympathetic to the cause.[67]

However, when terrorist organizations expose a population to a culture of martyrdom, there may be less need for intense indoctrination. After decades in which children have existed in conflict settings with cultures of martyrdom, many have grown up with an appreciation of death, without the requisite isolation and brainwashing from the processes discussed above. This environment is based on an extreme appreciation of the afterlife and the certainty that it will be better than one's temporal existence.

The first step in preparing children for martyrdom requires that death be portrayed as more attractive and desirable than life. The children are trained for this from an early age—in many cases, much earlier than the terrorist organization would need to involve them. In Lebanese and Palestinian summer camps (called Paradise Camps), children as young as eight are trained in military drills and taught about suicide bombers. Children wear faux "suicide belts" to rallies and celebrations to show their enthusiasm. To paraphrase the jihadi viewpoint often repeated in the organizations' propaganda, "The difference between the West and the Islamic world is that 'they love death more than we love life.'"[68] By fetishizing the afterlife and emphasizing the benefits of martyrdom, it has become easier for terrorist organizations to convince young people to volunteer for suicide missions. The culture of martyrdom requires religious sanction and the promise of religious justification or reward.[69]

This contrasts with what we see in recent conflicts in Syria, Pakistan, and Afghanistan, in which the children are trained early as militants but are also deployed while still very young—well before they have genuinely absorbed the ideology of the movement or the goals of the organization. The use of children in this way creates powerful messages about the willingness not just of youth to engage in violence but of their parents to provide the terrorist organizations with access. It is here where we see variation between conflicts in terms of the coercive mechanisms at play for forcing children (or coercing their parents). Examples in Afghanistan and Iraq detailed in chapter 4 suggest that in many instances, the children may be unaware of the mission and have been duped into carrying out suicide attacks—with little understanding that they were a mere instrument for the explosive device.

Part of constructing a culture of martyrdom is to constantly show martyred children as a calculated strategy. Children killed on purpose or by accident serve as powerful mobilization tools for adults in the community, and through social media, they can impact people thousands of miles from the conflict zone. The killing of innocent children can rally people behind the cause. Likewise, images of children killed by an occupying force—for example, the iconic images from the Palestinian-Israeli conflict—speak to a different audience and can incentivize a community to take action against the brutal state.[70] The use of children's images to mobilize people to join terrorist movements is especially successful throughout the Middle East and North Africa. These children become martyrs in their community and are celebrated and admired far and wide. Interestingly, such images have cross-national appeal, and thus a picture of a slain Palestinian baby might have as much resonance in Algeria or Morocco as it does more locally in the Occupied Territories. There are both political and psychological reasons why this is effective as a tool for mobilization.

The bombers' last-will-and-testament videos provide compelling footage, as do interviews with their families. The bombings produce graphic images, and in a world in which "if it bleeds, it leads," suicide bombing is always newsworthy. The marches and celebrations after each attack, and naming of streets and parks after the martyr, all serve to elevate the violent actions into sanctified behavior worthy of respect and emulation. The media extol the virtues of the bombers as the martyrs' parents state on camera that they wish they had more than one child to give to the cause. According to one mother, "I was very happy when I heard. To be a martyr, that's something. Very few people can do it. I prayed to thank God. I know my son is close to me."[71]

In interviews with the families of suicide bombers, the parents rarely express remorse or guilt over what their children have done. According to a *Jerusalem Post* reporter, of the parents interviewed in an earlier article in the *Chicago Tribune*,

> not one parent owned up to contributing to a culture in which suicide bombers were teen idols. They wouldn't admit that photographing their children in studio portraits dressed up as suicide bombers and exposing them to the death chants popular on TV shows and in summer camp had contributed to their children's decisions.[72]

During the course of our research on IS, we observed an interesting dynamic with regard to martyrdom propaganda. The official channels of the so-called Islamic State (Dabiq, Amaq, Nashir) produce copious amounts of propaganda revolving around the theme of martyrdom. This includes last-will-and-testament videos and photos of adults and children who are eulogized in the propaganda as martyrs; images of non-IS civilians killed by Russian, US, or Turkish aerial bombardment or by Assad's barrel bombs; and a series dubbed "the smiling martyr."[73] The images of civilian casualties are among the most graphic that

IS disseminates, and often include before-and-after photos of dead children to heighten the viewer's reaction. In fact, one of the ways in which IS recruiters lure Western emigrants (especially Western women) to the Islamic State is by insisting that they can help prevent such atrocities and help these victimized children. The series of smiling martyrs comprises exclusively adults—images of deceased corpses that look serene, to convey the idea that death is peaceful and welcome. Interestingly, IS has only once (in October 2017) ever shown an image of a dead Cub of the Caliphate. Virtually every other eulogized image is of the children while they are alive. The dead children in the propaganda are overwhelmingly non-IS youth (victims) and adult smiling martyrs. This has been consistent over two years of monitoring the daily propaganda produced by the organization and collecting over 350 images of eulogized children and youth (under sixteen) and over one hundred last-will-and-testament videos.[74]

Not all martyrs are treated equally. IS differentiates between martyrs (victims) and its "Caravan of Martyrs" suicide bomber unit (those who chose to die). The organization seeks to whip up religious sentiment and to outrage its audience by showing extremely graphic images of dead children. It is a highly effective tactic since no one can view such images without having an emotional reaction. But it is curious that IS propagandists have deliberately avoided ever showing the remains of an IS Cub fighter, although they routinely show the adults (in the smiling martyrs series).

From IS videos we have learned about the process of selection for martyrdom. The children compete with one another for this honor. This is comparable to the youth wing, the Bakuts of the LTTE in Sri Lanka, who competed for the honor or the right to be chosen as a Black Tiger (suicide bomber). Once chosen, the cadre would have a celebration for the would-be martyr, and some prospective martyrs would have the privilege of meeting the leader and having Villupillai Prabhakaran cook their last meal. In the context of IS, videos have recently emerged of young Cubs drawing straws or playing a game in which the winner is selected for the operation. The other members of the group all congratulate him and comment on his luck. Brooks argues that in addition to portraying these honors as a euphoric win, there is likely an addictive quality to the process:

> Suicide bombing is the crack cocaine of warfare. It doesn't just inflict death and terror on its victims; it intoxicates the people who sponsor it. It unleashes the deepest and most addictive human passions—the thirst for vengeance, the desire for religious purity, the longing for earthly glory and eternal salvation. Suicide bombing isn't just a tactic in a larger war; it overwhelms the political goals it is meant to serve. It creates its own logic and transforms the culture of those who employ it.[75]

Child psychology corroborates this viewpoint. "Violence is self-perpetuating; it's like a drug. It sparks excitement, and an adrenaline rush, and so demands a repeat performance, in the same way that a drug becomes addictive."[76] The culture of martyrdom affects all members of a society. The older members are theoretically capable of making their own judgments and choosing their own paths, whereas children are too young to consent. While most religious authorities have promoted jihad only to adults, a few have sanctioned and encouraged children's participation.

In an interview with the Egyptian weekly *Al-Ahram al-ʿArabi*, Sheikh Akrama Sabri stressed that the new generation will carry on missions "with determination." He added that there was a religious need for child martyrs to "liberate" Jerusalem and the rest of Palestine:

> The child martyr suggests that the new generation will carry on the mission with determination. . . . The younger the martyr, the greater, and the more I respect him. . . . The mothers [who cry in joy when they hear of their sons' martyrdom] willingly sacrifice their offspring for the sake of freedom. It is a great display of the power of belief.[77]

Sheikh Muhammed Nassar, a well-known cleric, extolled the virtues of child martyrs during the time of the Byzantines in an interview on al-Nas television:

> Abu Qudama was the commander of the army of the Muslims, when they fought the Byzantines. The Byzantines had a very, very large army, whereas the Muslims did not have many fighters. So Abu Qudama walked down the alleys and streets, among the poor, calling: "Come join the Jihad," "Come join the Jihad." A woman said to him: "Abu Qudama, I have a boy. I will give him to you. Take him with you to war." He asked: "Is he still a boy?" She said: "He is 15 years old, and his father was martyred in the previous war. Since his father's martyrdom, he sits day and night, praying that Allah grant him martyrdom." . . . Sa'id, the 15-year-old child, was martyred for the sake of Allah. He died happy.[78]

Cultures of martyrdom glamorize violence—convincing children that their deaths are more valuable than their lives. The groups target children from a young age through religious teachings, exposure to mass media (including television programs aimed specifically at children), education (including textbooks that subtly influence ideology), community pressures, and charismatic entrepreneurs who shift societal norms. As was the case with the first suicide bomber, Mohammed Hossein Fahmideh, young bombers become folk heroes; their pictures are plastered in town squares and parks are named after them.

As explored in this book, the role of the community and sources of authority is especially important in fostering an environment in which children believe they want to be martyrs. The role of families remains highly contentious. While there are intense community pressures for families to support the martyrdom operations of their children, parents are increasingly voicing their opposition to terrorist operations regardless of whether they were aware of their children's involvement or even genuinely supported it. Many groups deliberately separate children from anyone who might influence them positively and could prompt them to change their minds.[79] That said, cultures of martyrdom affect parents as well as youth and explain how parents might willingly provide terrorist groups access to their children. Some parents might even go so far as to promote the idea of their children making the ultimate sacrifice. In this way, the social ecology surrounding youth is key to sustaining the culture of martyrdom.

For Palestinian children, exposure to a culture of martyrdom begins at an early age. In chapter 3 we explored how some Palestinian children's textbooks have shown a bias against certain groups (Jews or Israelis) and extolled the virtues of martyrs. Hamas has developed television shows targeting children specifically; as we mentioned in chapter 1, *Tomorrow's Pioneers* features a Mickey Mouse–like character (Farfour) who tells children that the ultimate goal is to be a *shahid*. According to Israeli analysts, the incitement of schoolchildren dates back to 1998, well before there were suicide bombers in the Israeli-Palestinian conflict:

> Indeed, martyrdom is instilled in [children] as an ideal. . . . Clips abound of young teenagers vowing martyrdom on Palestinian television, but the most dramatic and world renowned, which was played and replayed by the world media, concerned Muhammad al-Durra.[80]

According to Raphael Israeli, the events surrounding the death of al-Durra, the young boy caught in a crossfire between Palestinian police and the Israel Defense Forces (IDF), has been reenacted on television, and was repeatedly aired during the al-Aqsa Intifada to mobilize Palestinian youth. The televised clips were produced by the Ministry of Information and Culture and by the Palestinian National Fund. Rather than focus on the graphic images of al-Durra's death, which were captured by a French film crew, the public service announcements (PSAs) portrayed al-Durra in heaven, in what Israeli describes as "beautiful, peaceful places, running along the beach, or through the Plaza of the Aqsa Mosque, or alongside wonderful fountains, flying a kite in a green pasture, approaching a giant wheel." These images were accompanied by a soundtrack that regaled viewers with stories of a children's paradise. In the video, Muhammad talks to his father: "Till we meet, my father, till we meet! I go with no tears, with no fears, how sweet is the fragrance of the martyrs!!! I shall go to my place in Heaven, how sweet is the fragrance of the martyrs!!!" The narrator continues: "How sweet is the fragrance of the martyrs, how sweet is the fragrance of the earth, its thirst quenched by the gush of blood flowing from the youthful body."[81]

It appears that the PSA's message addressed what children might fear most: being separated from family and friends. It portrayed the afterlife of the martyr as idyllic and serene (the same message conveyed by IS's smiling martyrs). Given the day-to-day violence most Palestinian children encounter, such a depiction could resonate positively. From the start of the intifada to early November 2007, Israeli forces were documented as having killed 889 Palestinian children. In 2006 alone, 124 children were killed, during the IDF operations Summer Rains and Autumn Clouds in Gaza.[82] In two incidents in Gaza in August 2007, the IDF shot and killed five children under twelve.[83] According to one preempted bomber interviewed in jail, "Israel does not kill Palestinian children by accident, Israelis kill intentionally. They smash into a house in Gaza with a bulldozer and bring the house down on its residents. What's that?"[84]

Beyond their religious justification, cultures of martyrdom are also derived from secular sources. The organizations turn what are ordinarily mundane and innocent venues into recruitment tools. Chris Huebner lists diverse sources that include jihadi rap music, music videos that allegedly entice children to become combatants, comic books about Islamic martyrs, and teen-oriented stories of "classic martyrs," as well as biographical accounts of contemporary martyrs.[85] On their encrypted platforms, new media extolling martyrs have appeared, including video games and IS-specific memes, emojis, and stickers.[86]

Statements by children aired on Palestinian state television in which they discuss how they want to become martyrs, and statements by political leaders (both religious and secular) extolling the virtues of martyrdom, reinforce this message. "Martyrdom," Brooks observes, "has replaced Palestinian independence as the main focus of the Arab media."[87] Huebner adds, "The market for martyrs is growing at a striking rate."[88]

While a culture of martyrdom comprises tangible and intangible elements, taken together they create powerful incentives for children to aspire to involvement with militant groups and give the impression that the children in fact concede to involvement. While clearly the children are too young to consent, the culture of martyrdom plays an important role in convincing communities, parents, and other sources of authority that death is superior to life and that children can contribute to the cause. It is an insidious social ecology that propagates hatred, intolerance, and trauma.

EXPERIENCES, APPRENTICESHIPS, AND CAREERS IN TERROR

> **My mission was just to choose the place and to bring the Martyrdom-seeker (i.e., the suicide bomber). [I made] the general plan of the operation, but carrying it out was entrusted to the Martyrdom-seeker.**
>
> Ahlam al-Tamimi, Palestinian who aided and abetted the Sbarro Pizzeria bombing, October 2011

In chapter 2 we explored how children occupy various roles within a movement, ranging from the traditional role of support to more active engagement in violence, and we differentiated between roles involving formal (official) engagement and those that seemed spontaneous. In this chapter, we examine the multiple pathways into terrorism in greater detail. There is no single explanation for why or how anyone becomes involved in terrorism, and, so far, this book has endeavored to demonstrate the variety and nuances of involvement. While these explanations are not theoretically parsimonious, they reflect the reality of involvement. This dynamism and variation not only is found across different organizations but might also reflect the multiplicity of pathways into and experiences inside the same group.

If there are different types of pathways *into* terrorism, there are also multiple routes *through* terrorism—not everyone's experiences are the same, in part because not everyone's expectations and subsequent role(s) in the movement are the same. Children do not join terrorist organizations ready to embrace a new role. They have to be socialized and to learn what the commitment to that role entails. Children have to learn how to think in new ways about what they do, and how to feel about it. The previous chapters explored the mechanisms through which children become involved in terrorism. Here, we examine what happens next. We trace how the socialization process introduced in chapter 2 becomes more focused after the initial mobilization. To do this, we must recognize the psychological mechanisms through which commitment is shaped, and how a new child recruit can move from one type of role to another. To fully explain how children are transformed from passive bystanders into full-fledged fighters, we present a model drawing from the concept of community of practice.

Most of the research on child soldiers has focused on the factors driving supply and demand, variation in child-adult ratios across different groups (e.g., Andvig and Gates),[1] or the experiences of children undergoing demobilization, reintegration, and rehabilitation. Models of child soldiering draw on labor economics to understand whether, for instance, children represent a substitute or a complementary good as far as violent groups are concerned. But such models are abstract, and to further complicate matters, certain cases are overrepresented. Andvig and Gates point out that most of the findings regarding child soldiers were derived from a small number of cases in Central and West Africa.[2]

Despite these limitations, we have learned a great deal about the processes of involvement, and about the factors that drive children's involvement in terrorism. The various influences identified from analyses of child soldiering, from the broad to the specific, help us understand why a child might initially become involved in terrorism, or at least be drawn to it, through exposure or broad acculturation. However, neither the child soldiering literature nor the adult terrorism literature reveals much about how a child is shaped to become a member of a terrorist group. These factors help us understand how a child reaches the door, but not what happens once he or she passes through it.

First, we must clarify what constitutes involvement in terrorism. When we conjure up images of terrorists, we imagine masked figures, stealthily moving from operation to operation, wreaking the maximum amount of havoc and destruction. Yet even the smallest and most obscure terror group functions thanks to the execution of multiple jobs, tasks, or roles. Not all of the roles involve violence, though all of them might be essential for the survival of a group or movement. By imagining that all terrorists engage in violence, we miss a wide variety of nonviolent actors without whom the group would cease to function, or would be very limited in its capabilities. These key personnel include recruiters, commanders, financiers, spokespersons, and those involved in logistical support and other critical tasks. As such, engagement with a terrorist group doesn't simply involve fulfilling one distinct role; a full-fledged member might hold more than one role at any given time. A would-be child suicide bomber, may, for instance, also be responsible for peer recruitment.[3] Some roles, such as leader versus follower, are also distinguished by their seniority.

However, we know less about how particular roles such as recruiter or suicide bomber might be perceived by potential recruits or by those already in training. We know little about how particular roles are realized, whether new recruits seek out specific roles, or how a child might move from one role to another. Is it the child who decides his or her role? Does the recruiter decide—giving the child little to no say? Or are roles decided based on the immediate circumstances and exigencies of the day? Perhaps a child might audition for a particular role, and be judged for suitability? A looming battle that threatens the very existence of the group might require coordination between otherwise diverse personnel into one singular function, such as physically repelling invaders in battle, where even those fulfilling nonviolent roles have to take up arms. Autobiographical accounts of former terrorists suggest that would-be recruits often have a specific function in mind when they first fantasize about joining the group. One such example in IS propaganda is a ten-year-old boy from Belgium who, according to Meira Svirsky, expressed on camera that "he wants to be a jihadist so that he can kill infidels in Europe, all infidels."[4] Subsequent circumstances, however, mean that some roles are not always available. The day-to-day demands, unexpected battles, and other challenges to survival require even the most belligerent of groups to be flexible when allocating jobs, tasks, or roles.

For these and other reasons, it is not always easy to understand what being "involved" with a terror group actually entails. It is a dynamic process subject to how individuals experience their roles (perhaps because they perform them well, or conversely, and perhaps based on feedback, because they are selected for a different kind of position altogether). In any event, we need a way to understand the process through which new recruits are shaped, mentored, and made ready to embrace their status as full-fledged members.

In ideal circumstances, terrorist groups select recruits based on specific pre-determined criteria. In his study of al-Qaeda recruitment, Jacob Shapiro found evidence that the group used elaborate application forms to screen potential applicants.[5] The group requested such information as the applicant's knowledge and experience of foreign languages, technical skills, aviation skills, and engineering skills.

Early accounts of child soldiers suggest that militias appreciated the need for youth to fill multiple roles. Boys who fought for George Washington in the American Revolution, some as young as seven, served mostly in auxiliary functions.[6] Allan Stover documents how during the American Civil War (1861–65), seven children under sixteen received the Medal of Honor for heroism; the youngest of them was Willie Johnson, age eleven. Peter Singer explains that while US Army regulations from 1802 onward specified that "no person under the age of twenty-one could enlist without his parents' permission, there was *no minimum age* [emphasis added] if the child had his parents' consent."[7] Young boys, he writes, served in a variety of roles, including "musicians, powder monkeys, and midshipmen (teenage gentlemen officers in training.)"[8]

Contemporary child soldiers also fill multiple roles, including, according to Michael Wessells, "porter, laborer, spy, cook, medic, bodyguard, and combatant."[9] Wessells notes that these jobs are "highly fluid and contextual, as children may perform multiple roles in the same day . . . [and] juggle multiple roles simultaneously."[10] This is supported by evidence from other cases. In March 2015, Human Rights Watch highlighted the increasing recruitment and deployment of children in Yemen, by both al-Qaeda and Houthi militants, as "scouts, guards, runners, and fighters."[11]

Inside the Islamic State, children may be assigned one of several roles. These range from media person (*'ilmi*), a recruit who documents battles, and whose eulogized last-will-and-testament image features the child with a camera; to suicide bomber (*istishhadi*); to commando (*inghemasi*), which involves engaging in high-risk missions as part of mixed child-adult units. Suicide bombing is ostensibly the most violent role for which children are involved, yet there are multiple nonviolent support roles filled by children, such as giving blood or serving as medics or recruiters of other children. IS child recruiters deliver speeches, typically via public performance, to lure other children, but they simultaneously perform a second function: in the fall of 2016, the Islamic State began using child preachers to deliver sermons from the pulpit, castigating and shaming adult men for not being more devoted to the cause and mobilizing themselves into action. Images of these child preachers were subsequently widely circulated in propaganda material disseminated by the Amaq and Nashir official news channels. Children are also given power over adults in selecting who lives and who dies. In November 2013, six guards in the IS-run "Islamic Court" were twelve to sixteen years old.[12]

Assessing how individual recruits fit into particular roles, and whether or not this reflects a choice made by the recruit or the group, becomes even more challenging when it comes to children. One popular view is that terrorist groups that use children do so specifically *because* they are children. There are several cases, for instance, in which children's physical attributes make them ideally suited for certain jobs. Nicholas Pelham, of the Institute for Palestine Studies,[13] suggests that Hamas uses children to build tunnels because, "much as in Victorian coal mines, they are prized for their nimble bodies."[14] Of the 160 people Hamas has acknowledged as having died in the construction of tunnels, nine have been confirmed to be children.[15] Likewise, security experts in Nigeria propose that Boko Haram uses children as suicide bombers because the group has "mastered the technology of 'miniaturizing' their explosive devices, such that they could be concealed under children's clothing, in contrast to previous suicide bombings in the region involving vehicular bombs."[16] A 2014 report explained that Boko Haram exploits very young girls because they can infiltrate markets and public places by arousing less suspicion than adults or even boys: "By using young girls, they are further relaxing the alertness barriers in people, so that when these bomb-carriers melt into a crowd, they are least expected to be the source of any threat. It is an innocent way of delivering a lethal weapon."[17]

A child's ability to either go unnoticed or blend in reflects the same kind of logic as the increase in the deployment of female suicide bombers in other conflicts (e.g., Palestine, Chechnya, and Sri Lanka). Female bombers became the weapon of choice for al-Qaeda in Iraq because of their capacity for concealment. They could easily blend into the civilian population and derived additional concealment benefits because of their clothing. Long, flowing, traditional attire effectively masks even bulky improvised explosive devices.[18]

Recruitment and role allocation are often gender specific. While there might be overlap in the types of roles to which boys and girls are delegated, boys are typically sent to fight and girls often are viewed as having greater domestic value. Dyan Mazurana and Khristopher Carlson explain that

> during their time in captivity, adolescent boys are . . . more likely to be sent into heavy fighting. . . . However, girls are also forced to serve as sexual slaves to numerous males in forces, or they may be given to one male for his exclusive use as a captive "wife." Adolescent girls are also forced to provide the majority of domestic and agricultural labor that sustains the fighting forces.[19]

Singer likewise highlights this special function for female recruits. "While [girls] may be expected to perform the same dangerous functions as boy soldiers," he says, "many are also forced to provide sexual services."[20] Boko Haram (in contrast to IS) selects very young girls and much older women to be its suicide bombers, while girls of childbearing age (around fourteen to nineteen) are "kept" and impregnated.[21] These girls are more useful to Boko Haram by providing the next generation than by serving as bombers. Thus, they function in much the same way as bush wives have in conflicts such as the one Sierra Leone.[22] It is important to emphasize that variation in role allocation occurs not just from one group to the next but even within affiliated groups. Boko Haram (like the Taliban) exploits little girls as suicide bombers, whereas IS does not. Young girls rescued from Boko Haram often escaped the fate of girls captured by IS—that is, Boko Haram did not rape the ten- and eleven-year-olds under its control, whereas IS abused girls younger than eleven.[23]

In all cases, the nature of children's engagement (what types of roles they hold) is ultimately a function of the terrorist group's priorities. These priorities may be influenced simultaneously by tactical and strategic concerns and by local exigencies. But whatever the child's role, whether active on the front line or providing peripheral support, the United Nations does not define "child soldier" based solely on the type of activity. In 2007, the UN's Paris Principles on the Involvement of Children in Armed Conflict acknowledged the variety of possible roles included in the definition of children in combat: "A child associated with an armed force or armed group refers to any person below 18 years of age who is, or who has been, recruited or used by an armed force or armed group *in any capacity* [emphasis added], including but not limited to children, boys and girls, used as fighters, cooks, porters, spies or for sexual purposes."[24]

How Children Learn Terrorism

Though acknowledging the diversity of roles and functions within terrorist movements is important, it doesn't explain how children are transformed into militants. The study of learning has long been a major concern within terrorism research.[25] "Learning" covers quite a few questions, ranging from why groups use terrorism as a strategy at all to how they learn from past experiences, such as recovering from making major strategic errors or from some crisis. Michael Kenney argues that "many . . . researchers gloss over how . . . terrorists . . . actually *learn*, in the sense of acquiring, analyzing, and applying knowledge and experience."[26] Answering this question is essential if we are to truly understand the development of children's involvement in terrorism. A major component, Kenney argues, is the need to understand the relationships and context in which such learning unfolds. This includes, he notes, "informal apprenticeships, on-the-job training, communities of practice, and combat."[27]

In some ways, terrorist organizations face and manage the same challenges, threats, and stressors faced by any large organization.[28] As part of this process, they routinely systematize their practices and formalize their training regimes (perhaps counterintuitively), often preserving such knowledge in extensive documentation. But can this help us understand why a child, originally on the periphery of a terrorist movement, is gradually transformed into a full-fledged fighter? Not really. To do this, we need a different kind of model, one that combines an understanding of learning processes with an understanding of group psychology. To do so effectively, one must utilize a "community of practice" approach.

The community of practice model developed by Etienne Wenger-Trayner and Beverly Wenger-Trayner, which characterizes "groups of people who share a concern or passion for something they do and learn how to do it better as they interact regularly,"[29] allows us to understand how people learn. Originally the term, as coined by Jean Lave and Etienne Wenger, focused on apprenticeships. The key differences they found between typical "master-apprentice" models and detailed studies of apprenticeship were revealed in a "more complex set of social relationships through which learning takes place."[30] In other words, community of practice tries to appreciate how learning takes place beyond the classroom, school, or textbooks, and all the associated formal trappings of learning, by looking instead at the informal, subtle ways in which we acquire new information, practices, and identities.

The anthropologist Karsten Hundeide has criticized the early work on communities of practice. Hundeide argues that even community of practice models that highlight "informal" learning don't illuminate more than an abstract description of what might be going on for the learner.[31] In particular, early community of practice models missed several key features, including

1. the significance of expressive style to mark identity and/or belonging;
2. the "deep commitment" aspects of sacrifices and committing actions;
3. the emotional communion aspects of belonging in a community;
4. alternative reality construction or legitimation with (i) new values that are "worth living for"—a new existential dimension—and (ii) strict internal loyalty/solidarity and internal discipline as a way of life; and
5. the role of the charismatic guide into the new reality.

Without understanding these critical elements, Hundeide says, we are left with a model of learning that captures just basic skill acquisition. Of special interest to Hundeide are groups where membership involves conversion to a new "life," and not just new skills:

> Becoming a committed, loyal convert who embraces the expressive life-style, rituals and practices, values and opinions (including enemy image) of the inner circle that sets the standards and the goals of the movement—in other words, movements where commitment and conversion to a new life is more essential than the acquisition of some craft of skill.[32]

This model informs the transformation of children into terrorists—which is frequently characterized as brainwashing. But the term "brainwashing" doesn't suggest agency on the part of the child, and certainly doesn't capture the psychological effort required of children who are forcibly recruited.

Studies of coercive persuasion identify the early stages of brain development to be especially susceptible to embedding messages, due to the brain's plasticity. Thus younger children are easier to brainwash than older adults. According to Kathleen Taylor, cults emphasize the positive aspects of the group rather than the negative aspects of outsiders. In Taylor's case study of the People's Temple, whose members likewise joined in their teens, the group emphasized brotherhood, communal living, and social support. These match precisely the key themes we see in terrorist groups. Cults are youth oriented, emphasizing novelty and radicalism while imposing strict control over information. Cults foster an environment of paranoia and rejection of the outside world, translating into an apocalyptic vision of the outside world as evil and corrupt—all of which reinforces feelings of cohesion within the group.[33] This is perhaps one of the areas in which millenarian terrorist groups such as IS share common cause with cults, as both emphasize the looming apocalypse. Bruce Hoffman argues that

> for the religious terrorist, violence first and foremost is a sacramental act or divine duty executed in direct response to some theological demand or imperative. Terrorism assumes a transcendental dimension, and its perpetrators are thereby unconstrained by the political, moral, or practical constraints that seem to affect other terrorists.[34]

Taylor notes how cults endlessly repeat simple concepts, using "highly reductive, definitive phrases."[35] We can observe a similar pattern in the videos used in IS Cub training, in which a particular phrase or word is repeated over and over. There are some similarities between the *dhikr* in Sufism, in which the name of God is rhythmically repeated to induce a trancelike state and allow worshippers to achieve a kind of communion with the deity, and the ways in which children are required to repeat the same words or phrases. The call to arms, or *takbir*, is repeated obsessively in the videos. The father of two young boys enrolled in an IS-run school in Aleppo explained,

> A school . . . is a recruitment centre, no more and no less, where class hours are used to brainwash the students, especially the younger ones, and train them to take orders and carry them out without any objection, and to memorise the Qur'an robotically without comprehension, in addition to dozens of fatwas that incite murder and bloodshed.[36]

Furthermore, during brainwashing, the children are physically and emotionally drained (no sleep, no food, taking the children to the brink of exhaustion, love bombing, fear of transgressing and subsequent forgiveness), which induces the same reality-altering responses observed in cults. This is why even after their release, many children may retain positive associations with and memories of their experiences in the training camps, even though objectively they endured terrible conditions and exposure to traumatic events.

In addition to repetition and mental and physical duress, the groups inculcate a normative shift. As part of coercive persuasion, they accentuate ambiguous ethereal ideas. Taylor clarifies what she means by this: "Ethereal ideas are bloodstained values more highly prized than human life."[37] This facilitates the process of dehumanization, shifting the children's norms and behavior so that they can

justify committing atrocities or engaging in violence. All of this ultimately helps
to consolidate the child's identity as a full-fledged fighter, no longer afraid and
free of all doubt. One sixteen-year-old Maoist rebel fighter told Human Rights
Watch, "Once I was involved in a battle to release those in jail at the district head-
quarters of Jumla. The security forces had put many teachers and villagers into
jail, so we attacked to get their release. There were 300 Maoists; I carried a gun.
It was 10 at night; the battle lasted about an hour. I was very excited, very aggressive."[38] The trained recruit can find reward even in the minutiae of the role. A boy
soldier from Sierra Leone told Myriam Denov, "I was good at shooting people
even at distant positions. . . . It normally made me feel good whenever I hit my
target. All my friends and fellow soldiers admired my skill."[39]

Hundeide extended his view of the community of practice to include what he
calls communities of "terror." He illustrates his arguments with examples from
research on neo-Nazi groups and interviews with child soldiers from Sierra Leone
and Angola.[40] Drawing from these sources, he ascertains whether it is possible to
identify similarities between the apprenticeship of child militants and soldiers
and other groups engaged in violence. He outlines the stages of the process of
fostering the "deep commitment" that is typical of involvement in counterculture
groups:

1. Positive, rewarding contact with leading charismatic members of the
   group.
2. The new entrant joins as a "peripheral apprentice," adopting the style and
   identity markers of the group. Acceptance as a member of the family is
   sometimes recognized in a ceremony of initiation that includes markers
   such as style, clothing and uniforms, and other symbols of belonging,
   which identify the entrant as a full member of a group or organization
   (even if still only an apprentice).
3. A process of redefining the past (sometimes a destruction of past values)
   and the introduction to new values/styles/fighting the enemy.
4. A stage of further commitment mandating sacrifice, hardship, isolation,
   and dissociation from previous contacts and previous life. This is also
   associated with requests for demonstrations of loyalty.
5. Loyal participation in daily collective practices and rituals. Internal
   discipline, morality, and loyalty are all directed toward acquiring the
   standards and mentality of the insider.
6. Final test of loyalty, which includes committing extreme acts that make a
   return to one's previous contacts and way of life very difficult.
7. Achieving new status and a role/identity of respect inside the new
   community. The former apprentice is now a full "core" member.[41]

These stages are unmistakably present in the trajectories and engagement accounts of former child soldiers and, as we suggest with our six-stage socialization model later in this chapter, for IS Cubs as well.

Though many accounts of children's recruitment emphasize brutality, punishment is often accompanied by, or quickly followed by, some reward. Traumatic initiation was characteristic of African child soldier recruitment. One of Richard Maclure and Myriam Denov's boy soldier interviewees reported, "I was attacked at school and forced to join the movement."[42] Indoctrination was eased with promises of great rewards, both social and financial. Another boy soldier said, "I was told . . . that if the rebels succeeded . . . [the leader] would compensate each and every one of us with money. I was happy about this."[43] The very fact that the Revolutionary United Front (RUF) separated young children from their families meant that the boys were now "wholly dependent on their commanders for survival."[44] Similar accounts emerge from Nepal, where between 3,500 and 4,500 boys and girls were forcibly recruited as child soldiers in the Maoist militant ranks over a ten-year period.[45] The Maoists operated a strict "one family, one child" rule, where each family was required to surrender a child to perform service with the group. Failure to comply resulted in serious punishment.

Maclure and Denov's interviewees revealed that despite being recruited under sometimes-great coercion, peer mentoring played a role in acculturating them into the movement. Even children forcibly recruited into the group underwent this shift. With no opportunity for social interaction with anyone outside the group, Maclure and Denov observe, "the idea of the 'enemy' shifted imperceptibly from those who had captured and abused them to those who were perceived to be opposed to the RUF."[46]

Recruitment is not a simple issue. Some groups embrace a scattershot approach, opting to grow their ranks wherever and however they can. According to Human Rights Watch, the Nepali Maoist insurgents would kidnap individual children and even abduct large groups of children en masse. Yet that same group would also hold social and cultural "events" to lure children in as volunteers.[47] This would typically involve putting on public performances at mass gatherings, with "songs, dance and theatrical performances designed to appeal to children; often children [would] carry out these performances in order to attract other children."[48]

Cultivating a group of "committed insiders," as per Hundeide's framework, is a practice mastered by groups like the RUF. Susan Shepler's findings from Sierra Leone show that the child's need "to have someone to love and respect" was transferred to military commanders.[49] As mere apprentices, child soldiers there were given uniforms—adopting formal clothing enhances in-group cohesion, identity, and solidarity. Children in the Lord's Resistance Army (LRA) experienced harsh discipline, yet at the same time had such extensive exposure to religious and propaganda-based indoctrination that their beliefs and values were, according to Bernd Beber and Christopher Blattman, "fundamentally altered."[50] A former child soldier in the LRA told Beber and Blattman, "It is easy to convince a child of 12 years of anything. He will believe any promises made and does not know the difference between good and bad. But if you are mature, you know they will not overthrow the government."[51]

Identity markers are not limited to clothing. As part of becoming a full-fledged fighter, boys in the RUF would get tattoos, often featuring violent imagery. In fact, identity markers such as these would be reached long before children were permitted to handle firearms. Beber and Blattman found that child soldiers in the LRA would be entrusted with weapons only after (on average) three and a half months.[52] Being given a functional weapon was perhaps the key step in preparing to fight the enemy, as well as the culmination of many little steps toward fighter maturity. One RUF recruit reported, "I always felt powerful with a gun. . . . When you have a gun, you can force anyone to do anything for you. You can even capture five big men if you have a gun. Otherwise who was going to listen to me as a small boy?"[53]

IS videos released by al-Hayat Media Center also utilize symbolic markers. As discussed in chapter 4, children in a particular video are divided between those wearing Cub uniforms and those wearing regular civilian clothes. It is clear from the video that the children wearing Cub uniforms are privileged, whereas the other children have not yet made the cut. Cubs in uniform are given preferential treatment, and the other children look on and admire those who have achieved Cub status (marked by such symbols as beige camouflage uniforms, black IS headbands, and the children's carrying automatic weapons). In essence, the group seeks to evoke jealousy and competition, fostering the sense that the Cubs are insiders while the children not in uniform are outsiders.

Internal discipline and loyalty are common in child soldiering accounts. Every single child interviewed by Maclure and Denov in their study reported being subjected to physical abuse. Boy soldier indoctrination in the RUF was characterized by what Maclure and Denov call "an aura of menace, repeatedly manifested through verbal abuse and acts of wanton cruelty." Daily exposure to such violence resulted in both "deep-seated fear and unquestioning compliance" among boy soldiers, with the boys routinely witnessing "outrageous forms of brutality that were clearly intended as public displays of horror." One boy recalled, "My commander captured a girl with her [baby] sister and her mother. He shot the mother and the little baby dead. He left the adolescent girl alive but told her to remove her dress and he raped her. . . . We all had to watch."[54]

This process is evident elsewhere. A female Nepali child soldier told investigators from Human Rights Watch, "The Maoists then kept me locked in a room during the nights, my mother wanted to come see me, but they didn't let her. The two ladies took me back [and] they again threatened me and said I should not even think of fleeing again. . . . [Then] it was hard to run away because we walked at nights in the jungle, and I just wouldn't know where to go."[55] Such tests of discipline and loyalty are often accompanied by explicit threats as a deterrent against withdrawal. Another female child soldier in the Nepalese Maoists said, "The commanders told us never to surrender. They told us to throw the grenade that we had into the troops and run away. When I said that I wouldn't be able to do that, they said that the army would then arrest me, and if I surrender the army would torture and rape me."[56]

The normalization and routinization of violence does not emerge organically. It has to be taught and fostered. One boy reported that after committing violence, "commanders told us to sing and laugh . . . to show that we were happy over a job well done. They did not want to see anyone showing sadness. . . . It showed that [killing] was a good thing—we were brave enough to withstand killing and we were prepared to kill at all times."[57]

Promotion in the RUF was a reward for greater displays of aggression. According to Maclure and Denov, as they progressed, boys were transformed from "frightened and disoriented recruits . . . to ruthless destroyers who became steeped in a sense of collective purpose and power."[58] Andvig and Gates observe that "spending day and night together in life-threatening situations can create strong bonds between fellow soldiers,"[59] but in groups such as the RUF, even carrying out domestic chores contributes to the boys' esprit de corps.[60] For Dara Cohen, whether or not group cohesion results is very much tied to whether recruitment was coerced or voluntary. The more coercive the recruitment, the more likely that youth require violent group activities to foster the band-of-brothers feeling.[61] Testimony from child soldiers supports Hundeide's extended model of community of practice, but we can trace in detail a contemporary case of how these dynamics are shaped.

Case Study: Apprenticeships in the Islamic State

The Islamic State was officially proclaimed on June 29, 2014.[62] However, various other militant organizations, including dozens of militias, elements of the Free Syrian Army, and al-Qaeda-affiliated groups such as Jabhat al-Nusra (later renamed Jabhat Fateh al-Sham), were all active in the area from the outbreak of the Syrian Civil War in 2012. According to reports, Syrian children were recruited into front-line combat beginning in 2012, a year after the Arab Spring protests that triggered the war. According to Michael Weiss and Hassan Hassan, early in the conflict people moved within groups (taking on different roles at different times) and also moved from one group to another. While migration between roles seems to be more of a common feature of terrorist organizations than is appreciated, movement from one group to another (and occasionally back again) happens with far less frequency.[63]

The age estimates of these children vary. German children who emigrated with their families are reportedly as young as thirteen years old,[64] but even younger children have been featured in Islamic State propaganda that we downloaded and archived for this book—there, children perpetrate all manner of violence, from distributing knives for beheadings to carrying out executions. Not all children engage in violence, but there are now confirmed reports of children as young as eleven or twelve engaged in military-style training,[65] as well as eulogies of even younger boys "martyred" as suicide bombers, such as the al-Sinjari brothers mentioned in chapter 4 and the son of the Australian Khaled Sharrouf.[66]

In video propaganda, al-Hayat Media Center showed four-year-old Isa Dare pressing the detonator on a vehicle-borne IED, killing three prisoners inside. In January 2017, IS's Khayr Province released a video, "He Made Me Alive with His Blood,"[67] set in Deir Ezzor, Syria, featuring child executioners. The most shocking is a three-year-old who appears to shoot a Syrian Kurdish prisoner in the head. The child, previously featured in 2016 propaganda videos holding a plastic toy gun, brandishes the weapon after shooting the prisoner in a plastic carnival ball pit at what appears to be an abandoned amusement park. Another child, Abu Mouaz al-Shami, nine, slits a man's throat with a large knife after being ordered by an adult to carry out the sentence, and a third child, thirteen-year-old Khattab al-Kamishli, beheads a Kurdish prisoner.[68]

There is variation among the children as to whether they are prompted by adults to perform for the camera or are unaware that they are being staged for a photo opportunity. Ordinarily, when young children are "interviewed" in al-Hayat Media Center productions, they merely parrot what their parents tell them to say rather than display some genuine degree of radicalization.[69]

Children who disappear and join IS often do so without the knowledge and permission of their parents. There are dozens of instances in which teenage girls from the UK, France, or Canada have traveled to Syria in small groups;[70] in several European cases, distraught parents have approached authorities after realizing that their children have gone missing.[71] Some children wait until they reach Syria before contacting their families back home and informing them of their where-abouts,[72] and in the cases of many of the young girls, this occurs after they have been married off to foreign fighters.[73] Sarah Birke summarizes the combination of factors that have given rise to the rapid mobilization of foreign fighters. In part, she argues, it is because of "unprecedented use of social media to attract people, the relative ease of getting to and living in Syria, and coming at a time at which governments in the region and in the West lack convincing ideologies and are seen as corrupt by their inhabitants, Muslim or otherwise."[74] Potential fighters are lured by perceived benefits, such as the housing IS may assign them; according to Birke, some accounts suggest that "widows receive welfare benefits based on how many children they have."[75]

It is difficult to say how much time passes between the arrival of the children and their engagement in focused activity. Brenda Stoter suggests that "not all foreign children undergo military training immediately,"[76] and that there would appear to be at least some period of adjustment and socialization. A resident of Raqqa said, "Sometimes I see the young kids of foreign fighters play outside. They seem happy."[77]

Human Rights Watch's Fred Abrahams summarizes the process of child recruitment as "twisted, pressured and forced."[78] Abu Ibrahim Raqqawi, of the citizen journalist group Raqqa Is Being Slaughtered Silently,[79] points to the basic mechanisms through which children are formally lured to IS. Some children, he says, seek out involvement with the militants, in many cases "spurred by poverty." Others are "kidnapped off the streets," while some parents choose to enroll their children in IS-run schools because they receive financial compensation for every child under IS's care (up to $200 for each child).[80]

Raqqawi and Ash Gallagher explain that by seducing children and their families with the prospect of a free education,[81] IS has filled a void in a setting where there is no formal school system.[82] As we explored in chapter 3, IS does not "force" parents to send their children to IS-sponsored schools,[83] but by providing the only education opportunity, its "alternative curriculum" represents de facto coercive recruitment.[84] Still, reports are mixed as to whether participation with the Islamic State can ever be considered voluntary. Birke and Berlinger suggest that in Raqqa, IS has adopted a carrot-and-stick approach whose components range from forcing parents to surrender their boys to the group, to luring children with parties, to outright kidnapping.[85]

On the surface, IS appears to differentiate between what it considers to be age-appropriate involvement and what it doesn't. "Abu Mosa," an IS "press officer," was interviewed by Vice News about the structure of children's education and why some children are selected for training at militant camps while others are not. "Those under 15 go to a sharia camp to learn about their creed and religion," he said. "Those over 16, they can attend the military camp."[86] Children under thirteen are not allowed to participate in the training camps, but according to Sara Williams, they are "still being put to work as spies, being paid $100 per month to inform on family, friends and neighbors."[87] It is within these settings that IS selects the few outstanding candidates who will eventually become fighters. These children are permitted to learn science and mathematics, but only, Rashid Najm points out, "as part of their military training to help them identify areas and use rockets and such."[88]

The characteristically hierarchical and disciplined structure of IS is felt at all levels of the organization, including for children.[89] Raqqawi explains that by early 2015, there were three child-centric camps in Raqqa alone: the al-Khalifa Cubs Institute, the al-Farouk Cubs Institute, and the Sharia Camp for Cubs.[90] Each camp trains 250 to 350 children; the boys have been selected from local schools and attend camp for forty days of intense indoctrination and training.

Peer pressure is a constant feature of this process. Conformity, compliance, and blind obedience are hallmarks of the child's progression from regular schooling to full-fledged training. In one case, IS leadership figures at a camp asked children to sign a "volunteer list" for martyrdom operations; one boy, notes Sara Williams, "eventually signed the list because he felt social pressure to do so,"[91] The intense and brutal training of the boys is characterized by subjugation, one key element of which is physical separation from the family.[92] A former IS child militant recalled how for an entire month, he and about one hundred other children were, according to CNN's Arwa Damon, "kept isolated" and "not allowed even to see or speak to their families."[93] When the father of a boy protested his son's induction into a training camp, IS members threatened to behead him.[94]

The constant threat of violence also permeates the children's advancement from schooling to training. In 2015, Judit Neurink interviewed a young Kurdish boy, "Habib," who explained, "The teacher made us repeat every word. If we did not do well he would beat us with a stick. . . . It was too difficult and in Arabic, and we only know Kurdish. All we wanted to do was sleep."[95] The same year, one boy from Raqqa, aged thirteen, described his time in a camp: "For 30 days we woke up and jogged, had breakfast, then learned the Qur'an and the Hadith of the Prophet. . . . Then we took courses on weapons, Kalashnikovs and other light military stuff."[96] Another boy, aged 15, told his interviewer, "We used to crawl under webbing. There was fire above it, and we would be firing our weapons. We would jump through large metal rings and the trainers would be firing at our feet and telling us if we stop we will be shot. . . . I was very careful not to stop running, I didn't stop, even if I was exhausted, out of breath, I didn't stop."[97]

The children are traumatized not just in training but also by passive observation of violence all around them. They regularly witness all forms of punishment including capital punishment. Berlinger reports that "we saw a young man who did not fast for Ramadan, so they crucified him for three days, and we saw a woman being stoned because she committed adultery."[98] Another boy described his reaction to seeing a beheading for the first time: he couldn't eat for two days.[99] The socialization of children to routine violence is particularly evident from social media sources. Regular exposure to beheadings, Birke says, guarantees that the children "get accustomed to it."[100] Throughout the month-long military training, the Cubs' conditions are terrible. One boy recalled to a journalist, "We all had fleas and everybody was smelling so badly."[101] According to a report from the Associated Press, children are routinely subjected to violence in an effort to desensitize them:

> The children had all been shown videos of beheadings and told by their trainers . . . that they would perform one someday. First, they had to practice technique. The more than 120 boys were each given a doll and a sword and told, cut off its head. A 14-year-old who was among the boys, all abducted from Iraq's Yazidi religious minority, said he couldn't cut it right. He chopped once, twice, three times.
>
> "Then they taught me how to hold the sword, and they told me how to hit. They told me it was the head of the infidels."[102]

Despite these experiences, socialization to violence may provide a sense of reward. Some children who emerge from IS camps, according to Berlinger, feel "proud, strong and filled with a sense of purpose."[103] Just like adults who experience military boot camp, the boys develop a camaraderie; Damon reports that they "laugh, joke and talk about their training."[104] A medical student at the University of Damascus describes encountering children injured by artillery shrapnel or bullets: "Some of [them] seemed happy with their injuries and saw them as proof of 'jihad.' Some talked of death and martyrdom as if it is a picnic in a public or amusement park."[105] According to Sofie Vindevogel, "Children often see that being part of an armed group can give them a kind of respect or prestige."[106]

The varying length of training supports the argument that different children may have different experiences depending on where they are sent as well as what the prevailing climate dictates. Raqqawi points to two types of training programs: the "slow" and the "speedy," the operations of which appear to be determined by whether or not IS is involved in "major battles."[107] Slow training entails a forty-five-day military boot camp experience involving routine indoctrination and "brainwashing,"[108] followed by a three-month period of "intensive weapon training." The speedy option, Raqqawi says, only exists if IS anticipates or is already engaged in a "large-scale battle . . . where new fighters are always required." In this program, indoctrination and socialization lasts approximately three weeks, followed by a month of military-style boot camp experience. After this, Raqqawi concludes, the children "get pushed immediately into battle." Upon completion of either training track, the final step of their socialization into IS, they are assigned to one of three groups "decided by their mentors": a suicide bombers group, an explosives-manufacturing group, or a soldiers group.[109]

By mid-2017, the organization had deployed almost two hundred children as suicide bombers.[110] But some children who wear suicide vests are not necessarily intended to be suicide bombers or to be blown up in battle. Damon interviewed fifteen-year-old "Yasir," whose role in IS involved being "regularly strapped into an explosive vest and handed a pistol, an AK-47 and a radio to stand guard" at an IS-controlled facility.[111]

In the context of child soldiering, Singer notes that "brutality and abuses of the worst kind underscore each stage."[112] IS appears to at least begin with a softer touch, which makes it similar to terrorist groups such as the Liberation Tigers of Tamil Eelam, who would build playgrounds for children as an enticement for recruitment. At later stages, however, the similarities—including peer pressure, brutality, and the fact that, as Singer puts it, children "end up creating the same cycle for other children"—emerge more clearly.[113] IS uses children to recruit more children. In many respects, young people are effective recruiters because children might be less suspicious of their peers than of adult recruiters. The tactic of using children to lure other children underscores why deviant peer pressure is considered a highly effective way to influence a child's propensity for risk taking.[114]

As presented in figure 8, we summarize children's socialization into IS as comprising six stages: seduction, schooling, selection, subjugation, specialization, and stationing.

1. *Seduction*: Initial learning about IS ideas, norms, and practices through peripheral exposure to propaganda events, including via public events ranging from toy/candy giveaways and speeches to shows of strength and executions; indirect exposure to IS personnel.
2. *Schooling*: Direct exposure to personnel, including charismatic guides; intensive teaching via religious indoctrination. This marks the beginning of ideological commitment.
3. *Selection*: Screening for aptitude; special, focused attention from recruiters; "grooming" and preparation for military training and/or other roles (e.g., spying).
4. *Subjugation*: Isolation from family; brutalization through intensive physical and psychological training; donning of uniform as an identity marker; deepening of commitment through loyalty, sacrifice, discipline, and hardship; emergence of solidarity via shared hardship.
5. *Specialization*: Fostering expertise; specialized training.
6. *Stationing*: Role assignment and deployment; repeating the cycle as the children, now full-fledged members, participate in public events such as executions (filmed and nonfilmed).

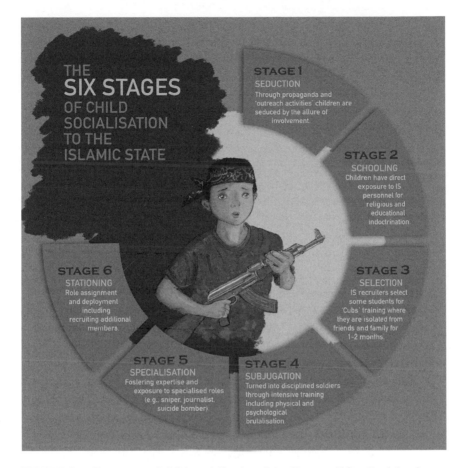

FIGURE 8.   Six stages of child socialization. John Horgan, "After the Islamic State," *CREST Security Review* (Spring 2017): p. 10.

These six stages capture a learning process with which the child engages, in both formal and informal ways. Individual pathways through this process will be contingent on circumstance, both the individual and his or her psychological and biological makeup, and the historical and actual social context. The concept of communities of practice offers a useful way of conceptualizing the social learning that takes place in such situations, and enables other concepts (such as notions of "affordance"—perceived or actual properties of an object or environment that enable an individual to perform certain actions[115]) to be embraced within a broad conceptual framework.

We do not attempt to offer an overarching explanation of IS's exploitation of children. Our objective instead is to describe the mechanisms through which IS involves and engages children and to understand how the group transforms

children from passive bystanders to full-fledged, active members of its organization. We must explicitly acknowledge other limitations. We do not yet have
the necessary data to begin to understand (with competing viewpoints and the
data necessary for hypothesis testing) *why* children become involved in IS, but
we can begin to explore *how* this occurs. As we have seen, children come to IS
from diverse and varied backgrounds, through at least five distinct pathways. The
socialization process, to an extent, flattens out any individual differences that
might exist. The only diversity that exists after training is that which emerges by
institutional design—that is, how and when children are assigned one particular role or function. There are tangible benefits to involvement (food, shelter)
and also social and psychological rewards in the form of status, significance, and
identity.

In this chapter we have traced the contours of children's progression into and
through terrorism. This transformation engulfs the child, redefining his or her
identity and sense of purpose. Considering the transformation through the lens
of community of practice shows us how the child's progression is shaped by both
positive and negative qualities. The transformation is decisively characterized by
increased, focused commitment, through both formal and informal acts, if not
tests, of loyalty. These qualities are apparent in different child soldiering contexts,
and appear to have been fully harnessed by contemporary groups such as IS.
A striking feature of IS's child soldiers is how ethnically diverse they are. Whether
the children are Uzbek, Yazidi, or Western, through a structured socialization
process, IS can transform an ethnically diverse population into an ideologically
homogeneous and organizationally cohesive group sustained by strong nonma-
terial rewards.

There are enough early accounts from escapees to begin building a picture
of this model, but many questions remain. We do not currently know about the
quality of training received by children in IS, nor do we know about the specific
kinds of battlefield actions they undertake. Even videos that focus exclusively
on documenting training (e.g., raids on houses and vehicles using GoPro head-
mounted cameras) present a limited glimpse into the training regimen. But it
appears that children serve multiple roles within the movement. This is consistent
with child soldier experiences in other regions, as well as with adult involvement
in terrorism more broadly. There are undoubtedly multiple roles, functions, or
"jobs" performed and executed even in the smallest of terror groups. The suicide bomber epitomizes for many the stereotypical image of today's terrorist,
yet even that individual is typically supported by a logistics operation made up
of others, perhaps including a driver, a handler, and a recruiter. In some cases,
these people may be nowhere near the actual terrorist operation when it unfolds,

whereas in others, they may compose a local cell where even individual roles and jobs are interchangeable and held simultaneously. In turn, those individuals may require more detailed support—from, for example, the person who supplies the actual suicide belt or purchases the cell phones operatives use to detonate the IED. Diving further into a terrorist network one finds other supporters, from the person who allows his or her house to be used by an organization to the financier who funnels low-level payments from sympathetic donors. These actors are all involved in terrorism in different ways, yet they might not all be immediately characterized as "terrorists," despite peripheral figures (e.g., financiers, recruiters) enjoying a far longer career trajectory than those directly involved in violent attacks. Though it is far less public and consequently less well understood, the role of support coordinator or recruiter may be of key importance to the sustenance of an organization.

Yet despite the current absence of data, it is not too early to begin thinking about the challenge of response. Though the structures and environment under IS authority suggest rigid control, some accounts of former IS Cubs have begun to emerge, as we have seen. These come from children who have run away from IS, or were pulled out by their parents. The next chapter explores the circumstances whereby children come to leave terrorism behind.

LEAVING TERRORISM BEHIND

A violently active, dominating, intrepid, brutal youth—that is what
I am after. Youth must be all those things. It must be indifferent to
pain. There must be no weakness or tenderness in it. . . . I intend to
have an athletic youth—that is the first and the chief thing. . . . I will
have no intellectual training. Knowledge is ruin to my young men.

Adolf Hitler, quoted in Helton Goodwin Baynes, *Germany Possessed*

Portrayals of children in conflict have been alleged to be a form of "war pornography." The British historian Antony Beevor, pointing to graphic accounts of suicides of young German children following the Soviet attack on Berlin, concedes that "there are things that you can't put in a book because they are too horrific," but adds, "And yet at the same time you wonder afterwards if you are chickening out by not putting them in."[1]

Beevor's sentiment comes to mind when we consider the impact of terrorism on children. We have illustrated how children are deliberately targeted as victims of terrorism, while at the same time nonstate actors are increasingly recruiting children for front-line activities. It would seem that children are ripe for exploitation, irrespective of the specific reason for targeting them. In this chapter, we examine how witnessing and/or participating in terrorist acts affects children, and what influence those effects might have on the child's capacity to disengage from violence. While considerable research exists on the indirect psychological impact of war on children, far less attention has been paid to the long-term effects of active participation in violence—much of which these children may be too young to comprehend. Some preliminary data suggests that the Albanian youth who joined IS and other jihadi groups witnessed their mothers being sexually violated by Serbian militias during the Kosovo war, and that decades later, jihadi recruiters exploited and channeled their feelings of helplessness as young children to persuade them to join the jihad.[2] One of the major challenges is that many countries in the developing world do not have a national framework to respond to childhood psychological trauma.[3]

Even when children are not directly engaged in terrorism, this manner of political violence has a profound impact on them. Perhaps the most sustained contribution of psychology to the study of terrorism has been examining how people survive it, tracing the clinical and psychological sequelae of trauma associated with living under the threat of terrorism, or coping with its impact.[4] Images of the aftermath of bombings and other atrocities (including, more recently, "about to die" images associated with terrorist martyrdom operations) are ubiquitous in the media. People respond to such events with varying levels of anxiety depending on their physical proximity, socioeconomic status, and perception of possible future attacks. According to the psychologist Andrew Silke,

> Intense media coverage by itself can have some damaging impact with some adults and children appearing to suffer serious psychological problems as a result of long exposure to media coverage of terrorist attacks. They often had trouble sleeping, suffered from nightmares, anxiety problems or depression. Yet, these people had not been at the scene when the attack occurred and they were not connected to direct victims. They had not lost family members, friends, neighbors or colleagues in the devastation, but they had witnessed a great deal of media coverage.[5]

This observation is borne out across multiple studies. Indirect exposure to terrorist violence via media coverage, Stephanie Thornton observes, can trigger "severe anxiety, sometimes amounting to PTSD [posttraumatic stress disorder]."[6] Six months after 9/11, 28 percent of children assessed in New York City demonstrated "at least one" diagnosable disorder—typically, according to Thornton, agoraphobia, separation anxiety, or PTSD. Such is the power of media that even children living on the other side of the United States, in Seattle, showed significant symptoms, including PTSD.[7]

We know more about children's indirect (and direct) victimization from terrorism than about the psychological effects of their participation. This is unsurprising given the historical focus on terrorism's impact on victims, and not on perpetrators. Yet children's involvement in terrorist violence suggests a profound and complex interplay of roles—namely, that between victim and perpetrator. Even when children are perpetrators, they must also be seen as victims, in the sense that they are targeted, groomed, and exploited to elicit violence in the service of others. Yet the fulfillment, sense of identity, and empowerment that children derive from being trained and deployed as operatives (fighters, suicide bombers, or executioners) only increase the likelihood that they will face injury or death. It is thus crucial to understand the impact of terrorism on children if we are to offer suggestions for preventing, disrupting, or otherwise reducing their involvement in the long term.

From studies of adult mobilization into terror groups, we know that recruits often find what they anticipated: adventure, camaraderie, excitement, and purpose, the various "pull" factors associated with becoming a terrorist. Similarly, they achieve a sense of belonging and the consolidation of a new identity, which are powerful sustaining influences on children's involvement and commitment to the movement. Children may revel in the feeling of power that accompanies executing someone if they come to believe that their victim "deserved" such a fate.[8] However, even for those whose initial recruitment may have been fueled by fantasy, such experiences can suddenly traumatize them. Unable to cope with the demands of involvement and the expectations of the group, some children struggle to adapt and are forced to conceal their disillusionment for fear of being disloyal or being considered a spy—and facing the prospect of execution.

How terrorists experience involvement, and how they are changed by their experiences, remains poorly understood, though there are preliminary efforts to examine this dynamic. In recent years, researchers have investigated the process whereby people disengage—how and why they leave terrorism behind. It might seem counterintuitive to assume that people leave terrorist groups. The leader of the German Baader-Meinhof Group (Red Army Faction), Andreas Baader, reportedly told new recruits that the only way for doubters would be "feet first."[9] Nevertheless, people can and do leave. Some leave voluntarily, either with the permission of the group or by running away. Others leave because they have to. They might have been excommunicated for some transgression, or unable to perform their duties or functions because of burnout or simply because of incompetence.

Terror groups often take a public stance against disengagement by promulgating the idea that nobody can leave. This tends to be an intentional effort to "hire right," essentially dissuading poor-quality prospects not up to the challenges of such commitment. The reality is that most terrorist groups do permit disengagement, to a degree.[10] When they do, there is a clear understanding that the soon-to-be-former member will not talk.[11] But such allowances are fluid. A group that permits limited disengagement at one point may at some later date threaten would-be defectors with execution. It is easier for a terrorist movement to permit disengagement during times of organizational strength, when recruits are plentiful, than when it is struggling to function and suffering from defections and losses in battle. Still, the ability to walk away from terrorism unscathed appears uncommon, or at least is rarely publicized. Accounts do exist, but they tend to be showcased as exemplars of the need to listen to apparent defectors.

Harry Sarfo, a German-born man who moved to the United Kingdom and joined the Islamic State, explained to the journalist Rukmini Callimachi of the *New York Times* in August 2016 how he had arranged his own escape. Upon seeing his comrades gleefully execute prisoners and painstakingly capture their deeds for propaganda purposes, Sarfo allegedly became so disillusioned that he began planning his escape, which "took weeks and involved sprinting and crawling in a field of mud before crossing into Turkey."[12] It is difficult to believe without question the narratives told by "formers." Despite his protestations, Sarfo was subsequently found to have participated in mass executions during his three months with IS. Ultimately he was charged with six counts of murder, and with violating human rights law, after videos emerged in which he was part of the team that carried out a public execution of six prisoners in Palmyra Square (which was videotaped). Sarfo, armed with a gun, guarded the prisoners to prevent their escape, and after the execution he fired at the bodies lying on the ground. These were details he neglected to include in his January 2016 interview with the *Independent*.[13] According to federal prosecutors in Germany,

> While failing to mention his own involvement in the atrocity, Sarfo named his worst memory of Syria as the "execution of six men shot in the head by Kalashnikovs," identifying it as one of the events that drove him to flee the terrorist group's "barbarity."[14]

Thus, Sarfo represents a cautionary tale about the nature of involvement that people admit to or might obfuscate, even after leaving a terrorist group. This has implications for how we understand the nature of involvement for youth as well as adults. The reasons for leaving a terrorist group are seldom straightforward. They can be as varied and overlapping as the motivations that pulled someone into terrorism in the first place. Just because someone becomes disillusioned with involvement in terrorism does not necessarily mean that he or she has either suddenly developed a conscience or embraced a nobler outlook on life. Sometimes even the group itself takes steps to remind its former members of this. In an unusual and highly publicized move, IS in late 2016 undermined the public's perception of Sarfo by releasing a video appearing to show him indirectly participating in an atrocity. The video was subsequently used as part of his prosecution.

We assume that because terrorists admit responsibility for their actions that they enjoy what they do, yet even this is not clear. In some of the earliest work on terrorist psychology, H. H. A. Cooper suggested that the life of a terrorist is hard and lonely.[15] Expressing such a sentiment seems inappropriate, and might be perceived as sympathizing with or romanticizing the terrorist. However, one of the stated reasons that former terrorists write autobiographical accounts is to help atone for their deeds and work through the shame, guilt, or remorse that many experience once free of these groups' vicelike grip.[16] Disillusionment and burnout are common in accounts of formers,[17] and even the most cursory examination of terrorist autobiographies shows that remorse and shame play key roles both in planting the seeds of disengagement and in influencing people to remain out of terrorism and embrace redemptory roles outside the group. Some formers embrace the role of the "ex-terrorist," at least for a certain period, and in hindsight are quick to offer cautionary tales about the high cost of involvement in terrorism. Such accounts are not just valuable for dissuading prospective future recruits, but are also probably crucial ways for the formers themselves to work through and make sense of the enormity of their prior actions.

However, despite the development of a robust literature on how, why, and when adults leave, accounts of children who have disengaged are virtually nonexistent. It is critical to develop these if we are to build appropriate resources for rehabilitation and reintegration—issues of equal importance for reducing the risk of recidivism. As a first step toward this, a key element is understanding how participation in terrorism specifically affects children.

Assessing Impact: From Exposure to Participation

Accounts of children's involvement have largely focused on those who have witnessed violence and on the psychological effects of this trauma, from children who witnessed the events of 9/11 to Palestinian or Tamil children in refugee camps. Studies have proposed that exposure to violence alone is no guarantee of long-term negative effects; the fact that, as one study puts it, "someone experiences or witnesses an act of violence" does not mean that he or she "will inevitably develop psychiatric morbidity."[18] However, it has been estimated that somewhere between 9 and 35 percent of those directly exposed to traumatic events such as terrorist attacks will develop significant posttraumatic psychological distress and perhaps PTSD.[19] The impact of 9/11 on children in New York City is well documented.[20] What has changed is that children are not just witnessing acts of violence that they see on TV or are exposed to in the media, but are encountering violence occurring in close proximity to their homes. In a study of girls and adolescents who experienced the effects of armed conflict in Peru, Eliana Barrios Suarez found that 81 percent had lost friends and neighbors from their community and a startling 61 percent had suffered the death of parents or other family members. However, Suarez was struck by how resilient the girls in the sample were, noting that only 5 percent reported symptoms likely associated with PTSD. She argued that the variance in effects was probably related to the degree of exposure to violence, combined with current (i.e., postconflict) stress.[21]

Children treated at the Pakistani rehabilitation center Sabaoon describe having witnessed torture, stonings, and beheadings while in the Pakistani Taliban. These children, rescued from the terrorist group by the army, exhibit multiple psychosocial problems, including attention deficit disorders, poor logical or reasoning skills, and problems trusting adults. Most recalled overwhelmingly negative experiences at the training camps (although some reported positive experiences). After performing menial tasks, they were locked in a four-by-five-meter room for the rest of the day. Some reported being repeatedly beaten and, in a few cases, assaulted by senior figures. The children had also suffered physical and sexual abuse, according to their doctors and therapists at Sabaoon.[22]

One child with whom we spent some time graduated from such deplorable conditions only to be "permitted" to become a martyr. The boy was given a suicide vest and directed to walk toward Pakistani military troops, but he changed his mind literally at the last second and surrendered to the authorities. That boy is now one of Sabaoon's brightest hopes for successful rehabilitation and reintegration, and a potential role model for younger children at Sabaoon. Nevertheless he remains traumatized by his experiences.[23]

Proximity to conflict is a major variable in children's experiences. A 2015 survey by Mercy Corps painted a grim picture of teenage life amid conflict. The study found that 80 percent of those surveyed refused go outside after dark, and 74 percent could engage in no other activity except for school. Over 40 percent of the teenagers needed hospitalization during 2014–15, and 20 percent suffered "serious health problems." These living conditions led the teenagers to engage in routine stealing and "rebelliousness," accompanied by depression.[24]

Many Palestinian children witnessed family members being killed, and homes, schools, and mosques being bombarded, during Israel's 2014 Gaza conflict, known as Operation Protective Edge. Some children suffered life-altering physical injuries.[25] The offensive also affected the unborn, as expectant mothers and fathers struggled with traumatic stress.[26] Following the operation, in which more than five hundred children were killed, Israeli commentators pointed out that many of those children were used by Hamas to indirectly contribute to the successful execution of terrorist attacks, while, Myer Freimann notes, "Hamas and its supporters display gruesome pictures of dead and wounded children in order to gain sympathy for their portrait of Israel as the villain intent on killing Palestinians."[27] A report issued by the Institute for Palestine Studies reported that Hamas officials acknowledged that "at least 160 . . . have been killed in the tunnels" that are used, Israeli officials claim, to launch attacks; these included at least nine children.[28]

Exposure to violence has led to high neuroticism and low self-esteem among children. A study of 108 Palestinian children aged eleven and twelve in the Gaza Strip showed that the more they participated in the Intifada and the more traumatic their experiences, the more concentration, attention, and memory problems they suffered afterward. Traumatic experiences also increased neuroticism and risk taking, and Intifada participation overall decreased self-esteem.[29] This might seem to stand in marked contrast to the descriptions in the previous chapter about the benefits children derive from participation in the Islamic State, but we would do well to carefully consider these findings. What might initially be reported as positive (especially when children are still in close proximity to the group) may ultimately be reported, and perhaps reinterpreted, as negative later on.

Child socialization into IS is characterized by conformity, compliance, and blind obedience. These are the hallmarks of progression from exposure to training and deployment. This becomes most apparent to child recruits upon their selection for training as Cubs. Separation and isolation from family members is a vital element of the training, marked by a period of intense physical and psychological mistreatment.[30] One former IS child soldier recalled how for an entire month, he and approximately one hundred other children were, according to CNN's Arwa Damon, "kept isolated" and "not allowed even to see or speak to their families."[31] The *New York Times* quotes a family counselor who reports that

> these children are put under constant stress, being told you will burn, you will be tortured if you do not do this—if you do not kill this infidel, you will end up in hell, your mother will end up in hell. It is a constant psychological torture.[32]

In the previous chapter, we explained that there existed a pervasive threat of violence that permeated the children's progression through the socialization process. In 2015, Judit Neurink interviewed "Habib," a young Kurdish boy, who explained, "The [IS] teacher made us repeat every word. If we did not do well he would beat us with a stick. . . . It was too difficult and in Arabic, and we only know Kurdish. All we wanted to do was sleep."[33] The same year, one boy from Raqqa, aged thirteen, described his time in an IS training camp: "For 30 days we woke up and jogged, had breakfast, then learned the Qur'an and the Hadith of the Prophet. . . . Then we took courses on weapons, Kalashnikovs and other light military stuff."[34] Another boy, aged fifteen, told his interviewer, "We used to crawl under webbing. There was fire above it, and we would be firing our weapons. We would jump through large metal rings and the trainers would be firing at our feet and telling us if we stop we will be shot. . . . I was very careful not to stop running, I didn't stop, even if I was exhausted, out of breath, I didn't stop."[35]

While we can assume that the pressure on children to carry out their missions is intense, some are able to exercise individual choice in the final seconds before a planned detonation and refuse, as discussed in chapter 4. There are numerous examples of children coerced into perpetrating an act of terror who allow themselves to get caught at the last minute or refuse to carry out the operation. Usam Sadiq al-Amin and Dionne Searcey of the *New York Times* describe the scene in which two of the three girls sent to the Dikwa refugee camp by Boko Haram carried out their suicide missions, but "one of the would-be bombers recognized her parents and siblings in the camp and decided not to detonate her device. . . . Instead, the girl surrendered to the authorities and warned that future attacks were being planned for the camp."[36] This was likewise the case with fourteen-year-old Usaid Barho (discussed in chapter 4), who, at the last minute, refused to detonate his suicide belt and instead approached a police officer, explaining, "I'm a Muslim and don't have any intention to kill Muslims. I want to go back home to see my mother. Can you help me?"[37]

As we explore the nature of children's coercion into carrying out deadly attacks, further complicating matters might be the fact that, as we discussed in the previous chapter, initial negative experiences may culminate in an overall positive experience for the child.[38] Among the children we met in Pakistan at the Sabaoon facility, some reported positive experiences, in contrast to the ones who spoke with horror of witnessing beheadings and being locked in closets or forced to clean bloodstained floors. When involvement was characterized as a family affair, the adventure, camaraderie, and sense of purpose proved all too real for the children. Nevertheless, we should not let such examples overshadow the overwhelmingly negative effects of involvement in violence. Peter Singer has bluntly pointed out that upon disengaging, significant numbers of child soldiers "run at every opportunity to escape their new lives; some do it out of terror, and some just miss their families."[39] The majority of child soldiers, he says, attempt at least one escape.[40]

Victim or Victimizer?

Reading accounts of children's experiences with terrorism might lead to the children's characterization as passive victims.[41] However, the reality is more complex and unsettling. In discussing the Hitlerjugend (Hitler Youth), the psychologist Rudolph Wittenberg understood the complexities of dealing with this population. "Our hostile feelings toward the children," he said, "will often be repressed, sublimated, or projected on to other objects."[42] The ways in which IS showcases its socialization of children in real time allows us to observe how this victim-offender cycle develops. In criminological terms, this is about understanding that neither role is fixed or predetermined;[43] today's victim can become tomorrow's offender, and vice versa. In an attempt to break out of victim status, a person may seek out ways to exact revenge, thus becoming a perpetrator in the process. Offenders who engage in high-risk behavior ironically increase the chances that they themselves will be victimized. The interchangeability of these roles not only serves as a reminder that thinking of "victim" and "offender" as fixed roles is misleading, but also complicates issues around the development of resources to manage or treat the person(s) in question.

This confusion is starkly illustrated by the case of a young Kazakh boy, Abdullah, who is depicted in a series of images taken over two and a half years and disseminated in IS's official propaganda (see gallery). Abdullah, whose age we do not know for certain, looks to be around ten. He first appears in a group setting; in the second video, he appears to be engaged in synchronized drilling and martial arts training in the IS propaganda video entitled "Race toward Good."[44] The boy was subsequently filmed shooting two alleged Russian FSB infiltrators, Zhanbolat Mamaev and Sergey Ashimov Nikolayavich, in the video "Uncovering the Enemy Within," posted by al-Hayat Media Center.[45] The image of Abdullah is now iconic on IS social media, where he is an avatar for many anonymous accounts on the group's preferred platform, Telegram.

In some cases, children's involvement is marked by such commitment that even direct intervention to remove them is unsuccessful. In Belfast, the teenager Conal Corbett was arrested in May 2015, charged with phoning in a bomb threat on behalf of dissident Irish Republican terrorists. According to an Irish television news report, Corbett was also charged with possessing documents "containing information likely to be useful to a person preparing an act of terrorism."[46] He was arrested six times over a period of eighteen months, but refused to acknowledge the legitimacy of the court or accept the clothing offered to him. Such an example illustrates the ineffectiveness of this type of intervention if a deep-rooted commitment to continuing involvement with the group is left unaddressed.

Despite this and other examples, however, it is important to remember that continued involvement in and sustained commitment to such groups may not always be by choice. For instance, Austria was a hotbed of IS terrorist recruitment that produced the case of two teenage girls, Samra Kesinovic, seventeen, and Sabina Selimovic, sixteen, who fled to join the group in Syria in 2014. When they subsequently tried to leave IS, the girls were killed; one was beaten to death and the other died under mysterious circumstances. Accounts of IS killing members who want to defect complicate our understanding of whether children can leave if they want to. Few have left unless with their parent(s), and we do not know to what extent the experience of being a member of IS will have long-term on their physical and mental health. Furthermore, far fewer children have been repatriated back to their home countries than adult males, according to a report by Joana Cook and Gina Vale.[47]. Charlotte McDonald-Gibson, in an opinion piece for the *New York Times*, tells of a nine-year-old boy who "came home in early 2016 with his mother—a convert to Islam who is now on trial—and found himself in a world he had been trained to hate, where he trusted nothing and no one."[48]

While such examples are easy to identify and might be illustrative, pinpointing the extent of the problem in order to develop resources for rehabilitation and reintegration is a broader challenge, and an overwhelming one. The true scale of the problem of child militancy is unknown, in terms of both the age range of the children and the number of children who are actually involved. An estimated six million people live under IS's control, two million of them under the age of fifteen (and naturally those numbers change as IS control of territory fluctuates).[49] It is impossible to know precisely how many children are involved with the group, how many will die in combat, and how many will grow up to become tomorrow's adult terrorists. Furthermore, as we have shown, every armed group in Syria deploys children (and subsequently, one presumes, victimizes other children using violence); combined, the other actors involved in the conflict outweigh the scale of IS child mobilization.

The three training camps in Raqqa that catered only to children had 250 to 350 children attending classes,[50] and one source in 2014 said that as many as five thousand European teenagers were believed to be fighting with the organization, though this was exaggerated.[51] The ages of these children vary considerably. Based on our data, children in IS may be as young as three or four in the propaganda or may even act as executioners; the group routinely releases images of children as young as ten who are car bombers, suicide bombers, or *inghemasi*. In more passive roles, children younger than ten have been featured in some capacity. For its 2014 report on the recruitment of children by several armed government and antigovernment groups in Syria, Human Rights Watch interviewed four former IS child militants. Abu Musafir said that his battalion had detained thirty children aged thirteen to fifteen who had fought with IS in a battle in Manbij in late 2013. "We found them in a training camp in Manbij, all of them were from Manbij," he said. "We kept them for two-and-a-half months. We put them in a rural area with a school and we tried to reverse the brainwashing of IS."[52] Such accounts, many more of which will likely emerge, raise questions about what can be done, and how best to treat children who have either witnessed or participated in violence. By 2016, the scale of IS's exploitation of child members was widely known. The *Washington Post* reported that the group was providing gun training to children as young as six.[53]

The extent of the indoctrination of children is comprehensive. A child's identity could be erased and supplanted with a new self, including one hostile to his or her original identity. Such was the case with the two al-Sinjari brothers, ethnically Yazidi, who after two years of intense indoctrination considered themselves to have been devil worshippers whose salvation was dependent on their becoming suicide bombers. Psychologists have seen firsthand the damage this indoctrination has caused. Jan Kizilhan, McDonald-Gibson writes, is a psychologist who "treats child soldiers in Iraq and boys from the Yazidi minority who were taken as refugees to Germany after being conscripted by the Islamic State. These children have witnessed rape, torture, murder—in some cases forced to take part in the atrocities themselves."[54] According to Kizilhan, the children manifest various symptoms of trauma: aggression, sleep problems, and sometimes even neurological problems resulting from their experiences. The rehabilitation of children from terrorist groups is an urgent and emerging challenge. To better understand how it can be dealt with, we look once again to the lessons learned from disarmament, demobilization, and reintegration (DDR) programs for child soldiers.

Rehabilitation and Reintegration

The NGO Save the Children chapter in Sweden has been working with militaries in Africa since 1998, teaching soldiers about children's basic rights as well as about the strategies they can adopt to protect and rescue children during armed conflict. This includes making soldiers aware of how "to incorporate child rights and protection . . . to minimize exploitation and abuse of children perpetrated by the military themselves . . . [and] to establish and strengthen child protection mechanisms within the military structures such as Child Protection Units (CPUs)."[55] A primary focus of its efforts is to shift how militaries in war zones actually perceive children. Child soldiers do pose a challenge for disciplined militaries; nevertheless, the child rights training urges restraint. One trainer in the Côte d'Ivoire Navy explained, "Children as combatants must be neutralized but not killed."[56] During the course of this book, we have maintained that there are important differences between how children are recruited as child soldiers (e.g., forcibly) and the nuanced processes of involvement for children associated with terrorist groups. While there are significant areas of divergence, rehabilitating and reintegrating children and youth might represent the area of greatest convergence between the two populations.

Michael Wessells identifies two major challenges regarding the child soldier phenomenon: preventing children from becoming involved in the first place and easing their transition back to "normal" life.[57] In the context of IS, it would appear that we have already failed the first challenge, since so many children have been involved in one capacity or another and even more children have been exposed to the atrocities committed by the terrorist organization. Whether there is sufficient social or political appetite to tackle the second still remains to be seen. But we are not without precedent in preparing for this, and the need to formulate a child-centric response has not fallen on deaf ears. Throughout 2015, the increasing visibility of child participants was reflected in calls for help. Early that year, Austria's "deradicalization hotline" reported calls from parents, teachers, and social workers about seventeen young boys and eleven young girls suspected of drifting toward extremism.[58]

There is twenty years of research on the efficacy of demobilizing and reintegrating child soldiers. In a systematic review of efforts aimed at exploring the effects of armed conflict on children, Theresa Betancourt and Timothy Williams propose two relevant paradigms: the psychosocial and the psychiatric. Psychosocial approaches, they say, focus on "restoring as much of the prior environment as possible or providing routines, predictability and engagement."[59] They stress the need to understand local culture and setting and focus on "local participation and restoring indigenous protective processes." Because of the emphasis on addressing the child's social and physical environment, psychosocial initiatives can be "commonly designed and implemented by non-mental health professionals,"[60] and may include providing vocational job training, economic opportunities, and spiritual support for those affected by conflict. Traditionally, the authors explain, the objective is to promote family reunification and community reintegration. In the case of the IS Cubs, however, promoting family reunification (which worked in cases of child soldiers in Africa) poses a conundrum. Many parents in Syria and Iraq were involved in providing IS with access to their children, facilitating recruitment, and permitting their use on the front lines.[61] In this context, the removal of children from their parents' influence might be a necessary first step, but this too carries a host of unintended consequences.

The second approach, which is not entirely separate from the psychosocial approach, is psychiatric intervention, which seeks to treat mental disorders stemming from conflict. Betancourt and Williams argue that in the immediate short term, psychosocial efforts merit prioritization because "their provision may lead to improvements in general symptoms among persons both with and without specific disorders."[62] They note, "The first line of response may be enough to reduce symptoms below a threshold of clinical significance for large proportions of the population."[63]

Fatima Akilu, lead psychologist for the Neem Foundation in Nigeria, points out that the psychological problems facing Boko Haram children are multi-layered. The children experienced trauma from witnessing violence and/or participating in atrocities, which may overlap with a preexisting psychological issue. As a result, underlying mental health problems are exacerbated by conflict. There are supplemental issues when the children suffer from "fractured identities" (i.e., multiple parts to their personality), especially those children unable to come to terms with what they have done.[64] According to Hamsatu Allamin (the regional manager of the Nigeria Stability and Reconciliation Program and the national executive member and coordinator of the Federation of Muslim Women's Associations in Nigeria), there are currently as many as five hundred children aged eight to fifteen who were part of Boko Haram and are either facing detention or undergoing psychosocial treatment in Nigeria. All of the children received weapons training, and "they have seen people slaughtered, or they slaughtered them themselves. There are 150 children in one IDP camp alone."[65] If the children are dealing with fractured identities, varied ideals, and different drivers of action, it can make treatment all the more challenging.[66] Akilu notes that of forty-three Boko Haram fighters arrested in 2017, twenty-one were immediately released and nine returned to the sect. Furthermore, there are thousands of women and children in Nigerian detention camps, and no way to separate the combatants from the displaced civilians. In Nigeria there is no probation or parole, and no way to track former fighters. There is no real risk assessment.[67]

In their study of former child militants in Sri Lanka, Pushpa Kanagaratnam, Magne Raundalen, and Arve Asbjørnsen explain why psychological research in war-torn areas remains scarce (an indisputable reality today): the lack of access to participants, researchers' reluctance to acknowledge that children play important roles as perpetrators of violence, and the theoretical complexity of the areas.[68] The authors set out to explore the connection between intense ideological commitment and PTSD in predicting possible future mental health outcomes. A particular feature of children's involvement in the LTTE was indoctrination. While children were involved in diverse roles, they were also explicitly taught how to "hate the enemy." The result of this was what the authors call "profound effects" on children: "All had seen wounded, seen dead bodies, had lost someone else, and had been in situations where they thought they were going to die."[69]

A third challenge, along with the two identified by Wessells listed above, is preventing former child militants from reengaging in violence. There is a need to identify lessons learned (or best practices) from current cases that can prevent the next generation of children from reengaging in violence. One of the primary challenges will be to ascertain whether, how, and when children are prepared to reenter civil society. The failure to systematically and comprehensively address this results in many demobilized child soldiers becoming, as Karsten Hundeide puts it, "even more disturbed than they were before."[70] Wessells stresses that the process of childhood socialization into armed groups "may reshape behavior, roles, values and identities."[71]

Despite identifying lessons learned from field research spanning multiple conflicts, Betancourt and Williams lament the lack of an evidence base from which child-focused interventions might be developed. Nonetheless, there are relevant initiatives that, although they are aimed mostly at adults, offer lessons for the reintegration and rehabilitation of children. As of 2017 there were approximately forty-five programs in countries around the world that could be characterized as deradicalization initiatives. Some of these are well known. The program in Saudi Arabia, for example, boasts of extraordinary success in rehabilitating former al-Qaeda members, and has offered tours to Western academics, journalists, and counterterrorism officials. Other programs operate in the shadows, with little desire for publicity. These programs vary in size, duration, resourcing, and transparency. Critical questions linger about their effectiveness, and to date, there have been no systematic evaluations of any of them. Some people (typically those involved in running the programs) claim they are not suitable for evaluation, yet will simultaneously claim widespread success in reducing the risk of recidivism.

Herein lies another conundrum. Recidivism is traditionally low, regardless of whether the individual has participated in a deradicalization program or not. Most people who serve prison sentences for terrorism and are released do not go back into terrorism. If an individual enters a program exhausted, disillusioned, and with no desire to return to the group, it is easy for any program to claim it has been effective in "preventing" reengagement or recidivism. However, each program, while often informed by others, tends to take a context-specific approach to the challenge of rehabilitation and reintegration. The Saudi program, for instance, in the words of Christopher Boucek, is a "Saudi solution to a Saudi problem."[72] In the absence of evaluation, there are strong reasons to suggest that the most effective programs will be grounded in local context and will adapt to changing social and political circumstances.

With few exceptions, these programs remain geared toward adults, and typically operate in prisons or other detention facilities. Youth-specific programs are needed because children have specific needs. In the case of the Islamic State, young people have been subjected to a level of deindividuation and "identity reshaping" so profound that it exceeds in focus and intensity what most adult IS recruits experience. Challenges will include taking steps to remove the child from further danger and providing services to facilitate rehabilitation, which may include the need to support reconciliation.

Despite the attention such programs receive, often via high-profile advocacy efforts, there is little substance behind them. Oliver Kaplan and Enzo Nussio, in their landmark 2016 study of recidivism among former militants, note that despite the international community having spent over half a billion dollars on "programs worldwide for around 1 million ex-combatants" in 2007, there is, it would appear, "little systematic evidence about who decides to 'go bad.'"[73]

Wessells insists that any program specifically for children must recognize the distinctive needs of children.[74] Viewing the challenge as one primarily of child protection, he recommends access to quality education and vocational and life skills training (to help prepare children for civilian life and teach them employable skills), as well as the use of interim care centers to assist with the reintegration process. Crucially, he says, existing efforts continue to fall short because of a recurring failure to include children's voices and perspectives in all aspects of the DDR process.[75]

Despite the scale of the child soldier phenomenon, efforts thus far to address the needs of former child soldiers have lacked substance, flexibility, scale, and effectiveness. In 2006, the United Nations released its Integrated Disarmament, Demobilization and Reintegration Standards. The UN's definition of youth comprises individuals between fifteen and twenty-four—people who are neither simply "children" nor "adults." The determination of this age range would appear to be deliberate, since according to the UN, "DDR programs have tended to treat those under 18 as child soldiers, ignoring the responsibilities they have often undertaken as providers and caregivers. Those over 18, by contrast, have often been offered job training and other support that neglect their need for remedial education."[76]

There are, in fact, a handful of promising child-specific efforts that exist in countries where the problem of children's involvement in terrorist violence has been especially acute. We can draw on some valuable insights and preliminary research from Sri Lanka, Colombia, and Pakistan to inform possible best practices about what to do with children who have been involved in terrorism (whether voluntarily or by coercion).

Over the course of Sri Lanka's nineteen-year civil war, an entire generation of children grew up knowing nothing but war and a culture of *thatkodai* (martyrdom and self-sacrifice). Kanagaratnam, Raundalen, and Asbjørnsen's study of former Tamil child soldiers showed that a strong ideological commitment can mitigate negative aspects, such as posttraumatic symptoms, among former child soldiers. The study's subjects were a highly diverse group of youth and children, all of whom reported that they "remember[ed], relate[d] to and interpret[ed] their past as child rebels," and who naturally differed depending not just on their degree of ideological commitment but on the roles they held within the movement and their subsequent experiences within those roles. This is not to say that every child exposed to violence will require psychiatric care; in fact, this approach might be counterproductive in non-Western societies, and may even be cultur-ally inappropriate as well.[77]

In a different study of former child militants in the LTTE by Daya Soma-sundaram, children exhibited an array of psychiatric conditions, ranging from "somatization, depression, and post-traumatic stress disorder to more severe reactive psychosis"; in sum, the children were "complete psychological and social wrecks."[78] Studies cite Somasundaram's research, which describes how, "com-pared to the direct war with the Sri Lankan State, the internal conflict between different Tamil rebel groups which led to Tamils torturing and killing their own people went deeper into their hearts, resulting in more and severe psychological problems."[79] In their research, Kanagaratnam et al. argue that ideological com-mitment in the present (which basically supported the children's actions in the past) protects against mental health problems, though this effect was most preva-lent for those with lower levels of war experience. One former child soldier with a strong commitment to ideology said,

> I saw and heard of many atrocities done to our people. When your sis-ters are raped and your mother is slaughtered what can you do? You are just 17. How would you feel? This is the reason for many youngsters joining armed groups. They are not brainwashed or anything like that.[80]

The authors note that the Sri Lankan children were a "highly heterogeneous group, differing vastly in their experiences depending on the context of war and on the unique characteristics of the culture to which they belong."[81] Curiously, the duration of military training was not necessarily linked to posttraumatic symp-toms; nor was the children's "length of exposure to combat" or "time elapsed since exposure to the last combat events."[82] The authors instead surmise that "quality of training" (though not measured in their study) might be of greater significance.

In cases of adult deradicalization, an intuitive generalization is that ideologi-cal retraining represents a key element in rehabilitating ex-terrorists and reduc-ing the risk of reengagement. However, a closer look suggests that in reality this matters far less than one might expect in the case of children. This isn't truly sur-prising, especially if the child's involvement was not originally characterized by intense ideological indoctrination. In fact, as explained above, exposure to ideol-ogy may actually strengthen children's resilience against psychological disorders. In examining the implications of this for practice, Tony Stanley and Surinder Guru urge the need to avoid "simplistic risk trajectory arguments."[83] Though they address the risk of initial involvement in terrorism, the same argument may be relevant for pathways out of terrorism (and potential pathways back in, for reengagement).

In their study, Oliver Kaplan and Enzo Nussio conclude that "recidivism is puzzling because there are multiple motivations to return to violent and illicit behavior, but there is little consensus about which pathways matter most since they have not been sorted through empirically."[84] Their review, which focused on adults, found that former militants were far more likely to return to illegal activities if they had "strong personal motives" for becoming involved with the group in the first place, "spent more time in such groups," did "not have children," were "in the vicinity of reemerging criminal bands," and "did not complete high school during their time in the reintegration program." Kaplan and Nussio argue that "recidivism can be thought of as repeat offending and is the clearest and most severe form of individual reintegration failure (and may drive broader collective remobilization). Although not all who fail to integrate are recidivists, all recidivists represent reintegration failures."[85]

A different perspective on child reintegration, however, comes from an examination of the Colombian case. More than half of the adults in the Revolutionary Armed Forces of Colombia (FARC) movement were recruited as minors.[86] A study of Colombia's child demobilization program by Evan Fagan and Evan Owens suggests positive outcomes, with neither boys nor girls reporting "major problems adapting to civil life."[87] Fagan and Owens highlight contrary views, however, citing one child's reservations: "They force us to push aside these things, to erase them, in order to create a new future that denies what we were and what we learned. They guide us to accept an identity that is not ours, to be bakers and cobblers."[88]

If, even within very specific cases, no consensus exists as to what constitutes rehabilitation, let alone what the appropriate recipe might be for creating a rehabilitation program, what hope is there for the thousands of children mobilized by the Islamic State? How will former children of IS come to think about and understand their past roles—as soldiers, as weapons deployed against fellow Muslims and apostates, or as unwitting participants in a religious cult? Or will they come to view themselves as victims of abuse? Regrettably, there are more questions than answers. Krjin Peters suggests that reintegration efforts struggle to take root in areas where conflicts continue.[89] But this has not prevented the development of innovative child-centered programs elsewhere (Sabaoon is a notable example, though presumably the role of the Pakistan Army in providing security for the initiative plays a major role in its sustainability). Exceptions aside, however, it is often simply impossible to create a local program until a conflict has ended, and even then this is hardly immediate. Jo Becker describes how UNICEF did not create a child soldier reintegration program in Afghanistan until two years after the conflict there "officially" ended.[90]

Most programs require that the conflict has ended and assume that children are to be reunited with their families, with subsequent engagement in educational or vocational programs. Becker strongly recommends that "keeping families together and reunifying separated children with family members also reduces recruitment risks and facilitates social reintegration of former child soldiers." She adds, "Armed groups perceive a public relations benefit from making public commitments not to recruit child soldiers, but often lack the political will or resources to actually demobilize children from their ranks. Commanders who are concerned with maintaining military strength may be reluctant to release young soldiers, particularly when alternatives for the children, including school or vocational training, are not available."[91]

Success may depend on continued monitoring and advocacy, practical assistance for demobilization and rehabilitation, effective use of political and military leverage by international actors, and an uncompromising commitment by local, national, and international authorities to hold perpetrators accountable.[92]

As we have explored in previous chapters, socialization into terrorist groups, and especially the Islamic State, follows an elaborate and relatively linear pathway. Similar dynamics are involved with the formal entry of children into the youth movements, schools, and camps run by militant groups, which the groups draw from for recruitment. There are significant differences between the entry dynamics of what have traditionally been called "child soldiers" and those of children who are involved in violent extremist groups that differ in size, scale, and aspiration. These differences are likely not merely a function of different labels (i.e., child soldier vs. child "terrorist"). In addition, and on another level, the experiences of children, regardless of the precise nature of the group, contrast with the far more diverse and dynamic pathways into violent extremism that characterize adult involvement, as well as the diversity of pathways that characterize child entry into other movements. Some children may be more overtly "ideological" than others in the sense of being able to articulate or parrot ideological content. Ideology remains very poorly understood in children and adults alike. Studies of adult terrorists typically view ideology in one of two ways: as a precursor to involvement in violent extremism (i.e., a stepping-stone) or as a by-product of involvement (i.e., whereby a person becomes more ideological after being recruited). After listening to accounts of child recruitment, it might seem logical to assume that children are more vulnerable to ideological commitment. But a child's parroting ideological content does not necessarily mean that the child fully grasps it. The more significant characteristics of childhood trajectories into violent extremism are probably the social and psychological aspects of those trajectories. The socialization process of children into militant movements, detailed in the previous chapters, involves fostering deep commitment in which both tacit and explicit acts of loyalty substitute for expressions of commitment.

Evaluations of deradicalization programs highlight just how important local context is to defining goals, outcomes, and expectations about what constitutes effectiveness. Betancourt and Williams's study, one of the few systematic and formal evaluations of such programs, showcases several programs in the Russian Federation and northern Uganda. Yet studies are limited by practical challenges, and are typically unable to incorporate large sample sizes. One intervention study of efforts to help Somali children with PTSD had a sample size of 6, whereas others (summarized by Betancourt and Williams) had sample sizes of between 55 and 314—tiny compared to the immense scale of the problem. Nevertheless, the focus of Betancourt and Williams's analysis appears to be on how systematic, evidence-based evaluations can be conducted. The authors concede that formal evaluations are "scarce," and they conclude with a call for "many more in-depth evaluations."[93]

Regrettably, the world appears ill equipped to deal with the nature and scale of children leaving the clutches of the Islamic State. In 2016 Nadim Houry highlighted the emerging bulge of "stateless" children, born of foreign fighters and most likely of rape.[94] These children do not have identification papers or birth certificates and as such are not able to prove their nationality. Statelessness brings "discrimination and lack of access to education, housing, healthcare and employment."[95] History has also shown that these children are more vulnerable to abuse, prostitution, child labor, trafficking, recruitment, and recidivism. Thus it is crucial to consider mechanisms for interrupting the cycle of violence.[96]

The steps required to rehabilitate children will demand a multipronged and comprehensive approach if we are to plan for a post-IS peace in the region. The scale of the challenge facing children affected or displaced by IS is staggering. DDR programs have historically been good at the *DD* part (disarmament and demobilization) but have fallen short in the *R* (whereby the R in DDR has come to represent either rehabilitation, reinsertion, or reunification), as funding tends to dry up by the time a conflict gets to this stage. This is why the threat of recidivism is high (even if the numbers of those who reengage in violence may be relatively low). Three-month programs are too short to guarantee any type of sustainable rehabilitation; much longer DDR programs will be needed if children who have been in IS are to be comprehensively rehabilitated and reintegrated.

In some cases, a multipronged psychosocial approach in which the children are provided with different types of treatment strategies works best. Aggression replacement training is a multimodal program composed of three elements:

moral reasoning, anger control, and the development of social skills. Social workers found that young children aged eight to fourteen did not respond to aggression replacement training by itself, partly because they were too young to fully comprehend what they had seen and done.[97] At one rehabilitation facility in Lebanon, therapists and social workers combined aggression replacement training with cognitive behavioral training.[98] In Lebanon they employed a variety of treatment approaches for the children, including using a Defense Mechanism Questionnaire to identify what triggers the children.

A key programmatic challenge in the rehabilitation of child fighters from IS will involve where precisely those children will experience rehabilitation. In many of the countries where IS children come from (and presumably might return to), there are few psychological resources available to children. In many countries, psychological services and psychosocial care are conflated. Because few of these countries have existing mental health services, it is difficult to know what portion of the psychological sequelae are a function of the conflict and which are underlying mental health problems exacerbated by the conflict. In many of these countries, there is no way to separate religion from politics and culture, since there is no way to disengage from the context. We know that ideological commitment plays a critical role in refugees' capacity to resettle in new countries. Inger Agger and Søren Jensen argue that the inability to retain strong ideological connections may give rise to deep psychological problems in the host country.[99] It will be essential to approach this dilemma from a variety of angles. The need to understand children's mobilization into violent extremism is pressing, and the challenge facing most governments in the immediate future will be what, if anything, to do with the children who want to return and live (hopefully) normal lives. In the next chapter we explore some preliminary solutions and best practices that have emerged from studying a variety of DDR programs around the globe, and suggest a few possible ways to move forward and in the right direction.

AN END OR A NEW BEGINNING?

Fighting terrorism is like being a goalkeeper. You can make a hundred brilliant saves but the only shot that people remember is the one that gets past you.

Paul Wilkinson

With guns you can kill terrorists, with education you can kill terrorism.

Malala Yousafzai

Terrorist organizations exploit children for tactical and strategic purposes. Children are vulnerable before, during, and even after conflict. Their continued exploitation, in a general sense, is a powerful expression of psychological warfare. On a day-to-day operational level, as we have described throughout this book, they may be used merely because they do not arouse suspicion and can effectively penetrate civilian "soft targets" as well as hardened military and security targets. Children are also used as human shields and will likely suffer longer-term effects than adults who experience the same trauma and witness the same atrocities.[1] However, researching children's involvement in terrorism undeniably raises more questions than we have been able to answer. This is perhaps understandable, but it is nevertheless frustrating, and it might leave the reader dissatisfied with this book.

The preceding chapters have highlighted how, despite occasional instances in which international norms have prevailed to mitigate the phenomenon of children in conflict, the extent of children's involvement in terrorism and unconventional warfare appears to have dramatically increased and expanded in recent years rather than decrease—as predicted in much of the literature. It will take time for even the most basic accounts to fully emerge, let alone the fruits of systematic research into the underlying processes of how, why, when, and where children enter and exit violent extremist groups. We understand the phenomenon of child soldiers better in hindsight than we did in the 1990s, when it was a common phenomenon across dozens of conflicts on every continent except Antarctica.[2] Unfortunately both the trend and the data on children in terrorist groups will continue to develop well after the publication of this book.

As with most developments in counterterrorism, it often takes a crisis to spur the general public's interest and the allocation of resources to the problem. The systematic recruitment, indoctrination, and utilization of children by the Islamic State have unquestionably been the primary catalyst for the current interest in children's involvement in terrorism, yet as we have shown here, children were involved in some capacity well before IS evolved out of al-Qaeda in Iraq. But because of the fascination with the Cubs of the Caliphate, questions are now emerging concerning how countries in the Middle East, North Africa, and the West might prepare a response to a problem of which we have only the most rudimentary understanding. Furthermore, the chronic use of very young children by Boko Haram in Nigeria and by local and transnational extremist groups in Pakistan, and the mounting use in Afghanistan by jihadi groups, illustrates the contagion of the tactic and necessitates a better understanding of ways to prevent it in the future.

The context for these concerns is hardly surprising, as the need for a response appears to be urgent. In many journalistic accounts, the children are variously and crudely characterized as "ticking time bombs," and are depicted as potential Manchurian candidates or as the "lost generation."[3] As we completed this chapter, local authorities were arresting children who had been featured in IS propaganda as well as orphaned children of IS fighters in Sirte, Libya, who are housed in makeshift orphanages without passports, citizenship, or future prospects. By the fall of 2017, the Islamic State was undeniably on the ropes. Suffering heavy military defeats in key battles in both Syria and Iraq, and diminishing influence in Libya,[4] the group lost control over most of the territory it had safely controlled in 2014 and 2015.[5] The symbolic nature of the territorial losses cannot be overstated, considering that the initial capture of the territory played such a pivotal role in the clarion call to recruits around the globe two and three years earlier. Now, however, the picture has changed. IS's ability to recruit foreign fighters has decreased, the quality (and volume) of its propaganda has deteriorated from its peak in 2015, and the number of defections and people attempting to escape the group has snowballed into an avalanche.[6] The movement was forced to reduce its remuneration to its fighters, and, as a result of significant external pressure on the Turkish government, the border between Turkey and Syria was finally tightened. Because of this and other enforcement measures, travel to the region has been disrupted, and IS relies mostly on what it has inside its physical borders. In recruiters' conversations with supporters online who express an interest in traveling to "Sham" (Syria and Iraq), new recruits are told to stay put and "do something (violent) locally."[7]

Outside Syria and Iraq, major concerns surround the potential threat posed by "returnees"—those men, women, and children who only a few years ago left home to embrace a new life in the caliphate. Faced with a crumbling dream and a harsh reality, those same travelers have begun to consider the possibility of returning to their homes while they still can. Some have already returned to face arrest or detention.[8] What will this mean for the security of their countries of origin, as some of these emigrants were encouraged to gleefully burn their passports to symbolically cement their break and send a public message of defiance to observers back home? Some countries preemptively invalidated the passports or revoked the citizenship of foreign fighters, including their young children, before facing the prospect of having to deal with returnees. According to the Soufan Center, not all IS fighters may be able to return to their home countries. They may migrate further, to the group's affiliates in Afghanistan, Libya, Egypt, and the Philippines.[9]

While IS issued birth certificates for children born inside the caliphate, no government currently recognizes these documents, much like the educational certificates mentioned in chapter 3, which are not valid outside IS-controlled territory.[10] For these stateless children, the immediate challenge is one of integration rather than reintegration, as they have no officially recognized country of origin. Furthermore, there are legitimate concerns that the flood of returnees might converge with IS's increasing strategy of low-tech, opportunistic attacks that require neither financing nor training.[11] According to the 2017 Soufan Center report authored by Richard Barrett, "While it will be hard to assess the specific threat posed by foreign fighters and returnees, they will present a challenge to many countries for years to come."[12]

In one interview with ITV News, a young IS fighter said that the organization had made plans to smuggle Cubs of the Caliphate into Europe along with refugees.[13] It is difficult, if not impossible, to assess the veracity of any individual account, especially when it appears in the Western media, but there are grounds for taking such statements seriously. The past two years have witnessed an alarming increase in "self-radicalized" or lone-actor events. Ramming attacks occurred in Germany, Spain, the UK, France, and the US after Abu Muhammad al-Adnani, IS's spokesman, called for attacks in the West using vehicles as weapons.[14] The July 2016 attack in Nice, France, illustrated the devastating consequences of driving a cargo truck into a crowded area: in seconds, eighty-six people were killed, and over four hundred injured. And the August 17, 2017, attack on Las Ramblas in Barcelona killed thirteen people and yielded one hundred casualties.

Alternatively, returnees might repatriate in shame, disillusioned by their experiences, desperate to reintegrate, or stigmatized and eager to hide.[15] In terms of scale, multiple countries face diverse challenges. A probable scenario is that countries that generated the largest quantities of emigrants will face higher volumes of returnees than those countries with comparatively smaller numbers of extremist travelers. Even those countries that generated few emigrants will face challenges depending on whether the returnees originated from a single region, and whether they made up a significant percentage of the population. For the respective countries, the scale of returning travelers is difficult to forecast, and each country has formulated its own policies about whether citizens are welcome to return at all. The range of dynamics associated with people's experiences inside the Islamic State will merit critical consideration. Not everyone who wishes to return will be permitted to do so. Many will die trying, either because IS has aggressively executed wannabe defectors,[16] including those merely expressing discontent, or via capture and probable torture and execution by local security forces. We are currently witnessing two-to-ten-minute trials in Syria and Iraq in which scores of women and children have been executed without any due process.[17] Some will be disenchanted, but it is equally evident that not everyone who is disillusioned will return home deradicalized. Many terrorists become disillusioned because of the strategic failures associated with the larger movement, not as the result of some "Pauline moment" where they suddenly realize the error of their ways. Being disillusioned is not synonymous with remorse, nor does it predict a lowered risk of reengagement in violence. Furthermore, not everyone who succeeds in returning is necessarily disillusioned. They may simply be trying to escape an inconvenient or meaningless death.

Host-country security services face the gargantuan task of assessing the risk of returnees' potential reengagement in terrorism or other illegal activity. The same skill set that makes for a successful militant in a terrorist organization can easily be applied to gang or other criminal activities. Thus, for the young people who have been trained by terrorist groups (or, at the very least, have been exposed to them), recidivism might include not only the risk of reengagement, but also the risk of their gravitating toward other forms of violence and criminality. Even if they are disengaged in the sense of no longer being involved in violent extremism, questions remain regarding whether genuine reintegration is possible. This is in addition to the children's palpable posttraumatic stress, which may not present itself for several years.

One essential principle is to get children back to a positive educational setting, with the goal of having them return to the level of education they lost because the conflict shuttered schools or because they were recruited by extremist groups and taken out of school. This is often the first and most difficult step, as it presumes that the infrastructure and resources to educate children are in place. Maurizio Crivellaro, Save the Children's Iraq county director, said in November 2016 that

> all displaced children will need to attend non-formal or catch up classes for at least the next few months before they are reassessed and referred to formal schools depending on their performance. . . . Children and parents tell us that during times of crisis, education is their priority. They tell us it's the key to their future and it can't be delayed. These children have missed out on enough of their childhoods.[18]

Even if the children receive an education, they still face problems of reintegration: their communities might reject the former child militants because of their involvement, even if that involvement was not strictly voluntary. Will local communities accept "formers" who might be perceived as traitors, future terrorists, or war criminals? Typically, risk is indefinable and unquantifiable. And there are supplemental questions regarding the allocation of resources and responsibility. Who will be tasked with monitoring returnees (the police, intelligence services, teams of social workers, mental health professionals, or community care workers), and how long will it take to ascertain whether an individual poses a risk? These and more concerns are relevant for just about all returnees, both adults and children, and many will ask whether the resources exist to adequately address even a fraction of these issues.

There is another aspect to consider. Sending IS Cubs back to school to educate them in a manner commensurate with their respective grade levels might have unintended negative psychological effects. As we have described in previous chapters, IS perverted the social hierarchies in the territories in which it governed, and empowered children by giving them the power of life and death over adults, training them like adults, and making the boys feel "manly." To this end, the children may not strictly perceive themselves as children, because they have been treated as adults from a young age. We cannot anticipate how their change in status will impact their psychological well-being.

What we can surmise is that those countries in the West (for example, the US, the UK, Germany, and France) that have the resources required to create comprehensive programs to address the far-reaching needs of children who have been recruited, trained, and brainwashed also have the least political will to do so. Paradoxically, these countries will likely face the fewest returning children, while the Middle Eastern actors from whence the majority of the adults came (Tunisia, Turkey, Libya, and Egypt) have the least resources to successfully reintegrate youth. A camp for displaced persons in Bartella near Mosul was created with the goal of providing its residents with what a September 2017 Vice News report calls "psychological and ideological rehabilitation." However, that report, drawing on interviews with Human Rights Watch staff members, describes the facility as little more than an "awful prison camp with minimal services."[19] Subsequent awareness of the camp led to its shutdown, but highlighted concerns about the ability of Iraqi authorities to deal with the overwhelming problems the country and the broader region face in attempting to achieve some kind of stability. Unfortunately, at least for the immediate future, this may be little more than aspirational. To say that mental health services are not widely available in Syria is a gross understatement. Prior to the broader crisis there, the country of some twenty-two million people had approximately one hundred psychiatrists. According to a physician with the Syrian American Medical Society, only five were child psychiatrists.[20] In a country devastated by war, food, medicine, and other basic supplies will inevitably take precedence, but the psychological impact of the war will be profound. In Nigeria there is no tradition of child psychiatry at all. Many of the countries have to create in a vacuum the infrastructure necessary for treatment.

In contrast to the Bartella camp, a detention facility in Erbil, the Women and Children's Reformatory, while overcrowded and underfunded, appears to show some promise. The social workers at this facility concentrate on the children's connections to the group before addressing education or their psychosocial needs. "The first thing we do in the institute," says its director, Diman Muhamed Bayiz, in a *Newsweek* report, "is change their clothes, shave their beard and cut their hair. We change their external appearance [first]."[21] Nevertheless, the program in Erbil mirrors the one at the Sabaoon facility in Pakistan, although the Women and Children's Reformatory is severely underresourced by comparison: the facility houses 475 people but was originally built for only 120. The curriculum for the children being rehabilitated includes sports, music, computer, and language courses. Bayiz provides the inmates access to social workers and psychologists. As in Pakistan, it is also necessary to address the children's distorted view of Islam, and so an imam teaches them the "real Islam."[22]

In some ways, the questions raised about the management of returnees are not entirely without precedent. Previous wars witnessed foreign fighters' return from Bosnia and Afghanistan. Numerous conflicts in Colombia and central and eastern Africa have seen peace and reconciliation efforts that have enjoyed varying degrees of success (reintegration is merely one measure of success), though not without presenting complications. In 2016, Dominic Ongwen, a former child conscript of the Lord's Resistance Army, appeared before the International Criminal Court at The Hague. Even though the Ugandan government granted a broad amnesty to those who left the LRA, not everyone benefited equally from this offer of clemency. Many of those considered to have played major leadership roles were deemed exempt. This included Ongwen, who was abducted into the movement at the age of ten and brutalized through years of coercion and socialization.[23]

Time will tell if the children of IS will be pursued as vigorously, but unlike Ongwen, whose identity was in question,[24] the fighters immortalized in IS propaganda efforts may ultimately come to be harmed by those videos, GIFs, and memes. In 2015, a young child was filmed by IS executing Muhammad Musallam, described as an "Israeli spy." The child was very clearly identified as an IS Cub, and the video achieved expected notoriety after the child shot Musallam. Also appearing in the video was an adult IS fighter, Sabri Essid (believed to be the boy's father). Essid himself was the stepbrother of the French IS militant Mohamed Merah.[25] The video was widely broadcast and covered by Western media, and was subsequently celebrated in multiple formats by IS itself. Just two years later, however, the young boy was photographed in the custody of Iraqi security forces. He had been easily identified because of the video, which also served as evidence of the atrocity.

It is imperative that the International Criminal Court treat the forced recruitment of children under the age of fifteen into terrorist organizations as a war crime. Since recruiting, training, and engaging child operatives under age fifteen is considered a crime against humanity, children involved in terrorist organizations, like child soldiers, must be immediately demobilized, even if the parties are still engaged in combat.[26] NATO has begun working on mainstreaming child protection— finding ways to operationalize United Nations Security Council (UNSC) Resolution 1612 because of the lessons learned from the war in Afghanistan.[27]

Today's concerns are not limited to the Islamic State. By the end of 2017, Boko Haram (Wilyata Ifriquiya) was coming to terms with its own declining influence. Over the course of that year, the IS African affiliate lost control of its territory in the Sambisa Forest and, through negotiations and unofficial channels, willingly returned many of the girls it had kidnapped in 2014 and 2015.[28]

Elsewhere, the Revolutionary Armed Forces of Colombia (FARC) disbanded and declared an end to armed hostilities. Children's involvement in FARC was stymied by overwhelming international condemnation. The general denunciation of children's involvement in armed forces has solidified the effect of previous UN resolutions against the use of children in war.[29]

We now stand at a crossroads. The power of groups that exploit children (such as IS) is decreasing, as they face a general consensus that terror groups should not involve youth—a consensus that might make us presume a future decline. At the same time, the emerging moral panic about what to expect from refugees who might pose a potential security risk to the countries to which they might return or flee contributes to an overwhelming popular belief that children in IS are all "radicalized" and could become future jihadis, Manchurian candidates waiting to be activated. Such fears, if left unchecked, may reinforce terrorist groups' use of children in this way. As we have said earlier, terrorist groups gain their power from using tactics that were once thought unacceptable, and the common strategic benefit of using children is that it produces not just shock but confusion, and ultimately despair.

To explore possible solutions, we can consider some best practices from other conflicts in which children were mobilized into violence. While there will likely be macrolevel programs sponsored by the United Nations whose efficacy is dubious, the best practices are likely observable by local grassroots organizations that have emerged to demobilize youth or reintegrate them into society. The major challenge in some of the African conflicts was how the army and police viewed youth as potentially dangerous—even well after the conflicts were resolved. Thus, some of the most successful programs have been opportunities for young people and the police or army to cooperate—everything from soccer leagues to sponsored joint harvesting events. While international efforts may or may not be as successful as the local ones, the UN is bringing attention and resources to local efforts to empower youth in order to prevent radicalization and involvement in terrorism.

On August 22, 2015, during the Global Forum on Youth, Peace and Security, the United Nations and civil society organizations announced the "Amman Youth Declaration" in Jordan under the auspices of the king of Jordan. The declaration called on the international community to engage young people as active proponents of a peace-and-security agenda. This two-day global forum brought together "500 government officials, policy experts, youth-led organizations, and young peacebuilders from over 100 countries aimed at helping shape a new international agenda on youth, peace and security."[30] It culminated with the declaration's adoption and included the results of consultations held with over ten thousand youth worldwide.

This initiative was followed a few months later by the adoption of UNSC resolution 2250 on youth, peace and security. In this resolution, adopted on December 9, 2015, the UN outlined five practical ways in which young people can meaningfully contribute to lasting peace in their communities, their countries, and the world. Member states stressed the importance of including their voices in the decision-making process. The resolution called for the inclusion of young people's views during the negotiation and implementation of peace agreements, and recognized that youth previously had been excluded from these processes and were often given no agency and no say. They had been regarded as a group to be managed rather than one to be respected and trusted as active collaborators in the fostering of peace.

The five pillars outlined in the resolution are as follows:

- Participation: increase inclusive representation of youth in decision-making for the prevention and resolution of conflict
- Protection: protect civilians, including youth, from all forms of sexual and gender-based violence
- Prevention: foster an environment in which young people are recognized and provided adequate support to implement violence-prevention activities, and support social cohesion to promote a culture of peace, tolerance, and intercultural and interreligious dialogue involving youth
- Partnership: increase political, financial, technical, and logistical support, accounting for the needs and participation of youth, and engage local communities and NGOs to develop ways to counter violent extremist narratives
- Disengagement and Reintegration: consider the needs of youth affected by armed conflict, through gender-sensitive employment opportunities and inclusive labor policies, and build young people's capabilities and skills through education designed to promote a culture of peace[31]

Subsequent to resolution 2250, in 2017 the UN unanimously adopted resolution 2368, in which the Security Council reaffirmed its resolve to combat terrorism and condemned abductions, the trafficking of children, and the use of children by terrorist groups.

Many examples of best practices for the prevention of young people's recruitment by and association with armed groups, and for the rehabilitation of youth after conflict, can demonstrate the practical application of resolution 2250—that is, to consider how the international community will handle the crisis of (re)integrating children who have been victimized and traumatized, we might explore what has worked in other contexts. The idea of best practices is a beguiling one, and in reality, when they can even be identified, the phrase is a proxy for what works at a particular time in a particular setting.[32] But principles can be set, lessons learned, and blueprints drawn for the development of programmatic efforts elsewhere. Although many of these initiatives were technically in place prior to the Amman Youth Declaration and the adoption of resolution 2250, the international community and the consensus around empowering youth can reinforce their success. Though they make imperfect analogies, they do provide a reference point for thinking about the challenges involved with the return of travelers from IS-controlled territory.

It is currently unknown how many returnees from the Islamic State are children, and how many of those who originally left as children might now return as young adults. Yet there is an urgent need to prepare for and respond to this challenge. Has IS truly created the so-called "next generation" of militants, or might these children simply get on with their lives if provided with the opportunity for rehabilitation and reintegration? Also unclear is whether different levels of risk might be associated with returnees from an earlier stage in the conflict, compared to those returning now or those who want to return in the future: is greater risk associated with having spent more time in Islamic State territory? Furthermore, might there be possible cohort effects to consider? That is to say, are children who were inducted into the movement earlier in IS's expansion (when the group enjoyed greater prominence, control, and authority) likely to be considered more "dangerous" than those inducted more recently, after IS's decline? And taken together, these issues are distinct from the more rudimentary question of what precisely constitutes a returnee. Will the children return to their countries as battle-hardened fighters or as disillusioned (and in some cases traumatized) escapees?

The first step in this process is to carefully consider the range of effects children have potentially been exposed to while in IS territory. Children who have engaged with IS will have lost people close to them, seen dead and wounded, killed or violently assaulted others, and faced death themselves. Such experiences have a profound and long-lasting psychological impact. War zones present children with multiple risks, and so one cannot reify the experience of one specific traumatic event (displacement, torture, death of a loved one); many of the children emerging from what remains of the so-called Islamic State likely experienced more than one trauma and more than one instance. There is no consensus on how to measure risk (or resilience), whether to simply aggregate all of the traumas experienced by the child, or whether the range of events, duration of exposure, or intensity matter more.[33] Studies of former LTTE children reveal an array of psychiatric conditions, including depression, posttraumatic stress disorder, and severe psychosis. Research into the effects of political violence on children has emphasized the pathological consequences. The history of research on children suffering from PTSD, according to Marla Buchanan and her coauthors, shows "a spectrum of psychological symptoms that include depressed affect, anxiety, fear of recurrence, guilt, insomnia, enuresis, delinquency, and post traumatic stress; acute stress reactions include nightmares, exaggerated startle reactions, somatic complaints, and sleep disturbances."[34]

The same will be true of many of those leaving IS. Conflict-related symptoms persist in the longer term where insufficient attention is paid to issues experienced after the conflict. While beyond the scope of this study, there is preliminary evidence that increased cortisol levels resulting from extended periods of stress might actually alter the neurobiology of young brains because of the brain's neuroplasticity—causing the children to experience paranoia, reduced impulse control, and the ability to assess risk later on in life. In essence, these studies have posited that unless treated, the children will be incapable of experiencing empathy.[35] Thus, exposure to violence at this young an age, and the resulting cortisol imbalances, might make treatment all the more difficult.

Issues such as personal loss during the conflict, family abuse or neglect, and the stigma of association with the conflict all lead to the internalization of negative psychological symptoms over time. Counterintuitively, Brian Barber and Benjamin Doty "contest the extent of this threat to the mental well-being of children and youth.... Most youth exposed to political violence show no sign of dysfunction, because their understanding of their war experiences depends on the specific nature and severity of those experiences and how they are interpreted."[36] In fact, Barber and Doty found that most children were highly resilient even under the most extreme and adverse circumstances. As a result of such divergent findings and opinions in the literature, each case will need to be assessed individually, especially since there is likely to be a delayed reaction, such that some traumatic events will be felt years or even decades after the events themselves. Other studies have found that "resistance" and "resilience" are relative terms in the context of repeated and chronic traumatic life experiences (such as those children experience in cases of occupation, war, or repeated violence). All of these assumptions presuppose that children will be able to avail themselves of such mental health services.[37]

Children who return from the Islamic State will have had different experiences, and will present different challenges, than children returning from other terrorist groups, or regular refugee children. Some will be traumatized, while others will not. The accounts of children involved in militancy will vary considerably; as we observed among the children in Sabaoon, some children had been traumatized by their involvement with the Pakistani Taliban, while a handful of children (unexpectedly) reported very positive experiences. It is important to mention that the children who had positive experiences had a more difficult time acclimatizing than those whose experiences were decidedly negative. We need to entertain the possibility that a percentage of the children will have felt empowered by their experiences in IS. This is also a reflection of IS's deliberate strategy of inverting social hierarchies by giving children the power of life and death over adults (and, in so doing, humiliating their enemies). Youth empowered in this way might consider their experiences to have been validating and positive. This can make their psychological recovery all the more challenging.

Former IS Cubs will need practical as well as psychological support. Access to quality education and vocational and life skills training (to help prepare them for civilian life and jobs) are essential, as is access to and use of interim care centers to assist with the reintegration process. To mitigate recidivism, we will need a way of determining whether, how, and when children are prepared to reenter society. The failure to properly address this results in many demobilized children becoming even more disturbed, especially given the cookie-cutter approach of set terms of treatment. We know that one proposed model of a mandatory three months of treatment, while cost effective, does not work for all populations or all individuals.

A further problem surrounds "stateless" children, born of foreign fighters, and some possibly of rape, whether in Syria, Iraq, Nigeria, or elsewhere. History shows us that these children are more vulnerable not only to discrimination and lack of access to resources but also to prostitution, trafficking, and recidivism.[38] The experiences of those women and children captured or kidnapped by Boko Haram and returned to their families and villages have shown that there is important variation between women returning to villages and those returning to urban centers. Whether or not their community accepts the children remains a lingering source of sensitivity. The children, while having no contact with their "Boko fathers," are assumed to be baby Boko Haram insurgents in the making. This same stigma was evident in the tens of thousands of children who resulted from mass rape campaigns and sexual violence in Rwanda and in the former Yugoslavia. Moreover, those children born of rape appear more likely to be abandoned, or aborted, although this varied significantly by context and by whether abortion was acceptable or legal in the country in which the sexual exploitation occurred.[39]

Many of the same long-term social-psychological sequelae in children born of rape are likely to impact the child returnees from IS. These include attachment difficulties, stigma, discrimination, problems with identity, and behavioral problems. Some additional consequences might occur depending on the children's age when they entered IS territory and on whether they have any preorganization memory. In one assessment by Tanya Zayed, slightly older children who had memories of a happy childhood prior to involvement in terrorist violence were able to hark back to a happy childhood in ways that younger children, with no lasting preinvolvement memories, could not.[40] Moreover, regarding the effect of witnessing versus participating in terrorist violence, it remains uncertain whether one is more difficult to forget than the other. For some children captured from IS and held in detention facilities, the perpetration of violence, including beheadings, was normalized by the group.[41]

In the short term, counterterrorism practitioners and local law enforcement have only started to identify the problems and possible remedies. In a report commissioned by the European Union's Radicalisation Awareness Network (RAN), Sharon Lambert and Orla Lynch acknowledge that the threat of violence posed by child returnees is "unknown and most likely unknowable."[42] Lessons on (re)integrating the children successfully can be identified from a variety of arenas.

Little is known about how individual countries (or regions) currently manage their returnees. Most countries have followed a practice of adjudicating on a case-by-case basis whether people are permitted to return. The European Union, through RAN, described the Dutch approach.[43] When authorities discover returnees, they are vetted by the police and may be subject to a comprehensive intelligence investigation. As part of that process, each returnee is assessed by a multidisciplinary case management team. These teams tailor suggestions for individual intervention, which may involve "criminal prosecution, care programs or a deradicalization program."[44] A major challenge for local police is in the monitoring of returnees. To effectively perform such a task, it is imperative for local authorities to determine who precisely constitutes a "potentially risky" individual.

RAN notes that children can be considered victims while simultaneously posing a risk to safety and security. The challenge associated with determining the level of risk in a child returnee is the need for both assessment and care. Both children and adults require constructive interventions as well as monitoring, and likely aftercare, as part of any program in which they participate. More so than adults, children face significant stigma upon their return. RAN's guidelines for practitioners dealing with child returnees highlight that this can involve everything from the children's needing to prove their ancestry or nationality via DNA testing to the stigma of being labeled a "terrorist" in their new schools. Gender accentuates the problem in terror groups because females are subjected to substantial gender segregation. This presents a basic challenge to reintegration if, for example, female returnees are not able to leave the house and are expected to do so.[45]

Practitioners have developed a variety of risk assessment tools. Given the tacit promise of what these tools are believed to offer, we cannot overstate the need to understand the limitations of such instruments. In terms of content, they typically encompass beliefs, intention, motivation, and other issues deemed pertinent to assessing the likelihood of continued or future engagement in political violence. But in essence, the tools are simply decision guides to help users determine whether a person may be moving in one direction or another—toward recidivism or toward successful reintegration. Mapping such change onto a judgment regarding risk or potential threat is problematic. If a person exhibits decreasing evidence of radical views over time, that could be interpreted as a possible lowering of risk of involvement in terrorism. It could also, however, if taken without additional inputs, suggest an effort to conceal true intention, which would signal increasing commitment. Ultimately the better goal might be to prevent any kind of reengagement, either in violence or criminal activity, since we know from studies of adults that addressing behavior is more realistic a goal than addressing what might be in someone's heart or mind. It is equally possible that the youth might never alter their behavior or their views.

Much has been said about identifying and harnessing the "protective factors" associated with radicalization. According to Michael Ungar, "A social ecological understanding of resilience decenters our understanding of resilience, arguing that much more of a person's positive development under stress can be accounted for by external rather than internal factors. . . . Recovery from trauma could be stimulated by engaging the individual in a process that promoted his or her expression of latent coping capacity."[46] However, in order to accomplish this, resources need to be mapped at all levels of a social ecology, from cultural beliefs down to basic needs. The leading expert on child soldier demobilization and reintegration, Theresa Betancourt, insists that children's rehabilitation requires many of the totems of a normal childhood, which include "a sense of safety; access to essential physiological needs, including sleep and food; family, biological or otherwise, and a connection to others who share a common identity; and economic security and education, which gives children the chance to seek a fulfilling life."[47]

Here again, gender matters. RAN notes that "masculinity, life as a warrior and the glorification of martyrdom" certainly represent strong focal points for males involved in the Islamic State. This contrasts with women's roles in IS, which focus on "perceived freedom from patriarchal traditions" by, ironically, offering women the opportunity to marry fighters and occupy auxiliary roles such as propagandist or recruiter. It is important to recognize the role of gender, as services provided may need to be gender specific, and the ways in which psychosocial interventions address gender-specific motivations and the subsequent experiences of those who became involved with IS need to be understood.[48]

Bronfenbrenner suggests that the family might be considered a key microsystem providing for the children's basic needs and for their protection.[49] The concentric circles of Bronfenbrenner's social ecological model assume three systems: a mesosystem (institutions) with which the child directly functions (e.g., schools or religious institutions), exosystems that impact the child (e.g., the parents' workplace), and macrosystems that involve language and cultural belief systems, which can create a blueprint for resilience. Thus children's needs are addressed at each level, by supporting families (in the immediate microcontext), providing opportunities for schooling and child-friendly spaces (in the mesocontext), and drawing on traditional belief systems to promote well-being and reintegration (in the macrocontext).[50] However, some assumptions of the social ecology may need to be reconsidered. Family support, ordinarily synonymous with resilience, is a key influence in preventing involvement in violent extremism. Yet this is questionable in cases where the children's families were central to their recruitment and initial involvement. Indeed, the only viable approach to protecting such children from recidivism or reengagement may be to remove them from their families and enter them into a different kind of care structure (e.g., extended family if it exists, or foster care). These are difficult and legally challenging recommendations to make. It might be plausible for the children to be treated in stages. Those children who merely witnessed violence might be easier to treat than those who engaged in it. It will be necessary to vet any refugee population given the current political climate and the very real concerns over security. All of these considerations will necessarily have to occur simultaneously, but building on successes can offer nongovernmental and international organizations the chance to show positive results. If the international community begins with the most difficult cases and fails, it is unlikely that any programs will expand to address the needs of children less impacted.

Preventing children from getting involved with violent organizations presents important challenges, and dealing with children who became involved presents a different set of challenges. To borrow from existing recommendations for future intervention, we start with the obvious principle from the Hippocratic Oath: "First, do no harm." The international community and individual states must be careful in how they engage children, and because of this, they have to be careful in how communities are approached and treated.

Where possible (which excludes family-initiated recruitment), intervention should include the wider communities of family and society to help provide the support that the children require. Programs should reduce risk and consider the specific contexts in which the children were traumatized, as well as the extent to which their traumas might have been layered and overlapping.

The children's basic needs must be addressed to provide security, safe schools, food, water, and shelter. IDP camps or refugee camps can become bases of recruitment (or re-recruitment) because the children are traumatized and experience new challenges after displacement, or dislocation in a postconflict setting. It is important to address all aspects of a child's well-being. Following the Sabaoon methodology, a multilayered, multipronged approach should address childrens' mental health, physical health, spiritual health, and employment opportunities.

There will be different approaches required depending on whether the child is older or younger, male or female, local or foreign. All of these factors should be considered as part of the treatment. While the international community can play a role (e.g., UNICEF, War Child, the United Nations Development Programme, Save the Children), local initiatives are crucial because they appreciate the context and understand the culture better than interventions brought in from outside. As we have maintained throughout this chapter, education is the most critical support mechanism for war-affected communities (whether impacted by IS or by other groups). Setting up child-friendly spaces will be crucial for creating educational opportunities and for providing a safe and secure environment. Fatima Akilu notes, however, that in countries with little experience of child psychology, psychosocial treatment and supportive initiatives are routinely conflated.[51] Communities can promote psychosocial well-being through education and afford children the ability to learn important coping mechanisms, emotional regulation, and how to manage peer interactions to avoid future antisocial behavior or violence.[52] This should be in addition to creating safe spaces and building afterschool programs.

Uncertain and imperfect knowledge, however, is no excuse for inaction, and already many governments in Europe have only just started to contemplate the inescapable challenge of returnees. The time will eventually come for identifying lessons for preventing future generations of children from becoming involved in terrorism. Certainly, engaging returnees will provide valuable opportunities for eliciting and documenting their experiences across multiple domains—from simply capturing accounts of their involvement to assessing the psychological impact. These details will help to ascertain and identify the bases of their needs for successful rehabilitation and reintegration. But for now, the overwhelming focus is on assessing the risk of future engagement in violent extremism by children returning from conflict zones.

In order to disrupt or prevent the mobilization of youth and the reengagement of returnees into extremist violence, we propose eight practical steps—summarizing many of our conclusions from previous chapters.[53]

1. Address the specific context and realities of communities affected by conflict, war, and terrorism, and broaden the focus of reintegration and rehabilitation efforts to suit local needs.
2. Be sensitive to the gendered nature of conflict, and prioritize gender in any rehabilitation and reintegration programs. Understand how processes likely impact girls differently than boys. This entails involving women in DDR program design early on.

3. Implement multidisciplinary treatments that combine good practices from other settings (gangs, cults, and child soldiers) and mix methods where appropriate. If one approach fails, pivot and try a combination. Understand that there will be no silver-bullet, one-size-fits-all solution. To get the right mix of local context and realities, involve as many local stakeholders—including educators, social welfare, local NGOs, and state institutions—as possible.

4. Ensure safe and coherent policies that are transparent, and make guidelines explicit, especially with regard to how states will accept child returnees. Those deemed acceptable for return must also be protected from retaliation, and stigma. If need be, institute human rights monitoring for child returnees to ensure they have the necessary support.

5. Build NGOs' and other local stakeholders' capacity for implementing psychosocial services, especially if these kinds of programs did not previously exist in the country.

6. Engage the families and communities of child returnees to better facilitate their reintegration. Aftercare in these situations will be critical, and will require follow-up visits by social workers to ensure its success.

7. Engage the public sector, such as the media, and include religious and secular education in dialogues. While there might not be root causes that constitute drivers for terrorism, it is clear that by the time the youth are fifteen, many might subscribe to an ideology, and it is important to take this seriously. Including educators and religious leaders in rehabilitation programs will therefore be crucial. In cases where children have been fed a steady diet of extremist (religious) ideology, debunking and addressing the false narratives will be necessary. Critical to this point is that secularization or Westernization is not a goal, nor is it a proxy measure for deradicalization.

8. Invest economically in countries after conflict; this is an important way to prevent reengagement, in particular youth transitioning into illegal criminal networks. Vocational training that offers children and youth an alternative pathway and the possibility of a bright future is a good investment and worth every penny, as we observed in the case of Sabaoon.

Up to now, the major focus of countering violent extremism (CVE) and preventing violent extremism (PVE) programs has been on the negative. Programs that proliferated in the aftermath of major terrorist attacks—such as 9/11 in the US, the Madrid train attack in 2004, and 7/7 in the UK—and following the emergence of jihadi offshoots over the past decade identify (if not always clearly) what

the West wants to combat. But these programs, along with government policies, NGOs, and civil society, have been less proficient at explaining what they are in favor of. The ability to win hearts and minds is what has allowed many of the extremists to operate, by providing social services and offering benefits where states have failed to, but also by outlining what they are for and whom they are against. This partly explains their relative success despite their limitations, a protracted war against terror, and the fact that the vast majority of Muslims oppose the violent ideology of groups such as al-Qaeda and the Islamic State.

Notes

1. WHAT IS A CHILD?

1. These are all negative terms IS uses to refer to its enemies: apostate, Shiite, and disbeliever.

2. Graphic video has been removed from http://zerocensorship.com/t/uncensored-isis-execution/136259-isis-child-soldiers-shooting-execution-in-palmyra-syria-graphic-video but can be found at Imogen Calderwood, "Slaughter in the Roman Amphitheatre: Horrific Moment ISIS Child Executioners Brutally Shoot Dead 25 Syrian Regime Soldiers in Front of Bloodthirsty Crowds at Ancient Palmyra Ruin," *Daily Mail*, July 5, 2015, (accessed June 2016).

3. Peter W. Singer, "Terrorists Must Be Denied Child Recruits," *Financial Times*, January 20, 2005.

4. *Baghdad Mosquito*, January 26, 2007, vol. 4, edition 1223, 5.

5. *Child Soldiers: Implications for US Forces*. Seminar Report, November 2002, Center for Emerging Threats and Opportunities, US Marine Corps, CETO 005-02, 10.

6. Ilene Cohn and Guy S. Goodwin-Gill, *Child Soldiers: The Role of Children in Armed Conflicts* (London: Oxford University Press, 1993), 9.

7. Ibid., 23.

8. Vera Achvarina and Simon Reich, "No Place to Hide," in *Child Soldiers in the Age of Fractured States*, ed. Gates and Reich (Pittsburgh: University of Pittsburgh Press, 2010), 56, reprinted from *International Security* 31, no. 1 (Summer 2006): 127–64, citing Martha Finnemore, *National Interests in International Society* (Ithaca: Cornell University Press, 1996), 158, and Ronald L. Jepperson, Alexander Wendt, and Peter J. Katzenstein, "Norms, Identity, and Culture in National Security," in *The Culture of National Security: Norms and Identity in World Politics*, ed. Peter J. Katzenstein (New York: Columbia University Press, 1996), 45.

9. Erik Stakelbeck, "Kiddie Jihad: Child Bombers Terror's Newest Weapon," CBN News, April 23, 2010, http://cbn.com/cbnnews/world/2010/April/Kiddy-Jihad-Child-Bombers-Terrors-Newest-Weapon (URL no longer active, accessed June 15, 2013). See also Brooke Goldstein and Alistair Leyland, *The Making of a Martyr*, A2B Film Productions, April 2006, further information at https://www.imdb.com/title/tt0932666/?ref_=ttpl_pl_tt.

10. Many countries decreased or limited child recruitment as a result of the Child Soldiers Prevention Act, signed into law in December 2008 by President George W. Bush.

11. Katie Zavadski, "ISIS's New Child Executioner Speaks English," *Daily Beast*, February 2, 2016, http://www.thedailybeast.com/articles/2016/02/04/isis-s-new-child-executioner-speaks-english.html.

12. We are grateful to James Fearon and Scott Gates for having suggested this approach in preliminary drafts of papers and chapters that led to this book.

13. Most of them also note that the phenomenon is not new, and that child soldiers existed in the United States and Europe for centuries before the rise of modern childhood.

14. Susan Shepler, "The Social and Cultural Context of Child Soldiering in Sierra Leone" (paper presentation, Techniques of Violence in Civil War workshop, Oslo, August 20–21, 2004), 5.

15. Peter Hammond, *The Children of Mozambique's Killing Fields* (Eureka Springs, AR: Center on War and the Child, 1989), quoted in Cohn and Goodwin-Gill, *Child Soldiers*, 26.

16. Alex Vines, *RENAMO Terrorism in Mozambique* (Bloomington: Indiana University Press, 1991), 95–96.

17. Jo Becker, *Campaigning for Children: Strategies for Advancing Children's Rights* (Palo Alto, CA: Stanford University Press, 2017), 112.

18. Save the Children, "Invisible Wounds: The Impact of Six Years of War on the Mental Health of Syria's Children," 2017, https://www.savethechildren.org.uk/content/dam/global/reports/emergency-humanitarian-response/invisible-wounds.pdf.

19. Joby Warrick, *Black Flags: The Rise of ISIS* (New York: Penguin, 2015), 285.

20. Save the Children, "Invisible Wounds," 7–10.

21. Save the Children, "Mosul's Children Mentally Scarred by Brutal Conflict," July 5, 2017, https://www.savethechildren.org.uk/news/media-centre/press-releases/mosuls-children-mentally-scarred-by-brutal-conflict.

22. Shepler, "Social and Cultural Context," 4–5.

23. Jamie Dettmer, "Steeped in Martyrdom, Cubs of the Caliphate Groomed as Jihadist Legacy," Voice of America, July 6, 2017, https://www.voanews.com/a/islamic-state-cubs-of-the-caliphate/3931042.html.

24. Becker, *Campaigning for Children*, 9.

25. Shepler, "Social and Cultural Context," 3.

26. Mia Bloom and Charlie Winter, "How a Woman Joins ISIS," *Daily Beast*, December 6, 2015, https://www.thedailybeast.com/how-a-woman-joins-isis.

27. Shepler, "Social and Cultural Context," 7.

28. Becker, *Campaigning for Children*, 6.

29. Ibid., 9.

30. Ibid., 8–9.

31. *Children of War: Report from the Conference on Children of War*, Stockholm, May–June 1991 (Lund: Raoul Wallenberg Institute, 1991), 18. According to the CRC, a child is "anyone under 18 unless under the law applicable to the child, majority is attained earlier." It is worth noting that the original definition for a child combatant was fifteen and was then raised universally to eighteen, although youth can volunteer for military service. See http://www.child-soldiers.org/international_standards.php.

32. In 2012, the court convicted Thomas Lubanga Dyilo, a rebel commander from the Democratic Republic of the Congo, of recruiting and using child soldiers.

33. Jean-Marie Henckaerts and Louise Doswald-Beck, eds., *Customary International Humanitarian Law* (Cambridge: International Committee of the Red Cross and Cambridge University Press, 2005), rules 136 and 156; Rome Statute of the International Criminal Court, adopted July 17, 1998, UN Doc.A/CONF.183/9 (1998), entered into force July 1, 2002, arts. 8(2)(b)(xxvi) and 8(2)(e)(vii).

34. Quoted in Cohn and Goodwin-Gill, *Child Soldiers*, 62.

35. Ibid., 64.

36. Ali Akbar Mahdi, *Teen Life in the Middle East* (Westport, CT: Greenwood, 2003), 2.

37. Cohn and Goodwin-Gill, *Child Soldiers*.

38. Shepler, "Social and Cultural Context," 2.

39. Kate Douglas, *Contesting Childhood: Autobiography, Trauma and Memory* (New Brunswick, NJ: Rutgers University Press, 2010), 6.

40. Chris Jenks, *Childhood* (London: Routledge, 1996), 127–28.

41. Cohn and Goodwin-Gill, *Child Soldiers*, 24.

42. Tanya Zayed (former deputy director, Roméo Dallaire Foundation, Child Soldiers Initiative), interview with Mia Bloom, December 2015.

43. The host Neal Conan observed on National Public Radio that "there are reasons for each of these apparently arbitrary milestones and arguments that some of these rights should be made dependent on an individual's ability to handle them or rather than a calendar, that instead of voting age or drinking age or driving age, we ought to decide on an age of responsibility." "When Does Responsibility Begin? 16, 18, 21?," *Talk of the Nation*, National Public Radio, October 7, 2009, https://www.npr.org/templates/story/story.php?storyId=113579236.

44. Betsy Perabo, "The Innocent Enemy: Children at War and the Boundaries of Combatancy," International Society for Military Ethics, accessed August 1, 2018, http://isme.tamu.edu/JSCOPE03/Perabo03.html.

45. Robert Tynes and Bryan R. Early, "Governments, Rebels, and the Use of Child Soldiers in Internal Armed Conflicts" (paper presentation, American Political Science Association, Seattle, September 2011). See also Robert Tynes, *Tools of War, Tools of State* (Albany: SUNY Press, 2018).

46. English Common Law formulated *doli incapax* in the work *Countrey Justice*, by Michael Dalton in 1619. Dalton. (1619). Countrey Justice (1619), 223–24. Crofts: Murdoch University, 2008, http://socyberty.com/issues/doli-incapax-an-issue-for-all-to-discuss/#ixzz1pITxBSwV. See also William Blackstone, *Commentaries on the Laws of England, Volume 4: A Facsimile of the First Edition of 1765–1769* (Chicago: University of Chicago Press, 1979), 23. For children between the ages of ten and fourteen, *doli incapax* is a rebuttable presumption, meaning that innocence will not be held if the prosecution can produce evidence contrary to the presumption of innocence. This means that the prosecution has the burden of proof, and if evidence is not produced to back up the accusations, the court will dismiss the charge.

47. Take, for example, the use of five-year-old Isa Dare to kill four IS prisoners by using a remote detonator on February 11, 2016. Maayan Groisman, "New ISIS Video Shows Child Soldier Blowing Up Four Alleged Spies," *Jerusalem Post*, February 11, 2016, https://www.jpost.com/Middle-East/ISIS-Threat/WATCH-New-ISIS-video-shows-child-solider-blowing-up-four-alleged-spies-444570.

48. We are grateful to Michael Jablonski, at Georgia State University, for conducting this analysis.

49. Franz Boas, "Museums of Ethnology and Their Classification," *Science* 9, no. 228 (June 17, 1887): 589.

50. P. W. Singer, "Books: *Children at War*," Q&A transcript, *Washington Post*, June 12, 2006, http://www.washingtonpost.com/wp-dyn/content/discussion/2006/05/22/DI2006052200785.html.

51. Becker, *Campaigning for Children*, 113.

52. "Children's Rights: Iran," US Library of Congress, last updated July 2, 2015, https://www.loc.gov/law/help/child-rights/iran.php.

53. This tracks with how children in the developing world are categorized in their school systems. For example, in Nigeria, *kole* students are ages four to fourteen, and *titiburi* students are ages fifteen through twenty. Virginia Comoli, *Boko Haram: Nigeria's Islamist Insurgency* (London: Hurst, 2015), 73.

54. Mahdi, *Teen Life*, 2.

55. Ibid.

56. Field notes from confidential interviews, Swat Valley, Pakistan, 2013.

57. Mia Bloom, *Dying to Kill: The Allure of Suicide Terrorism* (New York: Columbia University Press, 2005), chap. 4; Jan Goodwin, "When the Suicide Bomber Is a Woman," *Marie Claire*, January 16, 2008, http://marieclaire.com/world-reports/news/international/female-suicide-bomber; Mia Bloom, *Bombshell: Women and Terrorism* (Philadelphia: University of Pennsylvania Press, 2011), 209.

58. Becker, *Campaigning for Children*, 111.

59. Field research in Pakistan, February 3–6, 2013. Also see John Horgan, "Child Suicide Bombers Find Safe Haven," CNN, March 27, 2013, http://cnn.com/2013/03/27/world/asia/pakistan-anti-taliban/.

60. Sabaoon, *Confidential Annual Report* (Lahore, Pakistan, December 2014), 18.

61. Coalition to Stop the Use of Child Soldiers (website), "How Do Children Become Involved?" https://www.child-soldiers.org/FAQs/how-do-children-become-involved-in-military-organisations (accessed August 1, 2010).

62. United Nations General Assembly, "Promotion and Protection of the Rights of Children: Impact of Armed Conflict on Children," note by the secretary-general, August 26, 1996, http://www.un.org/ga/search/view_doc.asp?symbol=A/51/306.

63. *Child Soldiers: Implications for US Forces*, 7.

64. Singer, "Terrorists Must Be Denied."

65. Barry Ames, "Methodological Problems in the Study of Child Soldiers," in Gates and Reich, 14–26.

66. Human Rights Watch, "'Maybe We Live and Maybe We Die': Recruitment and Use of Children by Armed Groups in Syria," June 22, 2014, http://hrw.org/report/2014/06/22/maybe-we-live-and-maybe-we-die/recruitment-and-use-children-armed-groups-syria, documents that boys as young as fourteen assisted in support roles for the "Free Syrian Army" in 2012 onward. See also Human Rights Watch, "Armed Groups Send Children into Battle: Recruitment under the Guise of Education," June 22, 2014, http://hrw.org/news/2014/06/22/syria-armed-groups-send-children-battle.

67. For example, the UN documented nineteen child bombers for Boko Haram in 2016 when the actual number of bombers was five times that many. Sally Hayden, "Boko Haram: Huge Rise in Children Used as 'Human Bombs' by Islamists in Nigeria UN Warns," *Independent*, August 22, 2017, https://www.independent.co.uk/news/world/africa/boko-haram-child-suicide-bombers-west-africa-unicef-nigeria-islamist-terrorists-a7907166.html.

68. Nelly Lahoud, *Jihad's Path to Self-Destruction* (New York: Columbia University Press, 2010), chap. 5.

69. Sheikh Abdullah Azzam, *Defence of Muslim Lands: The First Obligation after Iman*, February 1, 2002, accessed at religioscope.com/info/doc/jihad/azzam_defence_3_chap1.htm.

70. Bloom, *Dying to Kill*; Mia Bloom, "Mother. Daughter. Sister. Bomber," *Bulletin of the Atomic Scientist* 61, no. 6 (November 1, 2005), http://journals.sagepub.com/doi/pdf/10.2968/061006015; Bloom, *Bombshell*, 2011.

71. Cord Jefferson, "Osama's Last Wish? For His Children Not to Become Terrorists," *Al-Anba'a*, May 5, 2011, http://good.is/post/osama-s-last-wish-for-his-children-to-not-become-terrorists/.

72. Quoted in Julia Glum, "Who Is Hamza bin Laden? Osama's Son Encourages Terrorist Attacks in New al-Qaeda Propaganda Video," *Newsweek*, May 13, 2017, http://www.newsweek.com/al-qaeda-hamza-bin-laden-608814.

73. Glum, "Who Is Hamza bin Laden?"

74. Isabel Kershner, "Palestinians Honor a Figure Reviled in Israel as a Terrorist," *New York Times*, March 11, 2010, https://www.nytimes.com/2010/03/12/world/middleeast/12westbank.html.

75. Goldstein and Leyland, *Making of a Martyr*, 2006.

76. Ami Pedahzur, *Suicide Terrorism* (Cambridge: Cambridge University Press, 2005), 132–35; Arnon Regular, "Six Suicides from Hebron: Friends in the Football Team," (Hebrew) *Ha'aretz*, May 29, 2003; Arnon Regular, "Hebron's Playing, Plotting Field," *Ha'aretz*, May 30, 2003, http://www.haaretz.com/hebron-s-playing-and-plotting-field-1.89861. See also

Ali Waked, "Hamas: Dimona Attack a 'Heroic Act,'" February 4, 2008, https://www.ynet news.com/articles/0,7340,L-3502461,00.html, and Israeli Foreign Ministry Spokesman, "Two Suicide Bombers Carry out Attack against Israeli Civilians in Dimona," February 4, 2008, http://mfa.gov.il/MFA/PressRoom/2008/Pages/Suicide%20bombers%20attack%20 citizens%20in%20Dimona%204-Feb-2008.aspx.

77. Regular, "Hebron's Playing and Plotting Field."

78. Israel Ministry of Foreign Affairs, "Participation of Children and Teenagers in Terrorist Activity during the 'al-Aqsa' Intifada," January 30, 2003, http://mfa.gov.il/MFA/ MFA-Archive/2003/Pages/Participation%20of%20Children%20and%20Teenagers%20 in%20Terrori.aspx.

79. Hannah Beech Farkhar, "The Child Soldiers," *Time*, July 13, 2002, cited in Betsy Perabo, "Innocent Enemy."

80. Director of the "Jihad Academy" in Tulkarm, attended by children ages eight to twelve and run by the Palestinian Islamic Jihad, interviewed in Goldstein and Leyland, *Making of a Martyr*, 2006.

81. Victoria Forbes Adam, *Child Soldiers Global Report 2008*, London, April 2008, http://childsoldiersglobalreport.org/content/occupied-palestinian-territory.

82. Goldstein and Leyland, *Making of a Martyr*, 2006.

83. Israel Ministry of Foreign Affairs, "Participation of Children and Teenagers," 2003.

84. Mia Bloom, "Armed and 'Innocent'?," *Monkey Cage* (blog), *Washington Post*, September 11, 2014, http://washingtonpost.com/blogs/monkey-cage/wp/2014/09/11/armed-and-innocent/. See also news.vice.com/article/islamic-state-releases-eid-greetings-video-purporting-to-show-foreign-fighters.

85. Aasmund Lok, interview, "In Mosul, ISIS' Youngest Recruits Still Face Brutality and an Uncertain Future," *PBS NewsHour*, November 22, 2017.

86. Mia Bloom, John Horgan, and Charlie Winter, *Depictions of Children and Youth in the Islamic State's Martyrdom Propaganda* (Combatting Terrorism Center report, February 18, 2016), https://ctc.usma.edu/depictions-of-children-and-youth-in-the-islamic-states-martyrdom-propaganda-2015–2016/.

87. John Horgan, *The Psychology of Terrorism* (London: Routledge, 2014), 137.

88. "PA Names Ramallah Street after Hamas Terror Mastermind," April 7, 2010, https:// www.haaretz.com/1.5471901.

89. Bloom, *Bombshell*, 29.

90. Arie Kruglanski has written extensively on a theory of goal systems and the "quest for personal significance" among Palestinian suicide bombers; see Kruglanski et al., "A Theory of Goal Systems," in *Advances in Experimental Social Psychology*, vol. 34, ed. M. P. Zanna (San Diego: Academic Press, 2002), 331–78, http://faculty.chicagobooth.edu/ ayelet.fishbach/research/advances.pdf.

91. Lloyd deMause, *The Emotional Life of Nations* (New York: Karnac Press, 2002), chap. 3.

92. "When Does Responsibility Begin?"

93. Stanley Milgram, "Behavioral Study of Obedience," Journal of Abnormal and Social Psychology 67 (1963): 371–78; Philip Zimbardo et al., "The Stanford Prison Experiment: A Simulation Study of the Psychology of Imprisonment Conducted August 1971 at Stanford University," slide show, https://web.stanford.edu/dept/spec_coll/uarch/exhibits/ Narration.pdf.

94. Emma Cardeli, Mia Bloom, Heidi Ellis, Sarah Gillespie, and Tanya Zayed, "Exploring the Social-Ecological Factors That Mobilize Children into Violence in Central American Gangs and Terrorist Groups" (working paper, 2018).

95. D. E. Woods, *The Conditions of Employment for Children at War* (Geneva: Quaker United Nations Office, 1991), 1.

96. Becker, *Campaigning for Children*, 112.

97. *Child Soldiers: Implications for US Forces*, 16–17.

98. Peter W. Singer, "Caution: Children at War," *Parameters* (Winter 2001–2): 40–56, http://carlisle-www.army.mil/usawc/Parameters/Articles/01winter/singer.htm.

99. "LTTE," South Asia Terrorism Portal, 2008, http://satp.org/satporgtp/countries/shrilanka/terroristoutfits/LTTE.HTM.

100. Associated Press, "Taliban Tricked Me into Wearing a Bomb, Boy Says," MSNBC, June 26, 2007, http://msnbc.msn.com/id/19420772/ns/world_news-south_and_central_asia/t/taliban-tricked-me-wearing-bomb-boy-says/#.T2NbNhyaK4A.

101. "Al-Qaeda Training Child Terrorists: US," *The Age*, February 7, 2008, http://theage.com.au/news/world/alqaeda-training-child-terrorists-us/2008/02/07/1202234020900.html.

102. Tynes and Early, "Governments," 2.

103. Associated Press, "Taliban Puts Afghan Boy in Suicide Vest," *USA Today*, June 25, 2007, http://usatoday.com/news/world/2007-06-25-afghan-boy-bomber_N.htm.

104. Interviews at Sabaoon conducted by the authors, Swat Valley, Pakistan, March 2013.

105. Thomas Ricks, *The Gamble: General Petraeus and the American Military Adventure in Iraq* (New York: Penguin, 2006), 169.

106. Archive of "Documenting the Virtual Caliphate," ONR project N00014-16-1-3174, Georgia State University (in progress).

107. Al-Qaeda Training Child Terrorists, 2008.

108. Milton Viorst and Patt Derian, "Iran Using Children to Clear Minefields," *The Age*, March 23, 1984, https://news.google.com/newspapers?nid=1300&dat=19840323&id=3kFVAAAAIBAJ&sjid=g5UDAAAAIBAJ&pg=2276,1118583&hl=en.

109. Ibid.

110. Terence Smith, "Iran: Five Years of Fanaticism," *New York Times*, February 12, 1984.

111. Efraim Karsh, *The Iran-Iraq War 1980–1988 (Essential Histories)* (London: Bloomsbury, 2002), 54–60. See also Joseph Cummins, *The War Chronicles: From Flintlocks to Machine Guns* (Beverly, MA: Fairwinds, 2009), 407.

112. Warrick, *Black Flags*, 289.

113. *The Paris Principles: Principles and Guidelines on Children Associated with Armed Forces or Armed Groups* (UNICEF, February 2007), 7.

114. Bloom, Horgan, and Winter, "Depictions of Children."

115. Miles Amore, "What to Do with Islamic State's Child Soldiers?," *Economist*, June 17, 2017, https://www.economist.com/news/middle-east-and-africa/21723416-cubs-caliphate-are-growing-up-what-do-islamic-states-child.

116. John Horgan, Mia Bloom, Chelsea Daymon, and Hicham Tiflati, "A New Age of Terror: Older Fighters in the Caliphate," *CTC Sentinel*, May 4, 2017, https://ctc.usma.edu/posts/a-new-age-of-terror-older-fighters-in-the-caliphate.

117. Nasra Hassan, "Arsenal of Believers: Talking to Human Bombs," *New Yorker*, November 19, 2001, http://newyorker.com/magazine/2001/11/19/an-arsenal-of-believers.

118. Israel Orbach, "Terror Suicide: How Is It Possible?," *Archives of Suicide Research* 8, no. 1 (2004): 115–30, http://informaworld.com/smpp/content~db=all~content=a714492255~frm=titlelink.

119. Ariel Merari, *Driven to Death: Psychological and Social Aspects of Suicide Terrorism* (London: Oxford University Press, 2010).

120. Carol Winkler, Kareem el Damanhoury, Aaron Dicker, and Anthony Lemieux, "The Medium Is Terrorism: Transformation of the About to Die Trope in *Dabiq*," *Terrorism and Political Violence*, June 13, 2017 https://www.tandfonline.com/doi/full/10.1080/09546553.2016.1211526.

121. David Brooks, "The Culture of Martyrdom: How Suicide Bombing Became Not Just a Means but an End," *Atlantic*, June 2002, http://theatlantic.com/magazine/archive/2002/06/the-culture-of-martyrdom/302506/.

122. Orbach, "Terror Suicide."

123. Philip G. Zimbardo, "A Situationist Perspective on the Psychology of Evil: Understanding How Good People Are Transformed into Perpetrators," in *The Social Psychology of Good and Evil: Understanding Our Capacity for Kindness and Cruelty*, ed. Arthur G. Miller (New York: Guilford, 2004), 21–51.

124. Mia Bloom, "Women and Terrorism," Oxford University Research Encyclopedia, January 17, 2017, http://politics.oxfordre.com/view/10.1093/acrefore/9780190228637.001.0001/acrefore-9780190228637-e-124.

125. Cindy Ness, *Female Terrorism and Militancy: Agency, Utility and Organization* (London: Routledge, 2008), 28–29.

126. Jeremy Cooke, "School Trains Suicide Bombers," BBC, July 18, 2001, http://bbc.co.uk/2/hi/middle_east/1446003.stm.

127. Brooks, "Culture of Martyrdom," 2002.

128. *Al-Hayat al-Jadida*, July 29, 2010, cited in Itamar Marcus and Barbara Crook, "Summer Camp Named after Terrorist Dalal Mughrabi," Palestinian Media Watch, July 29, 2010, http://palwatch.org/main.aspx?fi=549&doc_id=2826.

129. Mohammed Hanif, "Taliban's Main Fear Is Not Drones but Educated Girls," *Guardian* (UK), November 12, 2012, https://www.theguardian.com/commentisfree/2012/nov/04/pakistan-extremists-girls-education.

130. Quoted in "UK: Children Involved in Terrorism," CNN, November 13, 2007, http://www.cnn.com/2007/WORLD/europe/11/05/britain.threat/index.html.

131. "The Mental Trauma Caused by Prevent on Muslim Children," 5 Pillars UK, February 21, 2016, https://5pillarsuk.com/2016/02/21/the-mental-trauma-caused-by-prevent-on-muslim-children/.

132. "Lancashire 'Terrorist House' Row 'Not a Spelling Mistake,'" BBC, January 20, 2016, http://www.bbc.com/news/uk-england-lancashire-35354061.

133. Anwar al-Awlaki, "44 Ways to Support Jihad," NEFA Foundation, February 5, 2009, http://www.nefafoundation.org/miscellaneous/FeaturedDocs/nefaawlaki44wayssupportjihad.pdf.

134. John F. Burns and Miguel Helft, "YouTube Withdraws Cleric's Videos," *New York Times*, November 4, 2010, http://www.nytimes.com/2010/11/05/world/05britain.html?_r=1.

135. Amira Choueiki and Theodore Karasik, "Conduits to Terror—Classifying the Methods of Middle Eastern Terrorist Recruitment," Institute for Near East and Gulf Military Analysis, Special Report No. 11, November 2010, http://www.inegma.com/special-report detail.aspx?rid=27&t=Conduits-to-Terror---Classifying-the-Methods-of-Jihadist-and-Middle-Eastern-Terrorist-Recruitment.

136. Zoe Murphy and Yoko Sari, "Bali Bomber Ali Imron Becomes Comic Book Character," BBC News, August 6, 2010, https://www.bbc.com/news/world-asia-pacific-10893889.

2. CHILD SOLDIERS VERSUS CHILDREN IN TERRORIST GROUPS

1. However, an eighteen-year-old leader of the al-Aqsa Martyrs' Brigades in Palestine (recruited when he was twelve) is quoted as saying, "I think teens are better fighters than adults because of a teen's willingness to fight and resist the army is strong." Brooke Goldstein and Alistair Leyland, *The Making of a Martyr*, A2B Film Productions, April 2006, further information at https://www.imdb.com/title/tt0932666/?ref_=ttpl_pl_tt.

2. F. K. Owen, "Political Violence, Psychology and Youth" in *Political Violence, Organised Crime, Terror and Youth*, ed. M. Demet Ulusoy (Amsterdam: IOS, 2008), 36.

3. Ibid., 36–37.

4. Robert Tynes, *Tools of War, Tools of State: When Children Become Soldiers* (Albany: SUNY Press, 2018).

5. Special Representative of the Secretary-General Children and Armed Conflict report lists fifty-one armed groups and seven governments, https://childrenandarmed conflict.un.org/wp-content/uploads/2015/10/15-18739_Children-in-Conflict_FINAL-WEB.pdf.

6. Neil G. Boothby and Christine M. Knudsen, "Children of the Gun," *Scientific American* 282, no. 6 (2000): 60–66, cited in Fidan Korkut Owen, "Political Violence, Psychology and Youth," September 2007, 20, http://www.nato.hacettepe.edu.tr/nato/Nato/Papers/KOR KUT.Rev1.pdf.

7. Countries most often include Afghanistan, the Central African Republic, Eritrea, Iraq, the Philippines, Rwanda, and Thailand.

8. As discussed in chapter 1, there is a need to nuance what constitutes childhood. Some preliminary work is being done toward this end—for example, in Christina Rose Clark-Kazak, "Towards a Working Definition and Application of Social Age in International Development Studies," working paper, York University, Toronto, http://yorkspace.library. yorku.ca/xmlui/bitstream/handle/10315/7847/C-KTowardsSocialAge.pdf?sequence=1

9. Vera Achvarina and Simon Reich, "No Place to Hide: Refugees Displaced Person and the Recruitment of Child Soldiers," *International Security* 31, no. 1 (Summer 2006), 127–64.

10. Ilene Cohn and Guy S. Goodwin-Gill, *Child Soldiers: The Role of Children in Armed Conflicts* (London: Oxford University Press, 1993).

11. P. W. Singer, *Children at War* (Berkeley: University of California Press, 2006).

12. Peter W. Singer, "Western Militaries Confront Child Soldiers Threat," *Jane's Intelligence Review*, January 1, 2005, 2.

13. Former terrorists (names withheld), interviews with Mia Bloom, Belfast, Northern Ireland, October 2010.

14. Ibid.

15. Ted Galen Carpenter, "Al Qaeda and the Taliban: Not the Same Thing," *National Interest*, June 18, 2014, http://nationalinterest.org/feature/al-qaeda-the-taliban-not-the-same-thing-10691.

16. Mia Bloom, John Horgan, and Charlie Winter, *Depictions of Children and Youth in the Islamic State's Martyrdom Propaganda* (Combatting Terrorism Center report, February 18, 2016), http://ctc.usma.edu/posts/depictions-of-children-and-youth-in-the-isla mic-states-martyrdom-propaganda-2015–2016.

17. Anthony Cordesman, "The Changing Nature of War in the Middle East and North Africa," *Harvard International Review*, January 14, 2017, http://hir.harvard.edu/ article/?a=14493.

18. Rachel Stohl, "Targeting Children: Small Arms and Children in Conflict," *Brown Journal of International Affairs* 9, no. 1 (2002): 281, https://www1.essex.ac.uk/armedcon/ story_id/Targeting%20Children-%20Small%20Arms%20and%20Children%20in%20 Conflict.pdf.

19. Coalition to Stop the Use of Child Soldiers, accessed January 1, 2014, http://www. child-soldiers.org, citing Human Rights Watch, "Child Soldiers: Global Survey Shows New Trends." June 11, 2001, https://www.hrw.org/news/2001/06/11/child-soldiers-global-survey-shows-new-trends.

20. Elisabeth Schauer and Thomas Elbert, "The Psychological Impact of Child Soldiering," in *Trauma Rehabilitation after War and Conflict*, ed. Erin Martz (New York:

Springer, 2010), 311. See also Richard Gilbert, "Child Soldiers and Small Weapons of Mass Destruction," Public Address 2004, http://www.richardgilbert.ca/achart/public_html/articles/publications/child_soldiers.html ("The extraordinary increase in the number of child soldiers since the cold war is closely related to the equally large number of small arms flooding the world market, advertised as 'Cheaper than dirt' on the internet").

21. David M. Rosen, *Armies of the Young: Child Soldiers in War and Terrorism* (New Brunswick, NJ: Rutgers University Press, 2005), 5.

22. Lois Legge, "Fighting to Let Children Be Children." *Chronicle Herald*, April 12, 2013, http://www.childsoldiers.org/fighting-to-let-children-be-children/.

23. Mia Bloom, "Constructing Expertise: Terrorist Recruitment and 'Talent Spotting' in the PIRA, Al Qaeda and ISIS," *Studies in Conflict and Terrorism* 40, no. 7 (2017): 603–23, http://www.tandfonline.com/doi/full/10.1080/1057610X.2016.1237219.

24. Christopher Blattman, "What's Special about Being a Child Soldier? Estimating the Labor Market Impact of Involuntary Military Service Using a Survey of Young Ex-combatants in Uganda," PhD diss., University of California, Berkeley, 2007, 3.

25. Data collected from YPG news sources and Kurdish-language websites that promoted Kurdish *Peshmerga* (prepared to die) and fighters.

26. Syrian Observatory for Human Rights, "IS Organization Continues in Attracting Children, and Recruits More Than 400 Children from 'Ashbal al-Khilafah,'" March 24, 2015, http://www.syriahr.com/en/?p=15709.

27. Arwa Damon, "Taliban Brainwashes Kids with Visions of Virgins," CNN, January 6, 2010, cited in Kalsoon Lakhani, "Indoctrinating Children: The Making of Pakistan's Suicide Bombers," CTC Sentinel, June 2010, https://ctc.usma.edu/posts/indoctrinating-children-the-making-of-pakistan's-suicide-bombers, 11–13.

28. Bernd Beber and Christopher Blattman, "The Logic of Child Soldiering and Coercion," *International Organization* 67, no. 1 (January 2013): 65–104.

29. Jo Becker, "Child Recruitment in Burma, Sri Lanka, and Nepal," in *Child Soldiers in the Age of Fractured States*, ed. Scott Gates and Simon Reich (Pittsburgh: University of Pittsburgh Press, 2009), 108.

30. Gates and Reich, *Child Soldiers*, 111.

31. Child Soldiers International, *Louder Than Words* (London, 2012), 18. Syria is listed on a table on page 21.

32. United Nations, Report of the Secretary-General, General Assembly Security Council, *Children and Armed Conflict*, April 20, 2016, http://www.un.org/ga/search/view_doc.asp?symbol=s/2016/360&referer=/english/&Lang=E.

33. Our data showed forty-nine children during this same time period.

34. United Nations, Report of the Secretary-General, General Assembly Security Council, "Children and Armed Conflict," A/72/865–S/2018/465, May 16, 2018, http://undocs.org/en/s/2018/465; see also https://childrenandarmedconflict.un.org/countries-caac/syria/.

35. Jamie Dettmer, "Kurdish Militia Accused of Using Child Soldiers in Syria," Voice of America, July 15, 2015, https://www.voanews.com/a/hrw-kurdish-forces-using-child-fighters-despite-pledge-to-demobilize/2862390.html.

36. In theory, this would be the first time the United States is overtly arming Syrian rebels, but the Syrian Arab Coalition (SAC) is wholly dependent on the YPG, which by some estimates has 50,000 fighters. . . . "The U.S. will now help the YPG-SAC "advance toward" Raqqa, but not try to seize it," the *New York Times* reports. "Rather, the aim is to isolate Raqqa and cut it off from travel and supply lines northeast and northwest of the city." Kyle Orton, "Why Solely Backing the PYD against the Islamic State Is a Mistake," October 20, 2015, https://kyleorton1991.wordpress.com/2015/10/20/why-solely-backing-the-pyd-against-the-islamic-state-is-a-mistake/. The average age for the YPG fighters (of which we have coded seventy in total) was fifteen for both boys and girls.

37. Human Rights Watch, "Iraq: Armed Groups Using Child Soldiers," December 22, 2016, https://www.hrw.org/news/2016/12/22/iraq-armed-groups-using-child-soldiers-0.

38. We are extremely grateful for Tanya Zayed's assistance in securing UN data on these tallies. Children and Armed Conflict, https://childrenandarmedconflict.un.org/countries-caac/syria/.

39. The UN does explain the monitoring and reporting mechanism (MRM), but that mechanism does not function in every country where children are recruited, so data from certain countries is impossible to access or is not reliable. The NGO Watchlist (http://watchlist.org/the-countries) compiles the MRM information so the public can better understand the situation of children and conflict.

40. United Nations Office of the Special Representative and Secretary-General, Children and Armed Conflict, "Child Recruitment and Use," https://childrenandarmedconflict.un.org/six-grave-violations/child-soldiers/.

41. Orton, "Why Solely Backing." This also violates the US Child Soldiers Prevention Act. Jo Becker, *Campaigning for Children: Strategies for Advancing Children's Rights* (Palo Alto, CA: Stanford University Press, 2017), 126.

42. Orton, "Why Solely Backing."

43. Luis F. Fuentes, "You'll Have to Learn Not to Cry," ASPI editorial, March 11, 2008, http://www.airpower.maxwell.af.mil/apjinternational/apj-s/2008/1tri08/editorialeng.html.

44. Becker, *Campaigning for Children*, 115.

45. Barry Ames, "Methodological Problems in the Study of Child Soldiers," in Gates and Reich, *Child Soldiers*, 14.

46. Jack Moore, "More Than 31,000 Pregnant Women under Islamic State Rule in Iraq and Syria," *Newsweek*, March 7, 2016, http://www.newsweek.com/more-31000-pregnant-women-under-isis-rule-iraq-and-syria-434091.

47. Human Rights Watch ("Maybe We Live and Maybe We Die," June 22, 2014, https://www.hrw.org/report/2014/06/22/maybe-we-live-and-maybe-we-die/recruitment-and-use-children-armed-groups-syria) documented that boys as young as fourteen assisted the Free Syrian Army in support roles from 2012 onward. See also Human Rights Watch, "Syria: Armed Groups Send Children into Battle: Recruitment Under the Guise of 'Education,'" June 22, 2014, https://www.hrw.org/news/2014/06/22/syria-armed-groups-send-children-battle.

48. Bloom, "Constructing Expertise."

49. Aymenn Jawad al-Taymimi, "The Dawn of the Islamic State of Iraq and Ash Sham," *Middle East Forum*, January 2014, no. 27, http://www.meforum.org/3732/islamic-state-iraq-ash-sham.

50. As the concept is understood in criminology, a "deviant peer" is a child used to lure other children at the behest of adults.

51. Syrian Observatory for Human Rights, "IS Organization Continues."

52. The German Interior Ministry required doctors to register all newborns born with Down syndrome, deformities, or epilepsy for euthanizing. Olga Khazan, "Remembering the Nazis' Disabled Victims," *Atlantic*, September 3, 2014, https://www.theatlantic.com/health/archive/2014/09/a-memorial-to-the-nazis-disabled-victims/379528/. However, much of the Nazi programs were inspired by American racial policies in the 1920s and 1930s. For the American roots of eugenics, see Edwin Black, *War against the Weak: Eugenics and America's Campaign to Create a Master Race* (Westport, CT: Dialogue Press, 2012).

53. The allegation that IS has exploited children with disabilities has been verified by NGOs and human rights groups focused on the exploitation of children with disabilities in Syria. Khawla Wakkaf and Arlene S. Kanter, "Children with Disabilities and the Syrian Conflict," *Impunity Watch* 7 (2016–2017), http://impunitywatch.com/wp-content/uploads/2017/05/IW_Final_Review.pdf.

54. Emma Glanfield, "How Much More Depraved Can ISIS Get? Group's Sharia Judges Order Children with Down Syndrome and Other Disabilities to Be Killed in Chilling Echo of the Nazis," *Daily Mail*, December 14, 2015, http://www.dailymail.co.uk/news/arti cle-3358840/How-depraved-ISIS-Group-s-Sharia-judges-order-children-s-syndrome-disabilities-killed-chilling-echo-Nazis.html, cited in Wakkaf and Kanter, "Children with Disabilities."

55. Ammar al-Shammary and Nabeel Gilgamesh, "ISIL Grooming Children to Be Killers: Terrorists Cross a New Line, Groom Kids for Brutality," *USA Today*, March 12, 2015, international edition, March 13, 2015, https://www.pressreader.com/usa/usa-today-international-edition/20150313/281479274889935.

56. Becker, *Campaigning for Children*, 113.

57. Ishmael Beah, *A Long Way Gone: Memoirs of a Boy Soldier* (Sarah Crichton Books, 2007), http://www.alongwaygone.com.

58. Becker, *Campaigning for Children*, 111.

59. Jihad Anton Shomaly, *Use of Children in the Occupied Palestinian Territories: Perspective on Child Soldiers* (Ramallah: Defence for Children International, Palestine Section, July 2004). It is worth noting that Che Guevara advocated that the ideal age for the fighter was twenty-five to thirty-five; anyone younger than that did not have the physical and mental fortitude needed for guerrilla warfare. "An individual who sets out at that age, abandoning their home, children, and entire world," he said, "must have thought through their responsibility and made a firm decision not to retreat a step. There are extraordinary cases of children who have reached the highest ranks of our Rebel Army as combatants, but this is not common. For every one of them who displayed great fighting qualities, there were dozens who should have been returned to their homes and who frequently became a dangerous burden for the guerilla band," Ernesto Che Guevara, *Guerilla Warfare* (Melbourne, Victoria: Ocean Press, 2012), 56.

60. Vera Achvarina and Simon Reich, "No Place to Hide: Refugees, Displaced Persons, and the Recruitment of Child Soldiers," *International Security* 31, no. 1 (2006): 127–64; Alfred Babatunde Zack-Williams, "Child Soldiers in the Civil War in Sierra Leone," *Review of African Political Economy* 28, no. 87 (2001): 73–82.

61. Alfred Babatunde Zack-Williams, "Child Soldiers in Sierra Leone and the Problems of Demobilisation, Rehabilitation and Reintegration into Society: Some Lessons for Social Workers in War-Torn Societies," *Social Work Education* 25, no. 2 (2006): 119–28.

62. Michael D. Jackson, *In Sierra Leone* (Durham, NC: Duke University Press, 2004), 159; also cited in Susan Shepler, "The Social and Cultural Context of Child Soldiering in Sierra Leone" (paper presentation, Techniques of Violence in Civil War workshop, Oslo, August 20–21, 2004), 23.

63. Jessica Stern and J. M. Berger, "Raising Tomorrow's Mujahideen: The Horrific World of ISIS's Child Soldiers," *Guardian* (UK), March 10, 2015, https://www.theguard ian.com/world/2015/mar/10/horror-of-isis-child-soldiers-state-of-terror.

64. Interviews at Sabaoon conducted by Mia Bloom, Swat Valley, Pakistan, March 2013.

65. John Horgan, "Child Suicide Bombers Find Safe Haven," CNN, March 27, 2013, http://www.cnn.com/2013/03/27/world/asia/pakistan-anti-taliban/.

66. Confidential interviews with Mia Bloom, Malakand, Pakistan, February 2013.

67. Confidential interviews with Mia Bloom, Malakand, Pakistan, February 2013.

68. Izhar Ullah, "Smoking Dead Scorpions Is KP's Latest Dangerous Addiction," *Dawn*, April 15, 2016, https://www.dawn.com/news/1252264.

69. Confidential interviews with Mia Bloom, Malakand, Pakistan, February 2013.

70. The Refugee Law Project has done a lot of work on sexual violence against boys in conflict settings. Chris Dolan and Onen David, "Investigation Guidelines on Conflict Related SGBV against Men and Boys," February 29, 2016, Refugee Law Project, The Hague,

https://www.refugeelawproject.org/files/others/IICI_Guidelines_for_Investigating_Con
flict_Related_SGBV_against_Men_and_Boys.pdf.

71. Renee Lewis, "UN Report Condemns Torture, Sexual Abuse of Syrian Children,"
Al Jazeera International, February 5, 2014, http://america.aljazeera.com/articles/2014/
2/5/un-report-condemnsunspeakableatrocitiesagainstsyrianchildren.html.

72. Lucinda Woodward and Peter Galvin, "Halfway to Nowhere: Liberian Former
Child Soldiers in a Ghanaian Refugee Camp," *Annals of the Association of American Geographers* 99, no. 5 (2009): 1003–11, https://doi.org/10.1080/00045600903245698.

73. Indeed, there is still variation within the African militias: children who were with
their families and were separated, children who were abducted, children who volunteered
for many reasons, and children who fight with family (such as Mai Mai groups).

74. A UNICEF report stated, "All families in OECD countries today are aware that
childhood is being re-shaped by forces whose mainspring is not necessarily the best interests of the child; a wide public is becoming ever more aware that many of the corrosive
social problems have their genesis in the changing ecology of childhood." UNICEF, "An
Overview of Child Well-Being in Rich Countries," Innocenti Research Center, Report
Card 7, 2007, https://www.unicef.org/media/files/pdf_01.pdf, 5–6.

75. Shepler, "Social and Cultural Context," 4–5.

76. Stohl, "Targeting Children," 286.

77. Shepler, "Social and Cultural Context," 15.

78. Myriam Denov, *Child Soldiers: Sierra Leone's Revolutionary United Front* (New
York: Cambridge University Press, 2010), 100.

79. Tynes, *Tools of War*, 11.

80. This has even been depicted in *Yoali and Mambo*, a series of children's comic
books created by the Roméo Dallaire Initiative to help the children deal with trauma and
understand what happened to them.

81. Tanya Zayed, interviews with Mia Bloom, New York City, May 2015, June 2016,
April 2017.

82. David B. Ottaway, "Child POWs: Captured Young Iranians Languish in Iraqi
Prison," *Washington Post*, July 16, 1984.

83. "Wounded Childhood: The Use of Children in Armed Conflict in Central Africa,"
April 2003 Geneva: Switzerland, International Labour Office report, 52, https://www.ilo.
org/wcmsp5/groups/public/@ed_emp/@emp_ent/@ifp_crisis/documents/publication/
wcms_116566.pdf.

84. Becker, *Campaign for Children*, 134.

85. Virginia Comolli, *Boko Haram: Nigeria's Islamist Insurgency* (London: Hurst, 2015),
22, 30.

86. Ibid., 50.

87. Ibid., 4.

88. Becker, *Campaign for Children*, 150–51.

89. Stuart Maslen, "The Use of Children as Soldiers in Africa: A Country Analysis of
Child Recruitment and Participation in Armed Conflict" (Coalition to Stop the Use of
Child Soldiers, 1999), 66.

90. Mia Bloom, "How the Islamic State Recruits and Coerces Children," The Conversation, August 23, 2016, https://theconversation.com/how-the-islamic-state-recruits-and-
coerces-children-64285.

91. Joby Warrick, *Black Flags: The Rise of ISIS* (New York: Anchor Books), 289.

92. Mia Bloom, "Ethnic Conflict, State Terror and Suicide Bombing in Sri Lanka,"
Civil Wars 6, no. 2 (Spring 2003): 54–84, http://www.tandfonline.com/doi/abs/10.1080/
13698240308402526.

93. Richard Spencer, "The World's Five Worst Terror Attacks Involving Children," *Telegraph*, December 16, 2014, http://www.telegraph.co.uk/news/worldnews/11297108/The-worlds-five-worst-terror-attacks-involving-children.html.

94. Timothy McGrath, "3 Reasons Why the Pakistani Taliban Attacked the School in Peshawar," *Global Post*, December 16, 2014, http://www.pri.org/stories/2014-12-16/3-reasons-why-pakistani-taliban-attacked-school-peshawar.

95. It should be noted that the day care center in the Alfred P. Murrah Federal Building in Oklahoma City witnessed the deaths of nineteen children who were located in the nursery attached to the building, which was bombed by two extreme right-wing activists, Timothy McVeigh and Terry Nichols, in 1995, although the nursery was collateral damage and not the terrorists' main target.

96. Roger Thurow, "Uganda: Lessons of Aboke," Chicago Council on Global Affairs, June 23, 2014, http://pulitzercenter.org/reporting/africa-uganda-aboke-lords-resistance-army-girls-abduction-boko-haram.

97. Anjana Shakya, "Experiences of Children in Armed Conflict in Nepal," *Children and Youth Services Review* 33, no. 4 (2011): 557–63.

98. Gilbert, "Child Soldiers."

99. Mia Bloom and Yannick Veilleux-Lepage, "Documenting the Virtual Caliphate: Archive of Official ISIS Propaganda." Minerva N00014-16-1-3174 (in progress).

100. Quoted in Human Rights Watch, *Early to War: Child Soldiers in the Chad Conflict* 19, no. 9 (July 2007): 22, https://www.hrw.org/reports/2007/chad0707/chad0707web.pdf.

101. Tynes, *Tools of War*, 201.

102. Jill Trenholm, Pia Olsson, Martha Blomqvist, and Beth Maina Ahlberg, "Constructing Soldiers from Boys in Eastern Democratic Republic of Congo," *Men and Masculinities* 16, no. 2 (2013): 203–27; Becker, *Campaigning for Children*, p. 113.

103. The UN estimates that as many as 30 percent of fighters in the Yemeni conflict are children. Agence Press France, "Third of Fighters in Yemen Are Children, Says Unicef," *Guardian* (UK), April 9, 2015, http://www.theguardian.com/world/2015/apr/09/third-of-fighters-yemen-children-unicef.

104. Ali al Mujahed, "In Yemen, Children—Possibly Thousands of Them—Join Fight," *Washington Post*, May 11, 2015, http://www.washingtonpost.com/world/middle_east/why-so-many-children-are-fighting-in-yemens-civil-war/2015/05/10/7602d9be-e7a8-11e4-8581-633c536add4b_story.html; Priyanka Gupta, "The Child Soldiers of Yemen." Al Jazeera, March 4, 2015, http://www.aljazeera.com/indepth/features/2015/03/child-soldiers-yemen-150302081855823.html.

105. "In Mosul, ISIS' Youngest Recruits Still Face Brutality and an Uncertain Future," *PBS NewsHour*, November 22, 2017.

106. Shu Uchida, *Human Security and Child Protection in Armed Conflict: The Issue of Child Soldiers in 2010* (Saarbrucken, Germany: Lambert Academic, 2017).

107. *Child Soldiers Global Report 2004* (London: Coalition to Stop the Use of Child Soldiers, 2004), 54, http://www.essex.ac.uk/armedcon/story_id/child_soldiers_csc_nov_2004.pdf.

108. Bernd Beber and Christopher Blattman, "The Logic of Child Soldiering and Coercion," *International Organizations* 67, no. 1 (January 2013): 78, https://www.nyu.edu/projects/beber/files/Beber_Blattman_LogicOfChildSoldiering.pdf.

109. Ibid.

110. Myriam Denov and Richard Maclure, "Girls and Small Arms in Sierra Leone: Victimization, Participation and Resistance," and Felicity Szesnat, "Small Arms and Rape as a System of War: A Case Study of the Democratic Republic of the Congo," both chapters

in *Sexed Pistols: The Gendered Impacts of Small Arms and Light Weapons*, ed. Vanessa Farr, Henri Myrttinen, and Albrecht Schnabel (New York: United Nations University Press, 2009).

111. Richard Maclure and Myriam Denov, "'I Didn't Want to Die So I Joined Them': Structuration and the Process of Becoming Boy Soldiers in Sierra Leone," *Terrorism and Political Violence* 18, no. 1 (2006): 119–35.

112. Trenholm et al., "Constructing Soldiers," 217.

113. Dara Kay Cohen, *Rape during Civil War* (Ithaca, NY: Cornell University Press, 2016), 21.

114. Maslen, "Use of Children"; Charu Lata Hogg, "Sri Lanka: The Liberation Tigers of Tamil Eelam (LTTE) and Child Recruitment," Coalition to Stop the Use of Child Soldiers, Forum on Armed Groups and the Involvement of Children in Armed Conflict at Chateau de Bossey, Switzerland, July 4–7, 2006.

115. Blattman, "What's Special," 18.

116. Anthony Vinci, "The Strategic Use of Fear by the Lord's Resistance Army," *Small Wars & Insurgencies* 16, no. 3 (2005): 371.

117. Paul Richards, *Fighting for the Rain Forest: War, Youth and Resources in Sierra Leone* (Oxford: International Africa Institute, 1996), 29.

118. Maura Conway, "'At Risk' or 'A Risk': The Portrayal of 'Jihadi' Brides in the UK Press," paper presented at the University College Cork, Ireland, March 2015.

119. "Anything you obtain of war booty—then indeed, for Allah is one fifth of it and for the Messenger and for [his] near relatives and the orphans, the needy, and the [stranded] traveler." Having concubines is related to several things: First, if an Islamic state exists. Second, if the Islamic state makes offers for other territories to join Islam or enter into treaties with them. Third, if those territories refuse offers of peace, or if they announce war.

120. Mia Bloom, Frontline: The Predatory Nature of ISIS's Recruitment of Western Women, 2014, https://soundcloud.com/frontlinepbs/isis-panel-mia-bloom-on-women.

121. Mona Al-Lami, "Martyrs Wanted: ISIS' Devastating Defector Problem," *National Interest*, February 26, 2015, http://nationalinterest.org/blog/the-buzz/martyrs-wanted-isis-devastating-defector-problem-12330?page=2.

122. Conversation between Hani al-Siba'i and ISIS fighter on Telegram, https://justpaste.it/obw9.

3. LEARNING TO HATE

1. UN Secretary-General, *Children in Armed Conflict: Report of the Secretary-General*, UN Document A/70/836, April 20, 2016, par. 105. See also Jo Becker, *Campaigning for Children: Strategies for Advancing Children's Rights* (Palo Alto, CA: Stanford University Press, 2017), 151.

2. Billy Briggs, "One Million Iraqi Children 'Have Lost Out on Education under Islamic State,'" Their World, November 9, 2016, http://theirworld.org/news/one-million-iraqi-children-lose-out-on-education-under-islamic-state.

3. Becker, *Campaigning for Children*, 151.

4. Virginia Comoli, *Boko Haram: Nigeria's Islamist Insurgency* (London: Hurst, 2015), 70–72.

5. Wole Soyinka, "Wole Soyinka on Nigeria's Anti-Christian Terror Sect Boko Haram," *Newsweek*, January 6, 2012, http://www.newsweek.com/wole-soyinka-nigerias-anti-christian-terror-sect-boko-haram-64153.

6. This was allegedly the case until Boko Haram started to deploy female suicide bombers in June 2014.

7. See, e.g., Alan Kruger and Jitka Maleckova, "Education, Poverty, Political Violence and Terrorism: Is There a Causal Connection?" (NBER working paper no. 9074, July 2002, nber.org/papers/w9074).

8. Marc Sageman, *Understanding Terror Networks* (Philadelphia: University of Pennsylvania Press, 2004), and Marc Sageman, *Leaderless Jihad: Terror Networks in the Twenty-First Century* (Philadelphia: University of Pennsylvania Press, 2008).

9. Claude Berrebi, "Evidence about the Link between Education, Poverty and Terrorism among Palestinians," *Peace Economics, Peace Science and Public Policy* 13, no. 1 (2007). Also see Diego Gambetta and Steffen Hertog, *Engineers for Jihad: The Curious Connection between Violent Extremism and Education* (Princeton, NJ: Princeton University Press, 2016); Kruger and Maleckova, "Education, Poverty, Political Violence."

10. Kruger and Maleckova, "Education, Poverty, Political Violence."

11. Sabaoon Report, "Confidential Briefing," December 4, 2014; Darcy M. E. Noricks, "Disengagement and Deradicalization: Processes and Programs," in *Social Science for Counterterrorism: Putting the Pieces Together*, ed. Paul K. Davis and Kim Cragin (Santa Monica: RAND Corporation, 2009), http://www.rand.org/pubs/monographs/2009/RAND_MG849.pdf.

12. Sabaoon Report, "Confidential Briefing."

13. Sarah Lischer, "War, Displacement, and the Recruitment of Child Soldiers," Ford Institute for Human Security, 10, 14, https://www.files.ethz.ch/isn/28058/2006_4_War_Displacement.pdf.

14. Ilene Cohn and Guy S. Goodwin-Gill, *Child Soldiers: The Role of Children in Armed Conflicts* (London: Oxford University Press, 1993), chap. 2.

15. Sharmeen Obaid-Chinoy, interview with ejournal USA, "Terrorism and Children: An Interview with Sharmeen Obaid-Chinoy," May 31, 2007, http://sharmeenobaidfilms.com/24.

16. Ibid.

17. Brooke Goldstein and Alistair Leyland, *The Making of a Martyr*, A2B Film Productions, April 2006, https://www.imdb.com/title/tt0932666/?ref_=ttpl_pl_tt, cited by Children's Rights Institute, http://www.childrensrightsinstitute.org.

18. Obaid-Chinoy, "Terrorism and Children."

19. See Eli Berman, *Radical, Religious and Violent: The New Economics of Terrorism* (Cambridge, MA: MIT Press, 2009); and Sageman, *Leaderless Jihad*.

20. Jamie Dettmer, "Steeped in Martyrdom, Cubs of the Caliphate Groomed as Jihadist Legacy," Voice of America, July 6, 2017, https://www.voanews.com/a/islamic-state-cubs-of-the-caliphate/3931042.html.

21. It was later discovered that there was one case of a child returning to the Pakistani Taliban because his brother was a local commander and his family ties to the group prevailed over the deradicalization program. Interviews at Sabaoon conducted by the authors, Swat Valley, Pakistan, March 2014.

22. Stuart Maslen, "The Use of Children as Soldiers in Africa: A Country Analysis of Child Recruitment and Participation in Armed Conflict" (Coalition to Stop the Use of Child Soldiers, 1999).

23. Cohn and Goodwin-Gill, *Child Soldiers*, 25.

24. Jacob Olidort, *Inside the Caliphate's Classroom: Textbooks, Guidance Literature, and Indoctrination Methods of the Islamic State* (Washington, DC: Washington Institute for Near East Policy, 2016).

25. Cole Bunzel, "From Paper State to Caliphate: The Ideology of the Islamic State" (Brookings Institution analysis paper no. 19, Brookings Institution, Washington, DC, March 2015), 27, citing Aymenn al-Tamimi, https://www.brookings.edu/wp-content/uploads/2016/06/The-ideology-of-the-Islamic-State.pdf.

26. Khales Joumah, "Profiling Mosul's Extremist Celebrity the Minister of Education, the Man with Two Horns," November 20, 2014, Niqash, http://www.niqash.org/en/articles/society/3580/.

27. Rafaqat Ali Gohar, "ISIS Is Reportedly Using Saudi Arabia Textbooks in Schools because They Promote the Same Ideology as ISIL," YouTube video (1:49), posted September 25, 2006, https://www.youtube.com/watch?v=CqnOtpOCCrg.

28. Aymenn Jawad al-Tamimi, "Archive of Islamic State Administrative Documents," Aymenn Jawad al-Tamimi, Pundicity, January 27, 2015, http://www.aymennjawad.org/2015/01/archive-of-islamic-state-administrative-documents.

29. Joumah, "Profiling Mosul's Extremist Celebrity."

30. Emile Nakhleh, "The Islamic State's Ideology Is Grounded in Saudi Education," Inter Press Service News Agency, October 31, 2014, http://www.ipsnews.net/2014/10/opinion-the-islamic-states-ideology-is-grounded-in-saudi-education/.

31. Joumah, "Profiling Mosul's Extremist Celebrity."

32. Nikita Malik and Alexandra Bissoondath, "Islamic State: Children of the 'Caliphate,'" Newsweek, March 7, 2016, http://www.newsweek.com/children-caliphate-isis-islamic-state-cubs-iraq-syria-434192.

33. "The Islamic State's Educational Regulations in Raqqa Province," Aymenn Jawad Al-Tamimi Pundicity, August 28, 2014, no. 9, http://www.aymennjawad.org/2014/08/the-islamic-state-educational-regulations-in, cited in Malik and Bissoondath, "Islamic State."

34. Malik and Bissoondath, "Islamic State," 28.

35. "More Than 1 Million Children Living under ISIS in Iraq Have Missed Out on Education," Save the Children, November 6, 2016, https://www.savethechildren.org/us/about-us/media-and-news/2016-press-releases/more-than-1-million-children-living-under-isis-in-iraq-have-miss.

36. John Huddy, "'G' Is for Gun: Troops Find ISIS Textbooks Used to Brainwash Children," Fox News, March 7, 2017, http://www.foxnews.com/world/2017/03/07/g-is-for-gun-troops-find-isis-textbooks-used-to-brainwash-children.html.

37. "More Than 1 Million."

38. Niqash, "Back to School in Mosul: The ISIS Curriculum," Daily Beast, October 29, 2015, http://www.thedailybeast.com/back-to-school-in-mosul-the-isis-curriculum.

39. Judy Woodruff, "In Mosul, ISIS' Youngest Recruits Still Face Brutality and an Uncertain Future," PBS NewsHour, November 22, 2017.

40. John Horgan, Max Taylor, Mia Bloom, and Charlie Winter, "From Cubs to Lions: A Six Stage Model of Child Socialization into the Islamic State." Studies in Conflict & Terrorism 40, no. 7 (2017).

41. Lizzie Dearden, "ISIS Releases Video of Child Soldiers Training for Jihad in Syria Camp for 'Cubs of the Caliphate,'" Independent (UK), February 23, 2015, http://www.independent.co.uk/news/world/middle-east/isis-releases-video-of-child-soldiers-training-for-jihad-in-syria-camp-for-cubs-of-the-caliphate-10065239.html. See also Report on the Protection of Civilians in the Armed Conflict in Iraq: 11 December 2014–30 April 2015, 23, cited in Nikita Malik, Children of the Islamic State, 37, http://www.globalgovernancewatch.org/library/doclib/20160317_TheChildrenofIslamicState.pdf.

42. Tom Wyke, "Children Use AK47 Rifles in Choreographed ISIS Propaganda Video," https://www.dailymail.co.uk/news/article-2847831/Children-use-AK47-rifles-choreographed-ISIS-propaganda-video.html.

43. Loaa Adel, "Video: Child Recruited by Isis Reveals 'Cubs of Caliphate's Camps' Secrets," Iraqi News, November 22, 2016, http://www.iraqinews.com/iraq-war/video-child-recruited-isis-reveals-cubs-caliphates-camps-secrets/.

44. Leila Zerrougui, former Special Representative of the Secretary-General for Children and Armed Conflict from September 2012 to May 2017 interview with Mia Bloom, New York City, March 2016.

45. *Prima Facie* newsletter (Geneva: UNHCR Department of International Protection, April 2002), 4, cited in Lischer, "War, Displacement," 15.

46. Cohn and Goodwin-Gill, *Child Soldiers*, 31.

47. Fieldwork was conducted under the auspices of the MacArthur Foundation, December 2002–January 2003, in Tamil-controlled areas in the North.

48. In a partnership called the Global Coalition to Protect Education from Attack, UN agencies and NGOs have addressed attacks on students, teachers, schools, and other education institutions during armed conflict. The coalition's report, *Lessons in War 2015: Military Use of Schools and Universities during Armed Conflict*, details the practice globally since 2005. Human Rights Watch, "Schools as Battlegrounds: Protecting Students, Teachers, and Schools from Attack," March 19, 2010, http://www.protectingeducation.org/sites/default/files/documents/hrw_schools_battlegrounds.pdf.

49. Zama Coursen-Neff, "The Right to Education," *Harvard International Review*, February 25, 2016, http://hir.harvard.edu/12838-2/.

50. Zama Coursen-Neff, presentation of Human Rights Watch report to the Council on Foreign Relations, New York City, May 2016. See also Coursen-Neff, "The Right to Education."

51. Coursen-Neff, presentation to CFR, 2016.

52. United Nations Security Council Resolution 2143, "Children and Armed Conflict," S/RES/2143 (2014), March 7, 2014, http://unscr.com/en/resolutions/2143.

53. Rommel C. Banlaoi, "The Pull of Terrorism: A Philippine Case Study," in *Youth and Terrorism: A Selection of Articles*, ed. Datin Paduka Rashidah Ramli (Kuala Lumpur: Southeast Asia Regional Centre for Counterterrorism, 2014), 21–27.

54. Daniel Bar Tal, Sami Adwan, and Bruce Wexler, "Victims of Our Own Narratives: Portrayals of the Other in Israeli and Palestinian Schoolbooks," *Political Psychology* 37, no. 2 (June 2014): 1–3.

55. Ibid., 13.

56. Ibid., 1.

57. In 2014, Israel received $3.1 billion in total aid from the United States. Nick Thompson, "Seventy-Five Percent of U.S. Foreign Military Financing Goes to Two Countries," CNN, November 11, 2015, http://www.cnn.com/2015/11/11/politics/us-foreign-aid-report/.

58. Edward Wong, "U.S. to End Funding to U.N. Agency That Helps Palestinian Refugees," *New York Times*, August 31, 2018, https://www.nytimes.com/2018/08/31/us/politics/trump-unrwa-palestinians.html.

59. Foreign Relations Authorization Act, Fiscal Years 2006 and 2007, H.R. 2601, 109th Cong. (2005–2006).

60. Robert I. Friedman, "Kahane and the Plan behind the Fury," *Washington Post*, April 22, 1990, https://www.washingtonpost.com/archive/opinions/1990/04/22/kahane-the-plan-behind-the-fury/1c5f0521-42e7-43c7-8218-82bb530088fd/?utm_term=.7235ea272726.

61. Rafi Nets-Zehngut, "Israeli Approved Textbooks and the 1948 Palestinian Exodus," *Israel Studies* 18, no. 3 (2013): 41–68.

62. The twelfth-grade text *Arabic Language, Analysis, Literature and Criticism* reads, "Palestine's war ended with a catastrophe that is unprecedented in history, when the Zionist gangs stole Palestine and expelled its people from their cities, their villages, their lands and their houses, and established the State of Israel" (104) cited by *Jerusalem Post*, February 25, 2007.

63. Gerald Cromer, *A War of Words: Political Violence and Public Debate in Israel* (London: Routledge, 2005).

64. Mia Bloom, "Atrocities and Armed Conflict: State Consolidation in Israel, 1948–1956," *Journal of Conflict, Security, and Development* 1, no. 3 (December 2001): 55–78.

65. In fact, Rabin was assassinated by Yigal Amir, an Israeli right-wing extremist, in 1995. Lidar Gravé-Lazi, "Critics Say New Israeli Civics Textbook Whitewashes and Distorts Reality," *Jerusalem Post*, May 10, 2016, http://www.jpost.com/Israel-News/Critics-say-new-Israeli-civics-textbook-whitewashes-and-distorts-reality-453570.

66. Bar Tal and Adwan, "Victims of Our Own Narratives," 46.

67. The Armalite was the symbol of armed struggle, such that the IRA referred to its strategy as one existing "between the ballot box [voting] and the Armalite [armed struggle]." Danny Morrison, one of the leaders of Sinn Fein—the political wing of the IRA—said in 1981, "Who here really believes that we can win the war through the ballot box? But will anyone here object if, with a ballot box in one hand and the Armalite in the other, we take power in Ireland?" Evan Malgrem, "Desynchronized Irish Republican Political Strategy: The Dichotomy of the Armalite and the Ballot Box," https://www.earl ham.edu/media/1683298/desynchronized-irish-republican-political-strategy.pdf, cited in "IRA: War, Ceasefire, Endgame?," BBC News, 2001, http://news.bbc.co.uk/hi/english/static/in_depth/northern_ireland/2001/provisional_ira/1981.stm.

68. Roozbeh Shirazi, "Islamic Education in Afghanistan: Revisiting the United States' Role," *CR: The New Centennial Review* 8, no. 1, Cultures of Occupation (Spring 2008): 214–15. See also Hashem Sahraie and Janet Sahraie, "Educational Development in Afghanistan: History of the Teachers College, Columbia University Educational Assistance Program, 1954–1971," PhD diss., Teachers College, Columbia University, 1974.

69. There is a debate as to whether jihad constitutes the sixth pillar of Islam. While most devout Muslims object to this terminology, it has been used by the right wing and even by US military propaganda to allege that the lesser jihad (holy war) is a hidden sixth pillar.

70. Shirazi, "Islamic Education in Afghanistan," 211–33.

71. Ibid., 213.

72. Faegheh Shirazi, *Muslim Women in War and Crisis: Representation and Reality* (Austin: University of Texas Press, 2010), 59.

73. Christopher Candland, "Pakistan's Recent Experience in Reforming Islamic Education," in *Education Reform in Pakistan: Building for the Future*, ed. Shahid Javid Burki and Robert M. Hathaway (Washington, DC: Woodrow Wilson International Center for Scholars, 2005), 16.

74. David B. Ottaway, "U.S. Eyes Money Trails of Saudi-Backed Charities," *Washington Post*, August 19, 2004, http://www.washingtonpost.com/wp-dyn/articles/A13266-2004 Aug18.html.

75. Shirazi, "Islamic Education in Afghanistan," 222.

76. Quoted ibid., 223.

77. Horgan, cited in Craig Davis, "'A' Is for Allah, 'J' Is for Jihad," *World Policy Journal* 19, no. 1 (2002): 92–93.

78. Huddy, "G Is for Gun."

79. Quentin Sommerville and Riam Dulati, "An Education in Terror," BBC, August 2017, http://www.bbc.co.uk/news/resources/idt-sh/an_education_in_terror.

80. Jacob Olidort, interview with Mia Bloom, Washington, DC, August 2016.

81. Sommerville and Dulati, "Education in Terror."

82. Ammar Cheikh Omar and Saphora Smith, "Generation ISIS: When Children Are Taught to Be Terrorists," NBC News, October 21, 2017, https://www.nbcnews.com/storyline/isis-uncovered/generation-isis-when-children-are-taught-be-terrorists-n812201.

83. Niqash, "Back to School."

84. Omar and Smith, "Generation ISIS."

85. Jibran Ahmad, "Pakistan Province Rewrites Textbooks to Satisfy Islamic Conservatives," *Reuters*, October 30, 2014, https://uk.reuters.com/article/uk-pakistan-education/

pakistan-province-rewrites-text-books-to-satisfy-islamic-conservatives-idUKKBN0IJ1G
620141030.

86. Candland, "Pakistan's Recent Experience."

87. Shirazi, *Islamic Education in Afghanistan*, 227.

88. Vaishali Honawar, "Targeted for Violence, Schools Still Make Strides in Afghanistan," *Education Week*, June 20, 2007.

89. Becker, *Campaigning for Children*, 151.

90. Thomas H. Johnson and M. Chris Mason, "No Sign until the Burst of Fire: Understanding the Pakistan-Afghanistan Frontier," *International Security* 32, no. 4 (April 2008): 57. See also Global Coalition to Protect Education from Attack, "Education Under Attack 2014," http://protectingeducation.org/sites/default/files/documents/eua_2014_brochure_lowres_final_embargo.pdf.

91. Suzanne Goldenberg, "Why Women Are Poor at Science, by Harvard President," *Guardian*, January 18, 2005, https://www.theguardian.com/science/2005/jan/18/education sgendergap.genderissues.

92. Isobel Coleman, "The Payoff from Women's Rights," *Foreign Affairs* (May–June 2004): 80, http://link.galegroup.com/apps/doc/A116195631/WHIC?u=albertak12&xid=ee82c5cc. Coleman summarizes Larry Summers's argument made in his address to the Economic Development Institute of the World Bank, "Investing in All the People: Educating Women in Developing Countries." EDI Seminar Paper #45, World Bank, Washington, DC, 1994, http://faculty.ucr.edu/~jorgea/econ181/summers_women94.pdf.

93. Coleman, "Payoff from Women's Rights," 83–84. See also Summers, "Investing in All the People," 23.

94. The first madrassa was reportedly founded in Baghdad in 1067 by Mullah Nasiruddin Tusi. Candland, "Pakistan's Recent Experience," 4.

95. Wadad Kadi, "Education in Islam: Myths and Truths," *Comparative Education Review* 50, no. 3 (2006): 319.

96. Francis Robinson, "Knowledge, Its Transmission, and the Making of Muslim Societies," in *Cambridge Illustrated History of the Islamic World*, ed. Francis Robinson (Cambridge: Cambridge University Press, 1996), 242, quoted in Candland, "Pakistan's Recent Experience," 10.

97. Candland, "Pakistan's Recent Experience," 11.

98. Ranjit Sau, "Reconstruction of Afghanistan into a Modern Nation." *Economic and Political Weekly* 37, no. 2 (January 12–18, 2002): 119.

99. David Montero, "Pakistan: The Lost Generation," *FRONTLINE/World*, February 23, 2010.

100. Najibullah Quraishi, "Behind Taliban Lines," *Frontline/PBS*, transcript, February 23, 2010, https://www.pbs.org/wgbh/pages/frontline/talibanlines/etc/script.html.

101. Barnett R. Rubin and Andrea Armstrong, "Regional Issues in the Reconstruction of Afghanistan," *World Policy Journal* 20, no. 1 (Spring 2003): 38.

102. Peter W. Singer, "Pakistan's Madrassas: Ensuring a System of Education not Jihad" (Brookings Institution analysis paper no. 14, Brookings Institution, Washington, DC, November 2001), quoted in Tahir Andrabi, Jishnu Das, Asim Ijaz Khwaja, and Tristan Zajonc, "Religious School Enrollment in Pakistan: A Look at the Data," *Comparative Education Review* 50, no. 3 (August 2006): 449.

103. National Commission on Terrorist Attacks upon the United States, *The 9/11 Commission Report* (Washington, DC: Executive Agency Publications, July 22, 2004), sec. 12.2, 367. Others have questioned the connection between madrassa attendance and engagement in terrorism. See, for example, Peter Bergen and Swati Pandey, "The Madrassa Myth," *New York Times*, June 14, 2005.

104. Andrabi et al., "Religious School Enrollment in Pakistan," 447.

105. Candland, "Pakistan's Recent Experience," 6.

106. Ibid., 5–6.

107. Paul Watson, "In Pakistan's Public Schools, Jihad Still Part of Lesson Plan," *Los Angeles Times*, August 18, 2005.

108. Montero, "Pakistan."

109. Karin Brulliard, "In Pakistan, Reform School Attempts to Offer Child Fighters Chance at a New Life," *Washington Post*, March 29, 2010.

110. Quoted in Dettmer, "Steeped in Martyrdom."

4. PATHWAYS TO INVOLVEMENT

1. Alexander Smith, "Young Afghan Girl Wearing Suicide Vest Says Family Coerced Her to Target Police Checkpoint," NBC News, January 7, 2014, worldnews.nbcnews.com/_news/2014/01/07/22215719-young-afghan-girl-wearing-suicide-vest-says-family-coerced-her-to-target-police-checkpoint?lite.

2. Jason Straziuso, "Boy: Taliban Recruited Me to Bomb Troops," *Washington Post*, June 25, 2007, http://washingtonpost.com/wp-dyn/content/article/2007/06/25/AR20070 62501072_pf.html.

3. Associated Press, "Taliban Tricked Me into Wearing a Bomb, Boy Says." NBC News, June 26, 2007, http://nbcnews.com/id/19420772/ns/world_news-south_and_central_ asia/t/taliban-tricked-me-wearing-bomb-boy-says.

4. Associated Press, "Taliban Accused of Forcing 6-Year-Old to Wear Suicide Vest," AP archive video, June 23, 2007, YouTube Video (2:18), http://youtube.com/watch?v=fr ITHbxqrj4.

5. Mia Bloom and John Horgan, "New Terror Weapon: Little Girls," CNN, January 7, 2014, http://www.cnn.com/2014/01/07/opinion/bloom-horgan-afghanistan-girl/index.html.

6. Journeyman TV, "Taliban's Child Fighters," YouTube video (27:05), https://you tube.com/watch?v=arq0are-2Rg.

7. John Horgan, *The Psychology of Terrorism* (London: Routledge, 2014), 77.

8. Tore Bjørgo citing John Horgan, "Dreams and Disillusionment: Engagement in and Disengagement from Militant Extremist Groups," *Crime, Law and Social Change* 55, no. 4 (2011): 277.

9. Jeff Victoroff, "The Mind of the Terrorist: A Review and Critique of Psychological Approaches," *Journal of Conflict Resolution* 49, no. 1 (2005): 35, http://www.jstor.org/stable/30045097.

10. Zeina Karam, *Life and Death in ISIS: How the Islamic State Builds its Caliphate*, Associated Press, AP Editions, New York: Mango Media, November 16, 2016, chap. 13.

11. Martha Crenshaw, "Theories of Terrorism: Instrumental and Organizational Approaches," *Journal of Strategic Studies* 10, no. 4 (1987): 13–31; Bruce Hoffman, "Change and Continuity in Terrorism," *Studies in Conflict and Terrorism* 24, no. 5. (2001): 417–28.

12. Audrey Kurth Cronin, "How al-Qaida Ends: The Decline and Demise of Terrorist Groups," *International Security* 31, no. 1 (2006): 7–48.

13. Audrey Kurth Cronin, "How al-Qaida Ends: The Decline and Demise of Terrorist Groups," *International Security* 31, no. 1 (2006): pp. 7–48.

14. Seth Jones and Martin Libicki, *How Terrorist Groups End: Lessons for Countering al Qa'ida* (RAND, 2008), http://www.rand.org/content/dam/rand/pubs/monographs/2008/RAND_MG741-1.pdf.

15. Bryan C. Price, "Targeting Top Terrorists: How Leadership Decapitation Contributes to Counterterrorism," *International Security* 4, no. 36 (2012): 9–46.

16. According to Leila Zerrougui, the UN special representative for children and armed conflict, IS kidnapped four hundred (Sunni) children from Anbar Province and

80. Aasmund Lok, interview, "In Mosul, ISIS' Youngest Recruits Still Face Brutality and an Uncertain Future," *PBS NewsHour*, November 22, 2017.

81. Arwa Damon, "Child Fighter Tormented by ISIS," CNN, November 13, 2014, http://www.cnn.com/2014/11/12/world/meast/syria-isis-child-fighter/index.html.

82. RT, "Boys of War: ISIS Recruit, Kidnap Children as Young as 10 yo," July 2, 2014, http://rt.com/news/170052-isis-kidnap-recruit-children/.

83. "In Mosul, ISIS' Youngest Recruits."

84. Ali Hashem, "Teenage Suicide Bomber Hopes for Second Chance," Al-Monitor, January 6, 2015, http://www.al-monitor.com/pulse/originals/2015/01/islamic-state-sui cide-bomber-baghdad.html.

85. Ibid.

86. Tim Arango, "A Boy in ISIS. A Suicide Vest. A Hope to Live," *New York Times*, December 26, 2014, http://www.nytimes.com/2014/12/27/world/middleeast/syria-isis-recruits-teenagers-as-suicide-bombers.html.

87. Raja Razek, Nick Patton Walsh, and Nick Thompson, "A 13-year-Old Witness to ISIS' Beheadings and Crucifixion in Syria," CNN, December 30, 2014, http://www.cnn.com/2014/08/28/world/meast/syria-isis-atrocities-boy/index.html.

88. Ibid.

89. John Kerry, "Remarks at the Carnegie Endowment for International Peace," US Department of State (website), October 28, 2015, http://state.gov/secretary/remarks/2015/10/248937.htm.

90. Lauren Said-Moorhouse, "Iraq Stops Would-Be Child Suicide Bomber for ISIS," CNN, August 23, 2016, http://www.cnn.com/2016/08/22/middleeast/would-be-child-suicide-bomber-iraq/index.html. It is worth noting that different news sources listed the child's age as being between eleven and fifteen, although he was eventually determined to be thirteen.

91. Simon Cottee and Keith Hayward, "Terrorist (E)motives: The Existential Attractions of Terrorism," *Studies in Conflict & Terrorism* 34, no. 12 (2011): 963–86.

92. Arnold P. Goldstein, *The Psychology of Group Aggression* (West Sussex, UK: John Wiley and Sons, 2002); Jane L. Wood, "Understanding Gang Membership: The Significance of Group Processes," *Group Processes and Intergroup Relations* 17, no. 6 (2014): 710–29, https://doi.org/10.1177/1368430214550344.

93. Roméo Dallaire cited in Augustine Brannigan, *Beyond the Banality of Evil: Criminology and Genocide* (Oxford: Oxford University Press, 2013), 79.

94. Ian A. Elliott, "A Self-Regulation Model of Sexual Grooming," *Trauma, Violence, & Abuse* 18, no. 1 (2015): 83–97.

95. Catherine Bott, W. James Castan, Rosemary Lark, and George Thompson, *Recruitment and Radicalization of School-Aged Youth by International Terrorist Groups: Final Report* (Arlington, VA: Homeland Security Institute for US Department of Education, Office of Safe and Drug-Free Schools, April 2009).

96. Mia Bloom, "In Defense of Honor: Women and Terrorist Recruitment on the Internet," *Journal of Postcolonial Studies* 4, no. 1 (2013): 153.

97. Kumar Ramakrishna, "Understanding Youth Radicalization in the Age of ISIS," *E-IR* (February 11, 2016), http://e-ir.info/2016/02/11/understanding-youth-radicalization-in-the-age-of-isis-a-psychosocial-analysis/.

98. Thomas Hegghammer, "The Recruiter's Dilemma: Signalling and Rebel Recruitment Tactics," *Journal of Peace Research* 50, no. 1 (2013): 3–16.

99. Clark McCauley and Sophia Moskalenko, "Mechanisms of Political Radicalization: Pathways toward Terrorism," *Terrorism and Political Violence* 20, no. 3 (2008): 415–33.

100. Ibid., 420.

101. Ramakrishna, "Understanding Youth Radicalization."

102. John Horgan, *Walking Away from Terrorism: Accounts of Disengagement from Radical and Extremist Movements* (London: Routledge: 2009).

103. Hegghammer, "Recruiter's Dilemma."

104. Damon, "Child Fighter Tormented."

105. John Horgan and Mia Bloom, "This Is How the Islamic State Manufactures Child Militants," Vice News, July 8, 2014, http://news.vice.com/article/this-is-how-the-islamic-state-manufactures-child-militants.

106. US General Accounting Office, *Succession Planning and Management Is Critical Driver of Organizational Transformation* (GAO-04-127T) (Washington, DC: US General Accounting Office, 2003), http://gao.gov/new.items/d04127t.pdf.

107. Cynthia D. McCauley, Lorrina J. Eastman, and Patricia J. Ohlott, "Linking Management Selection and Development through Stretch Assignments," *Human Resource Management* 34, no. 1 (1995): 93–115; Sim B. Sitkin, Kelly E. See, C. Chet Miller, Michael W. Lawless, and Andrew M. Carton, "The Paradox of Stretch Goals: Organizations in Pursuit of the Seemingly Impossible," *Academy of Management Review* 36, no. 3 (2011): 544–66.

108. Logan, "Child Suicide Bombers."

109. John Horgan and Max Taylor, "Disengagement, De-radicalization, and the Arc of Terrorism: Future Directions for Research," in *Jihadi Terrorism and the Radicalisation Challenge: European and American Experiences*, ed. Rik Coolsaet (Farnham, UK: Ashgate, 2011), 173–86.

110. Ben Rossington and Ben Russell, "Security Services Probe Whether 'British' Child Carrying out ISIS Execution Is Son of Jihadi Sally Jones," August 26, 2016, The Mirror (UK), https://www.mirror.co.uk/news/world-news/security-services-probe-whether-british-child-8714031.

111. Taryn Tarrant Cornish, "ISIS Recruiter Sally Jones' Son JoJo Still Alive in Jihadist Training Camp," November 15, 2017, Express, https://www.express.co.uk/news/world/879723/ISIS-Syria-Sally-Jones-son-JoJo-Dixon-killed-airstrike-terror-training.

112. Tom Wyke and Darren Boyle, "ISIS Release Shocking New Video of Child Soldiers from Kazakhstan Being Trained with AK47s," *Daily Mail* (UK), November 22, 2014, http://dailymail.co.uk/news/article-2845531/ISIS-release-shocking-new-video-child-soldiers-Kazakhstan-trained-AK47s.html?ito=embedded.

113. Ibid.

114. Global Voices, Advox, "Kazakh Authorities Censor Videos of Children in ISIS Training Camps," November 26, 2014, http://advox.globalvoices.org/2014/11/26/kazakh-authorities-censor-videos-of-children-in-isis-training-camps/. For the original posting, see http://kloop.kg/blog/2014/11/24/video-islamskogo-gosudarstva-deti-iz-kazahstana-ugrozhayut-ubivat-nevernyh/, November 24, 2014.

115. Ian A. Elliott, "A Self-Regulation Model of Sexual Grooming."

116. J. M. Berger, "Tailored Online Interventions: The Islamic State's Recruitment Strategy," *CTC Sentinel* 8, no. 10 (2015): 19–23.

117. Ibid., 22.

118. Özerdem and Podder, "Disarming Youth Combatants."

119. Stephen Webster, Julia Davidson, Antonia Bifulco, Petter Gottschalk, Vincenzo Caretti, Thierry Pham, Julie Grove-Hills, et al., *European Online Grooming Project: Final Report* (London: European Online Grooming Project, 2012), http://natcen.ac.uk/media/843993/european-online-grooming-project-final-report.pdf.

120. The extensive list of terrorist groups extends well beyond the official Foreign Terrorist Organization list of forty-nine groups. Based on data collected by Victor Asal, Karl Rathemeyer, and Jonathan Wilkenfeld (Big, Allied and Dangerous [BAAD] database, https://www.start.umd.edu/baad/database), over 580 groups can be defined as having used terrorist tactics.

121. Bloom, *Dying to Kill*, chap. 5.

122. James A. Piazza, "The Determinants of Domestic Right-Wing Terrorism in the USA: Economic Grievance, Societal Change and Political Resentment," *Conflict Management* 34, no. 1 (2015): 52–80.

123. Laurence Steinberg, "A Social Neuroscience Perspective on Adolescent Risk-Taking," *Developmental Review* 28, no. 1 (2008): 78–106; Charles F. Geier, "Adolescent Cognitive Control and Reward Processing: Implications for Risk Taking and Substance Abuse," *Hormones and Behavior* 64, no. 2 (2013): 333–42.

124. Horgan and Taylor, "Disengagement."

125. Horgan, *Psychology of Terrorism*.

126. Derek B. Cornish and Ronald V. Clarke, "The Rational Choice Perspective," in *Environmental Criminology and Crime Analysis*, ed. Richard Wortley and Lorraine Mazerolle (Cullompton, UK: Willan, 2008), 21–47; Richard Wortley and Stephen R. Smallbone, *Situational Prevention of Child Sexual Abuse*, Crime Prevention Studies 19 (Monsey, NY: Criminal Justice Press, 2006).

127. Zeina Karam and Vivian Salama, "Islamic State Group Recruits, Exploits Children," *Military Times*, November 23, 2014, http://militarytimes.com/story/military/2014/11/23/islamic-state-group-recruits-exploits-children/19444427/.

5. PATHWAYS TO INVOLVEMENT

1. Carl C. Bell and Esther Jenkins, "Traumatic Stress and Children," *Journal of Health Care for the Poor and Underserved* 2, no. 1 (Summer 1991): 175–85, http://www.giftfromwithin.com/pdf/children.pdf.

2. Samir Qouta, Raija-Leena Punamaki, and Eyad El-Sarraj, "Prevalence and Determinants of PTSD among Palestinian Children Exposed to Military Violence," *European Child & Adolescent Psychiatry* 12, no. 6 (2003): 265–72.

3. Jocelyn J. Belanger, Julie Caouette, Karen Sharvit, and Michelle Dugas, "The Psychology of Martyrdom: Making the Ultimate Sacrifice in the Name of a Cause," *Journal of Personality and Social Psychology* 107, no. 3 (2014): 494–515.

4. Keith Lewinstein, "The Reevaluation of Martyrdom in Early Islam," in *Sacrificing the Self: Perspectives on Martyrdom and Religion*, ed. Margaret Cormack (New York: Oxford University Press, 2002), 79.

5. David Cook, *Martyrdom in Islam* (New York: Cambridge University Press, 2007), 1.

6. K. M. Fierke, *Political Self Sacrifice: Agency Body and Emotions in International Relations* (Cambridge: Cambridge University Press, 2013), 5.

7. Diego Gambetta and Steffen Hertog, *Engineers of Jihad: The Curious Connection between Violent Extremism and Education* (Princeton, NJ: Princeton University Press, 2016).

8. Arie Kruglanski, Michelle Gelfand, Jocelyn Belanger, and Anna Sheveland, "How Significance Quest Impacts Violent Extremism," *Political Psychology* 35, Supplement 1 (2014): 69–93.

9. Fierke, *Political Self-Sacrifice*, 92.

10. Peter N. Stearns and Carol Z. Stearns, "Emotionology: Clarifying the History of Emotions and Emotional Standards," *American Historical Review* 90, no. 4 (October 1985): 813–36, quoted in Fierke, *Political Self-Sacrifice*, 94.

11. Elizabeth Castelli, *Martyrdom and Memory: Early Christian Culture Making* (New York: Columbia University Press, 2004), 33, 173.

12. Alan L. Kroeber and Clyde Kluckhohn, "Culture: A Critical Review of Concepts and Definitions," Philosophy and Phenomenological Research 14, no. 2 (1953): 270–71.

13. Castelli, *Martyrdom and Memory*, 198.

14. Ibid., 34.

15. Chris K. Huebner, "Between Victory and Victimhood: Reflections on Culture and Martyrdom," *Direction* 34, no. 2 (Fall 2005): 231, http://www.directionjournal.org/article/? 1402#15.

16. Farhad Khosrokhavar, *Suicide Bombers: Allah's New Martyrs* (New York: Pluto Press, 2005), 9.

17. Fierke, *Political Self-Sacrifice*, 37, 39, 48, citing Mark Juergensmeyer, *Terror in the Mind of God: The Global Rise of Religious Violence* (Los Angeles: University of California Press, 2003), 167.

18. Neil L. Whitehead and Nasser Abufarha, "Suicide Violence and Cultural Conceptions of Martyrdom in Palestine," *Social Research* 75, no. 2 (Summer 2008): 405.

19. Stanley Jeyaraja Tambiah, *Magic, Science, Religion, and the Scope of Rationality* (New York: Cambridge University Press, 1990), quoted in Fierke, *Political Self-Sacrifice*, 39.

20. Alex P. Schmid, "Violent and Non-Violent Extremism: Two Sides of the Same Coin?" Research paper, May 2014, International Centre for Counter-terrorism (ICCT), The Hague. See also Leonie Huddy, Stanley Feldman, Charles Taber, and Gallya Lahav, "Threat, Anxiety, and Support of Antiterrorism Policies," *American Journal of Political Science* 49, no. 3 (July 2005): 593–608.

21. Fierke, *Political Self-Sacrifice*, 18.

22. David Brooks, "The Age of Small Terror," *New York Times*, January 5, 2016, https:// www.nytimes.com/2016/01/05/opinion/the-age-of-small-terror.html; and Matthew Bowen and Angelica Chang, "Combat Addiction: Revisited and Reaffirmed," *Journal of Psychology and Clinical Psychiatry* 7, no. 6 (2017), https://medcraveonline.com/JPCPY/JPCPY-07-00 463.pdf.

23. Belanger et al., "Psychology of Martyrdom," 495.

24. Castelli, *Martyrdom and Memory*, 33.

25. Huebner, "Between Victory and Victimhood," 229.

26. Michael Biggs "Dying Without Killing: Self-Immolations, 1963–2002," in *Making Sense of Suicide Missions*, ed. Diego Gambetta (New York: Oxford University Press, 2006), 173–208.

27. Marie Gillespie, Alasdair Pinkerton, Gerhardt Baumann, and Sharika Thiranagama, "South Asian Diasporas and the BBC World Services: Contacts, Conflicts, and Contestations," *South Asian Diaspora* 2 (1): 3–25.

28. Faisal G. Mohammed, *Milton and the Post-Secular Present: Ethics, Politics, Terrorism* (Palo Alto: Stanford University Press, 2011), 116.

29. Amy Waldman, "Masters of Suicide Bombing: Tamil Guerrillas of Sri Lanka," *New York Times*, January 13, 2003, http://www.nytimes.com/2003/01/14/-orld/masters-of-suicide-bombing-tamil-guerrillas-of-sri-lanka.html. Thaya Master reiterated this point in interviews with Mia Bloom, December 2002 in Killinochi, Sri Lanka.

30. Paul Gill, "A Multi-Dimensional Approach to Suicide Bombing," *International Journal of Conflict and Violence* 1, no. 2 (2007): 148, http://ijcv.uni-bielefeld.de/index.php/ ijcv/article/viewFile/12/12.

31. Fierke, *Political Self-Sacrifice*, 108.

32. "The Forgotten Hunger Strikes (a work in progress)," http://www.hungerstrikes. org/forgotten_strikes.html, accessed May 1, 2016.

33. George Sweeney, "Irish Hunger Strikes and the Cult of Self-Sacrifice," *Journal of Contemporary History* 28, no. 3 (July 1993): 421, https://www.jstor.org/stable/260640?seq= 1#page_scan_tab_contents.

34. Interviews conducted by Mia Bloom, Belfast, Northern Ireland, 2009.

35. Fierke, *Political Self-Sacrifice*, 128.

36. Ibid., 162.

37. Ibid., 181.

38. James Verini, "A Terrible Act of Reason: When Did Self-Immolation Become the Paramount Form of Protest?," *New Yorker*, May 16, 2012, http://www.newyorker.com/culture/culture-desk/a-terrible-act-of-reason-when-did-self-immolation-become-the-paramount-form-of-protest.

39. Reuters Africa, "Peddler's Martyrdom Launched Tunisian Revolution," January 19, 2011, http://af.reuters.com/article/libyaNews/idAFLDE70G18J20110119.

40. Verini, "Terrible Act."

41. Fierke, *Political Self-Sacrifice*, 219.

42. Gambetta, *Suicide Missions*.

43. Michael Hardt and Antonio Negri, *Multitude: War and Democracy in the Age of Empire* (New York: Penguin, 2004), 346, quoted in Huebner, "Between Victory and Victimhood."

44. Cook, *Martyrdom in Islam*, 14. However, Bilal was eventually saved by Abu Bakr and did not die.

45. Fierke, *Political Self-Sacrifice*, 195.

46. Ibid., 196.

47. Babak Rahimi, "Dying a Martyr's Death: The Political Culture of Self -Sacrifice in Contemporary Islamists" (paper presentation, meeting of the Association for the Sociology of Religion, San Francisco, August 14, 2004).

48. "Sahih al-Bukhari," no. 1909, "Daily Hadith Online, Wisdom of Prophet Muhammad in Arabic and English," https://abuaminaelias.com/dailyhadithonline/2012/08/04/hadith-on-martyrdom-a-muslim-who-sincerely-asks-for-martyrdom-will-be-given-the-status-of-a-martyr-even-if-he-dies-a-natural-death/.

49. Fierke, *Political Self-Sacrifice*, 204.

50. Syed Ali Asghar Razwy, *A Restatement of the History of Islam and Muslims: C.E. 570 to 661* (Stanmore, UK: World Federation of KSI Muslim Communities, 1997), https://www.al-islam.org/printpdf/book/export/html/27929. "The first victims of pagan attrition and aggression were those Muslims who had no tribal affiliation in Makkah. Yasir and his wife, Sumayya, and their son, Ammar, had no tribal affiliation. In Makkah they were 'foreigners' and there was no one to protect them. All three were savagely tortured by Abu Jahl and the other infidels. Sumayya, Yasir's wife, died while she was being tortured. She thus became the First Martyr in Islam."

51. Ziauddin Sardar, "The Party of Martyrs," *New Statesman*, April 28, 2003, https://www.newstatesman.com/node/194721.

52. Rahimi, "Dying a Martyr's Death," 1.

53. See, e.g., Shi'a TV, "The Culture of Martyrdom among Lebanese Shiites—Lesson for Parents!" June 1, 2010, http://www.shiatv.net/view_video.php?viewkey=12115470147 6d893aa0a.

54. Rahimi, "Dying a Martyr's Death," 3.

55. Ibid., 2.

56. Ziauddin Sardar, "On the Culture of Martyrdom," *New Statesman*, November 28, 2005, http://www.newstatesman.com/200511280014.

57. Several sources cite his age as either twelve or thirteen.

58. Elaine Sciolino, "Martyrs Never Die," *Frontline*, 2000, http://www.pbs.org/wgbh/pages/frontline/shows/tehran/inside/martyrs.html.

59. Joyce M. Davis, *Martyrs: Innocence, Despair, and Vengeance in the Middle East* (New York: St. Martin's, 2003), 49.

60. Ibid., 50.

61. Steve Inskeep, "In Tehran, the Idea of Violence Is Everywhere," National Public Radio, February 5, 2009, http://www.npr.org/templates/story/story.php?storyId=100240751.

62. Sciolino, "Martyrs Never Die."

63. Inskeep, "In Tehran."

64. Aida Ghajar, "The Lost Youth of Iran's Child Soldiers," July 21, 2017, Iran Wire, https://iranwire.com/en/features/4724.

65. Undated Iranian handbook, *The Martyr*, cited by Elaine Sciolino, *Persian Mirrors, the Elusive Face of Iran* (New York: Simon and Schuster 2001), 172.

66. While suicide terrorism has spread throughout the region and to other countries far and wide, it has shifted from being a largely Shia tactic to one overwhelmingly used by Sunni terrorist groups. Mia Bloom, *Dying to Kill: The Allure of Suicide Terrorism* (New York: Columbia University Press, 2005).

67. David Brooks, "The Culture of Martyrdom," *Atlantic*, June 2002, http://www.the atlantic.com/magazine/archive/2002/06/the-culture-of-martyrdom/2506/.

68. Dana Priest, "Fort Hood Suspect Warned of Threats within the Ranks," *Washington Post*, November 10, 2009, http://www.washingtonpost.com/wp-dyn/content/arti cle/2009/11/09/AR2009110903618.html.

69. David Cook, *Understanding and Addressing Suicide Attacks: The Faith and Politics of Martyrdom Operations* (New York: Praeger Security Studies, 2007), 142.

70. Motro H. Schary, "Living among the Headlines," Salon, October 7, 2000, https://www.salon.com/2000/10/07/jamal_2/.

71. Joseph Lelyveld, "All Suicide Bombers Are Not Alike," *New York Times Magazine*, October 28, 2001, 50.

72. Barbara Sofer, "Raising the Children of Terrorists," *Jerusalem Post*, February 26, 2005, http://www.aish.com/jw/me/40910762.html, citing Christine Spolar, "Palestinian Families Wonder: Were Suicide Attacks Worth the Loss of Our Children?" *Chicago Tribune*, February 6, 2000.

73. Steven Stalinksy and R. Sosnow, "Faces of Death—Part II," MEMRI, July 1, 2013, https://www.memri.org/reports/faces-death-part-ii-twitter-jihadis-disseminate-death-photos-martyrs-noting-their.

74. Collected as part of the Minerva Research Initiative, the raw data will eventually be part of the Office of Naval Research dataverse archive of IS propaganda.

75. Brooks, "Culture of Martyrdom."

76. Matthew Bowen and Angelica Chang, "Clinical Psychiatry Combat Addiction: Revisited and Reaffirmed," *Journal of Psychology and Clinical Psychiatry* 7, no. 6 (2017), https://medcraveonline.com/JPCPY/JPCPY-07-00463.pdf.

77. "PA Mufti of Jerusalem and Palestine Discusses the Intifada," *Al-Ahram al-'Arabi*, October 28, 2000, cited by Peter Singer, *The New Children of Terror*, in Forest, *Making of a Terrorist*, 111. See also Raphael Israeli, "Palestinian Women and Children in the Throes of Islamikaze Terrorism," Ariel Center for Policy Research policy paper 139, n.d., 7, http://www.acpr.org.il/pp/pp139-risraeli-E.pdf.

78. Yaacov Lappin, "Egypt Primes Children for Jihad," Ynetnews, July 5, 2006, http://www.ynetnews.com/articles/0,7340,L-3271274,00.html.

79. Davis, *Martyrs*.

80. Israeli, "Palestinian Women and Children," 6.

81. Ibid.

82. Summary of information from Defence for Children International—Palestine Section, September 28, 2000–November 5, 2007. See also *Visit of the Special Representative for Children and Armed Conflict to the Middle East*, United Nations report, UN doc. OSRSG/CAAC, April 2007, 9–20.

83. Humanitarian Monitor, OCHA/DCI information, July–August 2007, No. 16 2007, http://data.ochaopt.org/documents/humanitarian_monitor_august_2007.pdf.

84. Erik Schechter, "Where Have All the Bombers Gone?" *Upfront, Jerusalem Post Magazine*, August 5, 2004, 11–13.

85. Chris K. Huebner, "Between Victory and Victimhood: Reflections on Culture and Martyrdom," *Direction* 34, no. 2 (Fall 2005): 228–40.

86. Mia Bloom, Hicham Tiflati, and John Horgan, "Navigating ISIS's Preferred Platform: Telegram," *Terrorism and Political Violence*, July 11, 2017, http://www.tandfonline.com/doi/citedby/10.1080/09546553.2017.1339695.

87. Brooks, "Culture of Martyrdom."

88. Huebner, "Between Victory and Victimhood," 228–40.

6. EXPERIENCES, APPRENTICESHIPS, AND CAREERS IN TERROR

1. Jens Christopher Andvig and Scott Gates, "Recruiting Children for Armed Conflict," paper prepared for presentation by Scott Gates as the keynote address at the Dutch Flemish Association for Economy and Peace (Economen voor Vrede), the Foundation for Peace Sciences (Stichting Vredes Wetenschappen), and the Institute of Social Studies Seminar "Economics as a Science of Peace and Conflict" on the occasion of the Inaugural Lecture of Professor Dr. S. Mansoob Murshed, June 22, 2006, the Hague, Netherlands.

2. Ibid.; P. W. Singer, *Children at War* (Berkeley: University of California Press, 2006).

3. IS has two official child recruitment centers, in al-Mayadin and al-Bokamal, where it inducts children into IS units. Syrian Observatory for Human Rights, "IS Organization Continues Attracting Children and Recruit More Than 400 from Ashbal al Khilafah," March 24, 2015, http://www.syriahr.com/en/?p=15709.

4. Meira Svirsky, "Teaching to Kill: The Islamic State's Jihad Camps for Kids," Clarion Project, August 28, 2014, https://clarionproject.org/teaching-kill-islamic-states-jihad-camps-kids-26/.

5. Jacob Shapiro, *The Terrorist's Dilemma: Managing Violent Covert Organizations* (Princeton, NJ: Princeton University Press, 2015).

6. Allan C. Stover, *Underage and under Fire: Accounts of the Youngest Americans in Military Service* (Jefferson, NC: McFarland, 2014), 14.

7. Singer, *Children at War*, 13.

8. Ibid.

9. Michael Wessells, *Child Soldiers: From Violence to Protection* (Cambridge: Harvard University Press, 2006), 71.

10. Ibid., 72.

11. "HRW: Houthis Recruit, Deploy Yemen Children," *Yemen Post*, May 13, 2015, http://yemenpost.net/Detail123456789.aspx?ID=3&SubID=7992&MainCat=3.

12. Priyanka Motaparthy, "'Maybe We Live and Maybe We Die': Recruitment and Use of Children by Armed Groups in Syria," Human Rights Watch, June 22, 2014, https://www.hrw.org/report/2014/06/22/maybe-we-live-and-maybe-we-die/recruitment-and-use-children-armed-groups-syria.

13. Nicholas Pelham, "Gaza's Tunnel Phenomenon: The Unintended Dynamics of Israel's Siege," *Journal of Palestine Studies* 41, no. 4 (2011/2012): 6.

14. Cited by Jennifer Rubin, "If Liberal Elites Really Cared about Gazan Children . . . ," *Washington Post*, July 31, 2014, https://www.washingtonpost.com/blogs/right-turn/wp/2014/07/31/if-liberal-elites-really-cared-about-gazan-children/?utm_term=.e1b6799e4a10. See also M. Freimann, "Hamas Killed 160 Palestinian Children to Build Tunnels," *The Scroll* (blog), Tablet, July 25, 2014, http://tabletmag.com/scroll/180400/hamas-killed-160-palestinian-children-to-build-terror-tunnels.

15. Institute for Palestine Studies, "A Response to Netanyahu and a Correction from the *Journal of Palestine Studies*," news release, August 21, 2014, http://palestine-studies.org/sites/default/files/response%20to%20netanyahu%20and%20correction%2028%20Aug%2014.pdf.

16. Ibid.

17. "Nigeria: Stark Encounters with Teen Female Suicide Bombers," allAfrica, August 3, 2014, https://allafrica.com/stories/201408042114.html.

18. Bloom, *Bombshell*, 211.

19. Dyan Mazurana and Khristopher Carlson, *The Girl Child and Armed Conflict: Recognizing and Addressing Grave Violations of Girls' Human Rights* (United Nations DAW and UNICEF, EGM/DVGC/2006/EP.12, 2006), 5.

20. Singer, *Children at War*, 33.

21. Dionne Searcey, interview with Mia Bloom, April 2016.

22. Chris Coulter, *Bush Wives and Girl Soldiers: Women's Lives through War and Peace in Sierra Leone* (Ithaca, NY: Cornell University Press, 2009).

23. This is according to the Nigerian civil society activist Hafsat Mohammed, who rescued her children after they were kidnapped by Boko Haram. Mohammed, interview with Mia Bloom, Washington, DC, March 2016.

24. International Committee for the Red Cross, "Child Soldiers and Other Children Associated with Armed Forces and Armed Groups," policy brief, Geneva, Switzerland, 2010, https://www.icrc.org/eng/assets/files/other/icrc-002-0824.pdf.

25. Tim Pat Coogan, *The IRA* (New York: Palgrave, 2000); B. Jackson, J. Baker, P. Chalk, K. Cragin, J. Parachini, and H. Trujillo, *Aptitude for Destruction: Organizational Learning in Terrorist Groups and Its Implications for Combating Terrorism* (Santa Barbara, CA: RAND, 2005); Bruce Hoffman and Gordon McCormick, "Terrorism, Signaling and Suicide Attack," *Studies in Conflict and Terrorism* 27, no. 2 (2004): 243–81; Shapiro, *Terrorist's Dilemma*; M. L. R. Smith, *Fighting for Ireland: The Military Strategy of the Irish Republican Movement* (London: Routledge, 1997); Horacio R. Trujillo and Brian A. Jackson, "Organizational Learning and Terrorist Groups," in *Teaching Terror: Strategic and Tactical Learning in the Terrorist World*, ed. James J. F. Forest (Lanham, MD: Rowman and Littlefield, 2006).

26. Michael Kenney, *From Pablo to Osama: Trafficking and Terrorist Networks, Government Bureaucracies, and Competitive Adaptation* (State College: Pennsylvania State University Press, 2007).

27. Ibid., 145.

28. See, e.g., Shapiro, *Terrorist's Dilemma*.

29. Etienne Wenger-Trayner and Beverly Wenger-Trayner, "Communities of Practice: A Brief Introduction," Wenger-Trayner, April 15, 2015, 1, http://wenger-trayner.com/wp-content/uploads/2015/04/07-Brief-introduction-to-communities-of-practice.pdf.

30. Ibid., 4. Etienne Wenger later changed his surname to Wenger-Trayner.

31. Karsten Hundeide, "Becoming a Committed Insider," *Culture and Psychology* 9, no. 2 (2003): 121.

32. Ibid., 108.

33. Kathleen Taylor, *Brainwashing: The Science of Thought Control* (New York: Oxford University Press, 2006), 51.

34. Bruce Hoffman, "Holy Terror: The Implications of Terrorism Motivated by a Religious Imperative," *Studies in Conflict and Terrorism* 18, no. 4 (1995): 272.

35. Taylor, *Brainwashing*, 47.

36. Clerics say that al-Baghdadi's sermon shows ignorance of Islam, http://www.wikileaks-forum.com/iraq/448/al-baghdadis-sermon-shows-ignorance-of-islam-clerics-say/30905/msg63765#msg63765; see also http://www.newageislam.com/Print.aspx?ID=98295.

37. Taylor, *Brainwashing*, 41.

38. Human Rights Watch, *Children in the Ranks: The Maoists' Use of Child Soldiers in Nepal*, February 2007, 39, https://www.hrw.org/report/2007/02/01/children-ranks/maoists-use-child-soldiers-nepal.

39. Myriam Denov, *Child Soldiers: Sierra Leone's Revolutionary United Front* (New York: Cambridge University Press, 2010), 129.

40. Hundeide, "Becoming a Committed Insider," 108, 122.

41. Adapted from Hundeide, "Becoming a Committed Insider," 122.

42. Richard Maclure and Myriam Denov, "'I Didn't Want to Die So I Joined Them': Structuration and the Process of Becoming Boy Soldiers in Sierra Leone," *Terrorism and Political Violence* 18, no. 1 (2006), 124.

43. Ibid.

44. Ibid., 130.

45. Human Rights Watch, *Children in the Ranks*, 2.

46. Maclure and Denov, "I Didn't Want to Die," 125.

47. Human Rights Watch, *Children in the Ranks*, 5, 18.

48. Ibid., 26.

49. Susan Shepler, "The Social and Cultural Context of Child Soldiering in Sierra Leone" (paper presentation, Techniques of Violence in Civil War workshop, Oslo, August 20–21, 2004), 14.

50. Bernd Beber and Christopher Blattman, "The Logic of Child Soldiering and Coercion," *International Organizations* 67, no. 1 (January 2013): 65–104, https://www.cambridge.org/core/journals/international-organization/article/the-logic-of-child-soldiering-and-coercion/EB8CC2FE13CC49C2846EEDE4FFD432FE.

51. Ibid., 94.

52. Ibid., 85.

53. Maclure and Denov, "I Didn't Want to Die," 129.

54. Ibid., 126.

55. Human Rights Watch, *Children in the Ranks*, 48.

56. Ibid., 41.

57. Maclure and Denov, "I Didn't Want to Die," 126.

58. Ibid., 129.

59. Andvig and Gates, "Recruiting Children," 8.

60. Maclure and Denov, "I Didn't Want to Die," 128.

61. Dara Kay Cohen, *Rape during Civil War* (Ithaca, NY: Cornell University Press, 2016).

62. Matt Bradley, "ISIS Declares New Islamist Caliphate," *Wall Street Journal*, June 29, 2014, http://wsj.com/articles/isis-declares-new-islamist-caliphate-1404065263.

63. Michael Weiss and Hassan Hassan, *ISIS: Inside the Army of Terror* (New York: Reagan Arts, 2015).

64. Johnlee Varghese, "Children as Young as 13 Have Fled Germany to Join ISIS—Report," International Business Times, September 23, 2014, http://ibtimes.co.in/children-young-13-have-fled-germany-join-isis-report-609782.

65. Arwa Damon, "Child Fighter Tormented by ISIS," CNN, November 13, 2014, http://cnn.com/2014/11/12/world/meast/syria-isis-child-fighter/.

66. Joshua Berlinger, "ISIS' Child Soldiers: What Will Happen to 'Cubs of the Caliphate'?," CNN, May 20, 2015, http://edition.cnn.com/2015/05/20/middleeast/isis-child-soldiers/index.html.

67. Simon Cottee, "Why ISIS Are Using So Many Children in Their Propaganda Videos," Vice News, January 31, 2017, https://www.vice.com/en_uk/article/9adaye/why-isis-are-using-so-many-children-in-their-propaganda-videos. The graphic video is archived at the Clarion Project, https://clarionproject.org/warning-graphic-video-isis-children-4/, January 9, 2017 (1:58), accessed June 10, 2017.

68. Vishakha Sonowane, "ISIS Child Executioners? Video Allegedly Shows 3 Children Executing Men Accused of Spying for Kurdish Forces in Syria," International Business Times,

January 10, 2017, http://www.ibtimes.com/isis-child-executioners-video-allegedly-shows-3-children-executing-men-accused-spying-2472997. See also http://aranews.net/2017/01/isis-child-soldiers-execute-three-civilians-accused-spying-kurdish-ypg-forces/.

69. Svirsky, "Teaching to Kill."

70. Martin Robinson, "Is This ISIS' Youngest Foreign Jihadist?," *Daily Mail*, August 22, 2014, http://dailymail.co.uk/news/article-2731657/Is-ISIS-youngest-jihadist-Picture-eme rges-Belgian-boy-13-thought-joined-army-child-fighters-Syria.html.

71. Julia A. Heyer, "The Lost Children: France Takes Stock of Growing Jihadist Problem," *Der Spiegel*, November 6, 2014, http://spiegel.de/international/europe/france-strug gles-to-deal-with-young-jihadist-exodus-to-syria-a-1001254.html; Varghese, "Children as Young as 13."

72. Heyer, "Lost Children."

73. Kimiko de Freytas-Tamura, "Double Blow for Parents of Jihadists: Losing Children, Then Their Community," *New York Times*, December 27, 2014, http://www.nytimes.com/2014/12/28/world/double-blow-for-parents-of-jihadists-losing-children-then-their-community.html.

74. Sarah Birke, "How ISIS Rules," *New York Review of Books*, February 5, 2015, http://nybooks.com/articles/archives/2015/feb/05/how-isis-rules/?insrc=hpma.

75. Ibid.

76. Brenda Stoter, "Radicalized Western Mothers Lead Children into Islamic State," Al-Monitor, April 13, 2015, http://al-monitor.com/pulse/originals/2015/04/islamic-state-syria-western-women children-join.html.

77. Ibid.

78. Ash Gallagher citing Abrahams, "The Islamic State's Child Soldiers," Al-Monitor, April 2015, http://al-monitor.com/pulse/originals/2015/04/lebanon-islamic-state-child-soldiers-syria-iraq-hrw-afp.html.

79. Abu Ibrahim Raqqawi, "IS Boot Camps Rob Raqqa's Children of Their Childhood," Raqqa Is Being Slaughtered Silently, January 7, 2015, http://raqqa-sl.com/en/?p=150.

80. Sara E. Williams citing Raqqawi, "Cub Camps Turn Boys into Junior Jihadists," *Times* (UK), February 28, 2015, http://thetimes.co.uk/tto/news/world/middleeast/arti cle4367793.ece.

81. Gallagher, "Islamic State's Child Soldiers."

82. Rashid Najm, "Life under ISIL Caliphate: Recruitment of Child Soldiers," Al-Shorfa, July 15, 2015, http://al-shorfa.com/en_GB/articles/meii/features/2014/07/15/feature-01.

83. Birke, "How ISIS Rules."

84. Gallagher, "Islamic State's Child Soldiers."

85. Birke, "How ISIS Rules"; Berlinger, "ISIS' Child Soldiers."

86. Original interview with Abu Mosa, "The Islamic State," Vice News (42:31), https://news.vice.com/video/the-islamic-state-full-length, also cited in Svirsky, "Teaching to Kill."

87. Williams, "Cub Camps."

88. Najm, "Life under ISIL Caliphate."

89. Birke, "How ISIS Rules."

90. Williams citing Raqqawi, "Cub Camps."

91. Ibid.

92. Berlinger, "ISIS' Child Soldiers."

93. Damon, "Child Fighter Tormented."

94. Berlinger, "ISIS' Child Soldiers."

95. Judit Neurink, "ISIS Runs Prison Camps for Yezidi Women and Children," Rudaw, January 7, 2015, http://rudaw.net/english/kurdistan/07012015?utm_source=dlvr.it&utm_medium=twitter.

96. Berlinger, "ISIS' Child Soldiers."

97. Damon, "Child Fighter Tormented."

98. Berlinger, "ISIS' Child Soldiers."

99. Damon, "Child Fighter Tormented."

100. Birke, "How ISIS Rules."

101. Neurink, "ISIS Runs Prison Camps."

102. Zeina Karam, "In an IS Training Camp, Children Told: Behead the Doll," Associated Press, July 20, 2015, https://apnews.com/fcc0fe9b92bb49a2a5bc0f3bd401cc13/training-camp-children-told-behead-doll, quoted in Chas Danner, "How ISIS Abducts, Recruits, and Trains Children to Become Jihadists," Intelligencer, July 19, 2015, http://nymag.com/daily/intelligencer/2015/07/how-isis-abducts-recruits-and-trains-children.html.

103. Berlinger, "ISIS' Child Soldiers."

104. Damon, "Child Fighter Tormented."

105. Najm, "Life under ISIL Caliphate."

106. Quoted in Berlinger, "ISIS' Child Soldiers."

107. Raqqawi, "IS Boot Camps."

108. Also reported in Damon, "Child Fighter Tormented."

109. Raqqawi, "IS Boot Camps."

110. Berlinger, "ISIS' Child Soldiers."

111. Damon, "Child Fighter Tormented."

112. Singer, *Children at War*, 57.

113. Ibid., 64, 69.

114. Shelly S. McCoy, Laura M. Dimler, Danielle V. Samuels, and Misaki N. Natsuaki, "Adolescent Susceptibility to Deviant Peer Pressure: Does Gender Matter?" *Adolescent Research Review* (2017), https://doi.org/10.1007/s40894-017-0071-2.

115. Max Taylor and P. M. Currie, eds., *Terrorism and Affordance* (London: Bloomsbury, 2012).

7. LEAVING TERRORISM BEHIND

1. Keith Lowe, "Antony Beevor: 'There Are Things That Are Too Horrific to Put in a Book,'" *Telegraph* (UK), May 17, 2015, http://www.telegraph.co.uk/culture/hay-festival/11605822/Anthony-Beevor-There-are-things-that-are-too-horrific.html.

2. Adrian Shtuni, interview with Mia Bloom, Oslo, Norway, April 26, 2018.

3. Fatima Akilu, interview with Mia Bloom, Oslo, Norway, April 26, 2018.

4. Ed Cairns, *Children and Political Violence* (London: Wiley-Blackwell, 1996).

5. Andrew Silke, "The Psychological Impact of the Continued Terrorist Threat," American Academy of Experts in Traumatic Stress, n.d., http://www.aaets.org/article216.htm.

6. Stephanie Thornton, "Terrorism Reports: Looking at the Potential Impact on Children," *British Journal of School Nursing* 10, no. 2 (2015): pp. 79–81.

7. Ibid., p. 80.

8. Bertrand Venard, "How ISIS Terrorists Neutralise Guilt to Justify Their Atrocities," Conversation, October 6, 2016, http://theconversation.com/how-isis-terrorists-neutralise-guilt-to-justify-their-atrocities-66593.

9. Andrew Silke, ed., *Terrorists, Victims and Society: Psychological Perspectives on Terrorism and Its Consequences* (London: Wiley, 2003), 116.

10. Emma Disley, Kristin Weed, Anaïs Reding, Lindsay Clutterbuck, and Richard Warnes, *Individual Disengagement from Al Qa'ida-Influenced Terrorist Groups* (Cambridge: RAND Europe, 2011), https://www.rand.org/content/dam/rand/pubs/technical_reports/2012/RAND_TR785.pdf.

11. John Horgan, *Walking Away from Terrorism* (London: Routledge, 2009), 106–7.

12. Rukmini Callimachi, "How a Secretive Branch of ISIS Built a Global Network of Killers," *New York Times*, August 3, 2016, http://www.nytimes.com/2016/08/04/world/middleeast/isis-german-recruit-interview.html.

13. Lizzie Dearden, "Former London Postman Charged with Murdering Syrian Captives in Isis Mass Execution," *Independent* (UK), July 19, 2017, https://www.independent.co.uk/news/world/europe/harry-sarfo-isis-germany-syria-london-postman-charged-murder-mass-execution-palmyra-video-massacre-a7849831.html.

14. Ibid.

15. H. H. A. Cooper, "What Is a Terrorist? A Psychological Perspective," *Legal Medical Quarterly* 1 (1977): 8–18.

16. Some accounts, however, are written by people who are unrepentant, so the existence of an autobiography is not itself an indicator of altered beliefs or remorse. See, e.g., Steve Almasy, "Reports: Former Guantanamo Detainee to Get $10 Million from Canada," CNN, July 5, 2017, http://www.cnn.com/2017/07/04/americas/canada-omar-khadr-reported-settlement/index.html; Michelle Shephard, *Guantanamo's Child: The Untold Story of Omar Khadr* (Toronto: Wiley, 2008).

17. Horgan, *Walking Away from Terrorism*, 152.

18. Peter S. Curran and Paul W. Miller, "Psychiatric Implications of Chronic Civilian Strife or War: Northern Ireland," *Advanced Psychiatric Treatment* 7, no. 1 (2001): 73–80, https://www.cambridge.org/core/journals/advances-in-psychiatric-treatment/article/psychiatric-implications-of-chronic-civilian-strife-or-war-northern-ireland/3993FF749DB382604CBC0B3CBAD6E2D2.

19. Judith J. Mathewson, "The Psychological Impact of Terrorist Attacks: Lessons Learned For Future Threats," in *The Homeland Security Papers: Stemming the Tide of Terror*, ed. Michael W. Ritz, Ralph G. Hensley, and James C. Whitmore, 192, USAF Counter Proliferation Center, February 2004, http://www.au.af.mil/au/awc/awcgate/cpc-pubs/hls_papers/mathewson.pdf. Research conducted by the American Red Cross shows that there were more than 237,000 mental health contacts related to all three terrorist attacks from people in New Jersey, Connecticut, Massachusetts, California, and several other locations. The Pentagon, as of June 6, 2002, had 8,136 mental health contacts. Current studies show that 52 percent of the World Trade Center first responders suffered from both mental health issues and respiratory problems. Susan Klitzman and Nicholas Freudenberg, "Implications of the World Trade Center Attack for the Public Health and Health Care Infrastructures," *American Journal of Public Health* 93, no. 3 (2003): 400–406.

20. It may be difficult to assess rates of PTSD following acts of terrorism. Many individuals experience symptoms of intrusion, avoidance, and arousal without meeting the event exposure criteria of intense fear, helplessness, or horror. PTSD requires distress or dysfunction in addition to symptoms of hyperarousal, intrusion, and avoidance/numbing. Several studies following the 9/11 attacks indicated that exposure through watching events on television could be associated with symptoms of PTSD, although many question whether such exposure meets the event criteria. Thomas A. Grieger, "Psychiatric and Societal Impacts of Terrorism," *Psychiatric Times* 23, no. 7 (June 1, 2006), http://www.psychiatrictimes.com/disaster-psychiatry/psychiatric-and-societal-impacts-terrorism.

21. Eliana Barrios Suarez, "Two Decades Later: The Resilience and Post-traumatic Responses of Indigenous Quecha Girls and Adolescents in the Aftermath of the Peruvian Armed Conflict," *Child Abuse and Neglect* 37, no. 2-3 (2013): 200–210.

22. From 2013 to 2015, the authors made several trips to Malakand to talk with doctors, therapists, and social workers at the Sabaoon facility.

23. John Horgan, "Child Suicide Bombers Find Safe Haven," CNN, March 27, 2013, http://www.cnn.com/2013/03/27/world/asia/pakistan-anti-taliban/.

24. "Adolescents in Syria: No One Hears Us," Mercy Corps, August 7, 2015, https://www.mercycorps.org/research-resources/adolescents-inside-syria-no-one-hears-us. See also "Teens in Syria," *Economist*, Data Team, August 19, 2015, http://www.economist.com/blogs/graphicdetail/2015/08/daily-chart-6.

25. Nick Logan, "Journalists Witness Gaza Beach Attack That Killed at Least 4 Children," Global News, July 16, 2014, http://globalnews.ca/news/1454641/journalists-witness-gaza-beach-attack-that-killed-at-least-4-children/.

26. Hashem Said, "Gaza's Kids Affected Psychologically, Physically by Lifetime of Violence," Al Jazeera America, July 31, 2014, http://america.aljazeera.com/articles/2014/8/1/health-gaza-children.html.

27. Myer Freimann, "Hamas Killed 160 Palestinian Children to Build Tunnels," *The Scroll* (blog), Tablet, July 25, 2014, http://tabletmag.com/scroll/180400/hamas-killed-160-palestinian-children-to-build-terror-tunnels.

28. Institute for Palestine Studies, "A Response to Netanyahu and a Correction from the *Journal of Palestine Studies*," news release, August 21, 2014, http://palestine-studies.org/sites/default/files/response%20to%20netanyahu%20and%20correction%2028%20Aug%2014.pdf.

29. Samir Qouta, Raija Leena-Punamaki, and Eyad el Sarraj, "The Relations between Traumatic Experiences, Activity, and Cognitive and Emotional Responses among Palestinian Children," *International Journal of Psychology* 30, no. 3 (1995): 289–304.

30. Joshua Berlinger, "ISIS' Child Soldiers: What Will Happen to 'Cubs of the Caliphate'?," CNN, May 20, 2015, http://edition.cnn.com/2015/05/20/middleeast/isis-child-soldiers/index.html.

31. Arwa Damon, "Child Fighter Tormented by ISIS," CNN, November 13, 2014, http://www.cnn.com/2014/11/12/world/meast/syria-isis-child-fighter/.

32. Charlotte McDonald-Gibson, "What Should Europe Do with the Children of ISIS?," *New York Times*, July 23, 2017, https://www.nytimes.com/2017/07/23/opinion/isis-children-european-union.html.

33. Judit Neurink, "ISIS Runs Prison Camps for Yazidi Women and Children," Rudaw, January 7, 2015, http://rudaw.net/english/kurdistan/07012015.

34. Berlinger, "ISIS' Child Soldiers."

35. Damon, "Child Fighter Tormented"; see also Berlinger, "ISIS' Child Soldiers."

36. Usam Sadiq al-Amin and Dionne Searcey, "Young Bombers Kill 58 at Nigerian Camp for Those Fleeing Boko Haram," *New York Times*, February 10, 2016, http://www.nytimes.com/2016/02/11/world/africa/suicide-bomber-girls-kill-58-in-nigerian-refugee-camp.html.

37. Ali Hashem, "Teenage Suicide Bomber Hopes for Second Chance," Al-Monitor, January 6, 2015, http://www.al-monitor.com/pulse/originals/2015/01/islamic-state-suicide-bomber-baghdad.html.

38. Berlinger, "ISIS' Child Soldiers."

39. P. W. Singer, *Children at War* (Berkeley: University of California Press, 2006), 92.

40. Scott Gates, "Why Do Children Fight? Motivations and the Mode of Recruitment," in *Child Soldiers: From Recruitment to Reintegration*, ed. Alpaslan Özerdem and Sukanya Podder (London: Palgrave, 2011), 29–49.

41. The case against Dominic Ongwen is the first at the International Criminal Court to put on trial a former child soldier who grew up in the ranks and became a perpetrator.

42. Rudolph M. Wittenberg, "Children under the Nazi System: Some Facts for a Social Diagnosis," *American Journal of Orthopsychiatry* 15, no. 3 (April 26, 1945): 443.

43. R. Carl Hanson and Andrew Harris, "Dynamic Predictors of Sexual Recidivism," 1998-1, Public Works and Government Services Canada, 1998, http://www.static99.org/pdfdocs/hansonandharris1998.pdf.

44. The video was released by al-Hayat Media Center, November 22, 2014, video embedded in Radio Free Europe, "Kazakhstan Moves To Ban 'Illegal' IS Video Showing Training of Kazakh Children," http://www.rferl.org/a/kazakhstan-islamic-state-recruitment-children-syria/26709628.html.

45. Jessica Elgot, "Islamic State's Most Sickening Video Yet Shows Men Being Shot Dead by Young Child," Huffington Post (UK), January 13, 2015, https://www.huffingtonpost.co.uk/2015/01/13/islamic-state-video-child_n_6462676.html?guccounter=1&guce_referrer_us=aHR0cHM6Ly93d3cuZ29vZ2xlLmNvbS8&guce_referrer_cs=xvQDrluqUBtQOjv47NPP-g.

46. "Teen Accused in Ardoyne Bomb Plot Remanded," Ulster Television, May 9, 2015, http://www.u.tv/News/2015/05/09/Teen-accused-in-Ardoyne-bomb-plot-remanded-36927.

47. Joana Cook and Gina Vale, "From Daesh to Diaspora: Tracing the Women and Minors of the Islamic State," International Centre for the Study of Radicalisation (ICSR) Report, July 23, 2018, https://icsr.info/wp-content/uploads/2018/07/ICSR-Report-From-Daesh-to-'Diaspora'-Tracing-the-Women-and-Minors-of-Islamic-State.pdf.

48. McDonald-Gibson, "What Should Europe Do?"

49. Souad Mekhennet and Joby Warwick, "For the 'Children of ISIS,' Target Practice Starts at Age 6. By Their Teens, They're Ready to Be Suicide Bombers," Washington Post, October 7, 2016, https://www.washingtonpost.com/world/national-security/for-the-children-of-isis-target-practice-starts-at-age-6-by-their-teens-theyre-ready-to-be-suicide-bombers/2016/10/06/3b59f0fc-8664-11e6-92c2-14b64f3d453f_story.html.

50. Sara E. Williams, "Cub Camps Turn Boys into Junior Jihadists," Times (UK), February 28, 2015, http://www.thetimes.co.uk/tto/news/world/middleeast/article4367793.ece.

51. Martin Robinson, "Is This ISIS' Youngest Foreign Jihadist?," Daily Mail, August 22, 2014, http://www.dailymail.co.uk/news/article-2731657/Is-ISIS-youngest-jihadist-Picture-emerges-Belgian-boy-13-thought-joined-army-child-fighters-Syria.html.

52. Human Rights Watch, "'Maybe We Live and Maybe We Die': Recruitment and Use of Children by Armed Groups in Syria," June 22, 2014, https://www.hrw.org/report/2014/06/22/maybe-we-live-and-maybe-we-die/recruitment-and-use-children-armed-groups-syria.

53. Mekhennet and Warwick, "For the 'Children of ISIS.'"

54. McDonald-Gibson, "What Should Europe Do?"

55. Save the Children 2009 report, 1, cited by Robert Tynes, Tools of War, Tools of State: When Children Become Soldiers (Albany, NY: SUNY University Press, 2017), 200.

56. Ibid., 41.

57. Michael Wessells, "Psychosocial Issues in Reintegrating Child Soldiers," Cornell International Law Journal 37, no. 3 (2004): 513–30.

58. "'Extremism Hotline' Swamped with Calls," The Local, January 21, 2015, http://www.thelocal.at/20150121/austrian-extremism-hotline-swamped-with-calls.

59. Theresa S. Betancourt and Timothy Williams, "Building an Evidence Base on Mental Health Interventions for Children Affected by Armed Conflict," Intervention 6, no. 1 (2008): 39–40.

60. Ibid., 40.

61. John Horgan and Mia Bloom, "This Is How the Islamic State Manufactures Child Militants," Vice News, July 8, 2015, https://news.vice.com/article/this-is-how-the-islamic-state-manufactures-child-militants. See also the case of a young boy, Abu Ubaidah, who allegedly died in battle with his father, http://www.dailymail.co.uk/news/article-2786403/

The-youngest-martyr-cub-al-Baghdadi-ISIS-boasts-10-year-old-fighter-killed-went-battle-father-Syria.html.

62. Betancourt and Williams, "Building an Evidence Base," 40.

63. Ibid., 41.

64. Akilu, interview with Bloom.

65. Hamsatu Allamin, interview with Mia Bloom, Oslo, Norway, April 26, 2018.

66. Akilu, interview with Bloom.

67. Akilu, interview with Bloom.

68. Pushpa Kanagaratnam, Magne Raundalen, and Arne E. Asbjørnsen, "Ideological Commitment and Posttraumatic Stress in Former Tamil Child Soldiers," *Scandinavian Journal of Psychology* 46, no. 6. (2005): 512.

69. Ibid., 512, 515.

70. Karsten Hundeide, "Becoming a Committed Insider," *Culture and Psychology* 9, no. 2 (2003): 119.

71. Michael Wessells, *Child Soldiers*, 57.

72. Christopher Boucek, "Extremist Reeducation and Rehabilitation in Saudi Arabia," Jamestown Foundation, August 16, 2007, https://jamestown.org/program/extremist-reeducation-and-rehabilitation-in-saudi-arabia/.

73. Oliver Kaplan and Enzo Nussio, "Explaining Recidivism of Ex-combatants in Colombia," *Journal of Conflict Resolution* 62, no. 1, (May 10, 2016): 2, http://journals.sage pub.com/doi/abs/10.1177/0022002716644326.

74. Wessells, *Child Soldiers*, 179.

75. Ibid., 160.

76. United Nations, *Operational Guide to the Integrated Disarmament, Demobilization and Reintegration Standards* (IDDRS), New York: Report 2014, http://unddr.org/uploads/documents/Operational%20Guide.pdf.

77. Kanagaratnam, Raundalen, and Asbjørnsen, "Ideological Commitment."

78. Daya Somasundaram, "Child Soldiers: Understanding the Context," *British Medical Journal* 324, no. 7348 (2002): 1268.

79. Ibid.

80. Kanagaratnam, Raundalen, and Asbjørnsen, "Ideological Commitment," 515.

81. Ibid., 518.

82. Ibid., 517.

83. Tony Stanley and Surinder Guru, "Childhood Radicalisation Risk: An Emerging Practice Issue," *Practice* 27, no. 5 (2015): 4.

84. Kaplan and Nussio, "Explaining Recidivism," 2.

85. Ibid., 3–4.

86. Doctora Natalia Springer, *Como corderos entre lobos: Del uso y reclutamiento de niños, niñas, y adolescentes en el marco del conflicto armado y la criminalidad en Colombia* (Bogotá: Springer Consulting Services, 2012), 27.

87. Evan Fagan and Evan Owens, "The FARC and Child Soldiers: A Question of Reintegration—So Near, Yet So Far," Council on Hemispheric Affairs, 2016, http://www.coha.org/the-farc-and-child-soldiers-a-question-of-reintegration-so-near-yet-so-far/, citing Springer, *Como corderos entre lobos*, 5.

88. Evan Fagan and Evan Owens, cited in V. Ladisch, "Child Soldiers: Passive Victims?" Al Jazeera, November 21, 2013, http://www.aljazeera.com/indepth/opinion/2013/11/child-soldiers-passive-victims-2013111853742192541.html; see also Fagan and Owens, "FARC and Child Soldiers."

89. Krjin Peters, "From Weapons to Wheels: Young Sierra Leonean Ex-combatants Become Motorbike Taxi-Riders" *Journal of Peace, Conflict and Development* 10 (March 2007): 3.

90. Jo Becker, "Children as Weapons of War," Human Rights Watch, January 25, 2004, https://www.hrw.org/legacy/wr2k4/download/11.pdf.

91. Ibid.

92. Jo Becker, "President Obama Fails Child Soldiers: US Again Allows Military Aid to Countries Using Children as Fighters," Human Rights Watch, September 29, 2016, https://www.hrw.org/news/2016/09/29/president-obama-fails-child-soldiers.

93. Betancourt and Williams, "Building an Evidence Base," 50.

94. Nadim Houry, "Children of the Caliphate: What to Do about Kids Born under ISIS," Foreign Affairs, November 22, 2016, hosted by Human Rights Watch, https://www.hrw.org/news/2016/11/23/children-caliphate.

95. Ibid.

96. Michael Wessells, "Child Soldiers," Bulletin of the Atomic Scientists 53, no. 6 (1997): 32–39.

97. Nancy Yamout, interview with Mia Bloom, Oslo, Norway, April 27, 2018. Nancy Yamout is known as one of the "Kamikaze Sisters"; a social worker active in Beirut, Lebanon; and the president of Rescue Me—Crime Prevention. Yamout's work was profiled in WorldCrunch, "Women In ISIS: Prison Study Reveals Face of Female Jihadists," June 4, 2017, https://www.worldcrunch.com/world-affairs/women-in-isis-prison-study-reveals-face-of-female-jihadists.

98. Nancy Yamout, interview with Bloom, April 26, 2018.

99. Inger Agger and Søren B. Jensen, "The Psychosexual Trauma of Torture," in International Handbook of Traumatic Stress Syndromes, ed. J. P. Wilson and B. Raphael (Boston: Springer, 1993).

8. AN END OR A NEW BEGINNING?

1. Karen McVeigh, "Scarred and Broken: Children Escaping ISIS in Mosul Suffer Waking Nightmares," Guardian (UK), July 5, 2017, https://www.theguardian.com/global-development/2017/jul/05/scarred-and-broken-children-escaping-isis-in-mosul-suffer-waking-nightmares.

2. "Twenty-three percent of the armed organizations in the world (84 out of 366 total) use children age 15 and under in combat roles. Eighteen percent of the total (64 of 366) use children 12 and under." P. W. Singer, "Child Soldiers: The New Faces of War," Brookings Institution, accessed August 20, 2018, https://www.brookings.edu/wp-content/uploads/2016/06/singer20051215.pdf, citing data from Rädda Barnen, Childwar Database.

3. Maya Wesby, "The Lost Children of ISIS," Wilson Quarterly, August 21, 2015, https://wilsonquarterly.com/stories/the-lost-children-of-isis/.

4. Tim Lister, "Islamic State 2.0: As the Caliphate Crumbles, ISIS Evolves," CNN, July 3, 2017, http://www.cnn.com/2017/03/22/europe/isis-2-0/index.html.

5. Paul Szoldra, "ISIS Is Losing Massive Amounts of Territory—Here's What They've Left Behind," Business Insider, February 22, 2017, https://www.aol.com/article/news/2017/02/22/isis-is-losing-massive-amounts-of-territory-heres-what-theyv/21719401/.

6. "ISIS Sees More and More Foreign Fighters Trying to Escape," Fox News, April 27, 2017, http://www.foxnews.com/world/2017/04/27/isis-sees-more-and-more-foreign-fighters-trying-to-escape.html.

7. Anonymous (encrypted) chats on Telegram, observed by Mia Bloom, between IS recruiters and individuals wanting to join IS.

8. Emma Vardy, "Jihadi Jack Charged with Being IS Member," BBC, October 28, 2017, http://www.bbc.com/news/uk-41784827; Justin Carissimo, "Virginia Man Mohammed Jamal Khweis Sentenced to Twenty Years in Prison for Joining ISIS," CBS News, October 27, 2017, https://www.cbsnews.com/news/mohamad-jamal-khweis-gets-prison-sentence-joining-isis/.

9. Ben Hubbard and Eric Schmitt, "ISIS, Despite Heavy Losses, Still Inspires Global Attacks," *New York Times*, July 8, 2017, https://www.nytimes.com/2017/07/08/world/mid dleeast/isis-syria-iraq.html.

10. "Documents Show How ISIS Functions as a Government," CNN, Aril 20, 2015, http://www.cnn.com/2015/04/20/middleeast/gallery/isis-documents/index.html.

11. Lizzie Dearden, "More Than 400 British ISIS Jihadis Have Returned to the UK," *Independent* (UK), October 24, 2017, http://www.independent.co.uk/news/uk/home-news/isis-british-jihadis-return-uk-iraq-syria-report-islamic-state-fighters-europe-threat-debate-terror-a8017811.html.

12. Richard Barrett, *Beyond the Caliphate: Foreign Fighters and the Threat of Returnees* (New York: Soufan Center, October 2017), 41, http://thesoufancenter.org/wp-content/uploads/2017/10/Beyond-the-Caliphate-Foreign-Fighters-and-the-Threat-of-Returnees-TSC-Report-October-2017.pdf; Robin Wright, "ISIS Jihadis Have Returned Home by the Thousands," *New Yorker*, October 23, 2017, https://www.newyorker.com/news/news-desk/isis-jihadis-have-returned-home-by-the-thousands.

13. John Ray, "Revelations of a Caliphate Cub," ITV News, July 6, 2017, http://www.itv.com/news/2017-07-06/revelations-of-a-caliphate-cub-teenage-boy-captured-by-isis-exposes-terror-training-and-tactics/.

14. Yara Bayoumi, "Isis Urges More Attacks on Western 'Disbelievers,'" *Independent* (UK), September 22, 2014, http://www.independent.co.uk/news/world/middle-east/isis-urges-more-attacks-on-western-disbelievers-9749512.html. See also Yannick Veilleux-Lepage, "How and Why Vehicle Ramming Became the Attack of Choice for Terrorists," The Conversation, https://theconversation.com/how-and-why-vehicle-ramming-beca me-the-attack-of-choice-for-terrorists-75236.

15. In neighboring countries such as Jordan, those who may have been associated with IS are continuously followed by government intelligence forces. These individuals are not permitted to work and face additional challenges in securing housing or education.

16. Deborah Amos, "Islamic State Defector: 'If You Turn against ISIS, They Will Kill You,'" National Public Radio, September 25, 2014, http://www.npr.org/sections/paral lels/2014/09/25/351436894/islamic-state-defector-if-you-turn-against-isis-they-will-kill-you.

17. Margaret Coker and Falih Hassan, "A 10-Minute Trial, a Death Sentence: Iraqi Justice for ISIS Suspects," *New York Times*, April 17, 2018, https://www.nytimes.com/2018/04/17/world/middleeast/iraq-isis-trials.html.

18. Billy Briggs, "One Million Iraqi Children 'Have Lost Out on Education under Islamic State,'" Theirworld, November 9, 2016, http://theirworld.org/news/one-million-iraqi-children-lose-out-on-education-under-islamic-state.

19. Sam Lees, "Inside an Illegal Reeducation Camp for Families with Possible Ties to ISIS," Vice News, September 5, 2017, https://news.vice.com/story/inside-an-illegal-re education-camp-for-families-with-possible-ties-to-isis.

20. Alexandra Bradford, "In Syria's War, 'Mental Health Is the Last Priority,'" Huffington Post, September 8, 2017, http://www.huffingtonpost.com/entry/in-syrias-war-mental-health-is-the-last-priority_us_59b316f9e4b0dfaafcf810f7.

21. Emily Feldman, "Can ISIS's Indoctrinated Kids Be Saved from a Future of Violent Jihad?," *Newsweek*, July 6, 2017, http://www.newsweek.com/2017/07/14/isis-kids-indoc trination-saved-violent-jihad-632080.html.

22. Ibid.

23. Samuel Okiror, "Kony's Killers—Are Child Soldiers Accountable When They Become Men?," IRIN News, December 5, 2016, http://www.irinnews.org/analysis/2016/12/05/kony's-killers—are-child-soldiers-accountable-when-they-become-men.

24. Stephanie van den Berg, "Defence Tactics Exposed in Ongwen Case at ICC," *International Justice Tribune*, December 6, 2016, https://www.justicetribune.com/blog/defence-tactics-exposed-ongwen-case-icc; Mark Kersten, "We Need to Talk about Ongwen: The Plight of Victim-Perpetrators at the ICC," Justice in Conflict, April 19, 2016, https://justiceinconflict.org/2016/04/19/we-need-to-talk-about-ongwen-the-plight-of-victim-perpetrators-at-the-icc/.

25. Charlotte Piret, Abdelghani Merah, "Dans la famille Merah, il y avait un terreau fertile à la haine," InterFrance (FR), October 2, 2017, https://www.franceinter.fr/justice/abdelghani-merah-dans-la-famille-merah-il-y-avait-un-terreau-fertile-a-la-haine.

26. *Child Soldiers: Implications for US Forces*. Seminar Report, November 2002, Center for Emerging Threats and Opportunities, US Marine Corps, CETO 005-02, 21

27. Ambassador Stephen Evans, NATO Assistant Secretary General for Operations at the United Nations Security Council, Intervention. Transcripts of Speech to NATO, March 27, 2015, http://www.nato.int/cps/en/natohq/opinions_118555.htm.

28. Dionne Searcey and Emmanuel Akinwotu, "Boko Haram Returns Dozens of Schoolgirls Kidnapped in Nigeria," *New York Times*, March 21, 2018, https://www.nytimes.com/2018/03/21/world/africa/nigeria-boko-haram-girls.html.

29. "In December 1996, the General Assembly welcomed the report in its resolution *A/RES/51/77* and recommended that the Secretary-General appoint a Special Representative on children and armed conflict." United Nations, Children and Armed Conflict, "Graça Machel and the Impact of Armed Conflict on Children." n.d., https://childrenandarmedconflict.un.org/mandate/the-machel-reports/.

30. United Nations, Office of the Secretary-General's Envoy on Youth, "Amman Youth Declaration Adopted at Global Forum on Youth, Peace and Security," August 24, 2015, http://www.un.org/youthenvoy/2015/08/amman-youth-declaration-adopted-global-forum-youth-peace-security/. Bloom learned about this forum from Michael McCabe, youth coordinator for USAID, when he spoke at the United States Institute for Peace conference on Expanding the Role of Youth in Building Peace, Security, in Washington, DC, August 8, 2017, https://www.usip.org/events/expanding-role-youth-building-peace-security.

31. "UNSCR 2250: Introduction," Youth4Peace Global Knowledge Portal, accessed August 21, 2017, http://www.youth4peace.info/UNSCR2250/Introduction.

32. Within the NGO community, the preferred term is "good practices"; this was formerly known as "best practices."

33. Chandi Fernando and Michel Ferrari, "Resilience in Children and War," in *Handbook of Resilience in Children of War*, ed. Chandi Fernando and Michel Ferrari (New York: Springer, 2013), 291.

34. Marla J. Buchanan, Kasim al-Mashat, Liliana Cortes, Branka Djukic, Behesta Jaghori, and Alanna Thompson, "Children of War in Colombia and Iraq," in Fernando and Ferrari, *Handbook of Resilience*, 107–16.

35. A. Karmiloff-Smith, "Nativism vs. Neuro-Constructivism: Rethinking the Study of Developmental Disorders," *Developmental Psychology* 45, no. 1 (2009): 56–63. See also the work of Jane MacPhail of Mercy Corps, who has been treating IS survivors in Jordan.

36. Brian K. Barber and Samuel Benjamin Doty, "How Can a Majority Be Resilient? Critiquing the Utility of the Construct of Resilience through a Focus on Youth in Contexts of Political Conflict," in Fernando and Ferrari, *Handbook of Resilience*, 233–52.

37. Steven E. Hobfoll, Robert J. Johnson, Daphna Canetti, Patrick A. Palmieri, Brian J. Hall, Iris Lavi, and Sandro Galea, "Can People Remain Engaged and Vigorous in the Face of Trauma? Palestinians in the West Bank and Gaza," *Psychiatry* 75, no. 1 (Spring 2012): 60–75.

38. UNHCR, *I Am Here, I Belong: The Urgent Need to End Childhood Statelessness*, November 2015, http://www.unhcr.org/ibelong/wp-content/uploads/2015-10-Stateless Report_ENG16.pdf. See also R. Charli Carpenter, *Forgetting Children Born of War:*

Setting the Human Rights Agenda in Bosnia and Beyond (New York: Columbia University Press, 2010).

39. "Tens of thousands of infants have been born of wartime rape or sexual exploitation in the last decade alone": R. Charli Carpenter, "War's Impact on Children Born of Rape and Sexual Exploitation: Physical, Economic and Psychosocial Dimensions," www.childsoldiers globalreport.org/content/facts-and-figures-child-soldiers, citing Kai Grieg, *The War Children of the World* (Bergen, Norway: War and Children Identity Project, 2001).

40. Tanya Zayed, interview with Mia Bloom, New York City, October 2016. See also Alasdair Wilkins, "Why Childhood Memories Disappear," *Atlantic*, July 6, 2015, https://www.theatlantic.com/health/archive/2015/07/why-childhood-memories-disappear/397502/.

41. Charlie D'Agata, "Behind the Lens: Children of ISIS," CBS News, August 1, 2017, https://www.cbsnews.com/news/behind-the-lens-children-of-isis/.

42. Sharon Lambert and Orla Lynch, RAN Issue Paper on Child Returnees from Syria and Iraq, November 2016, 2, https://www.researchgate.net/publication/314154734_RAN_Issue_paper_on_Child_Returnees_from_Syria_and_Iraq.

43. Radicalisation Awareness Network (RAN), "The Role of Police Officers in Dealing with Jihadist Returnees," March 30–31, 2017, https://ec.europa.eu/home-affairs/sites/home affairs/files/what-we-do/networks/radicalisation_awareness_network/about-ran/ran-pol/docs/ran_pol_role_of_police_officers_dusseldorf_30-31_03_2017_en.pdf.

44. Ibid., 6.

45. Ben Hubbard, "Wives and Children of ISIS: Warehoused in Syria, Unwanted Back Home," *New York Times*, July 4, 2018, https://www.nytimes.com/2018/07/04/world/mid dleeast/islamic-state-families-syria.html.

46. Michael Ungar, "The Social Ecologies and Their Contribution to Resilience," in *The Social Ecology of Resilience: A Handbook of Theory and Practice*, ed. Michael Ungar (New York: Springer, 2012), 13–31.

47. Betancourt interview with CNN, "The SAFE Model for Child Soldier Rehabilitation." CNN (1:16), https://www.cnn.com/videos/world/2015/04/25/theresa-betancourt-child-soldiers-safe-model.cnn cited by Wesby, "Lost Children of ISIS."

48. "Responses to Returnees: Foreign Terrorist Fighters and Their Families," Radicalisation Awareness Network (RAN) Manual, July 2017, https://ec.europa.eu/home-affairs/sites/homeaffairs/files/ran_br_a4_m10_en.pdf, 82.

49. Urie Bronfenbrenner, *The Ecology of Human Development: Experiments by Nature and by Design* (Cambridge, MA: Harvard University Press, 1979).

50. Fernando and Ferrari, *Handbook of Resilience*, 293–94.

51. Dr. Fatima Akilu, Interview with Mia Bloom, Oslo, Norway, February 27, 2018.

52. Fernando and Ferrari, *Handbook of Resilience*, 297–98.

53. Many of the suggestions below summarize the findings of the Prevention Project, a collaboration between nongovernmental and international organizations sponsored by the International Civil Society and Action Network and the Women's Alliance for Security Leadership.

Index